integraleyemovement.com

INTEGRAL EYE MOVEMENT TECHNIQUES:

The Definitive Guide

by Sonia Richards

first published 2021

ISBN 978-1-8384964-0-1

Cover Design and layout Rob Russell

Praise for Sonia Richards

"I highly recommend Sonia Richards as a trainer and therapist. With an intelligent and no-nonsense approach, Sonia shows the highest level of professionalism and competency in the delivery of her work and is someone I recommend without hesitation."

Andrew T. Austin, Creator of IEMT

"The structure of the course, the material and the presentation were excellent. An exceptionally efficient and effective therapy technique that can be used on its own or in conjunction with any therapy modality. Two days of intensive practical learning and lots of fun."

Dr Ioannis Dovelos, Professor of Psychology, Athens

"Sonia is a great presenter who really knows her stuff. The training was very informative but fun with lots of pf practical elements. I was impressed by how easy IEMT was to understand and how effective it is."

Jennifer West, President of the Midwives Alliance of North America

"It is very rare to find a method and teacher quite so excellent."

Margaret Motilal, Hypnotherapist, NLP Practitioner, HypnoBirthing Practitioner, USA

"Sonia is a first-class trainer. The course was immensely informative, practical and fun. I highly recommend this course."

Brien Lee Men Siong, NLP Trainer & Coach, Singapore & Malaysia

"I have used IEMT so far with every client that I have seen since the training and am very happy. I feel very confident using it. Many thanks for a great course and skill set."

Celia Hogan, Hypnotherapist, NLP Practitioner, Life Coach, UK

"I thoroughly enjoyed the course. Great material and a convincing trainer. It was good to see you at work. I think you dealt with a pretty challenging group of delegates very well. I've been so impressed with how quickly IEMT works."

Dr Mark Chambers, NLP Trainer, Hypnotherapist, GP, UK

"Sonia is a brilliant teacher/trainer because she makes learning fun and interesting, whilst getting the message across. I have stopped using other eye movement therapies in favour of IEMT since my training as I have found it to be the best way to create change for the client. Sonia does things to the highest standards. My life has changed due to my training and so has my clients. Highly recommended!"

Paul Bridge, Counsellor, Psychotherapist,
EMDR Practitioner, UK

"Sonia is professional, knowledgeable, friendly and approachable. The IEMT course was both informative and hands on, allowing participants to practice techniques learned. I highly recommend this course and Sonia too."

Christine Gallier, mental health care professional, UK

"Sonia is an excellent trainer and so much skill and experience that the course far out stripped my expectations."

Mark Peters, NLP & Hypnotherapy Trainer, Tai Chi Trainer, UK

"I've attended both the Practitioner and Advanced Practitioner IEMT courses delivered by Sonia. She has a very wide breadth of knowledge allowing participants to explore a far broader utilisation of the IEMT methods and their uses in therapy than one would normally expect from such a course. She also has a significant depth to her knowledge that allows for a deep understanding of key points throughout the course. All of this delivered with an infectious style that really engages with the attendees and ensures a high level of practical participation."

Pete Linforth, NLP Trainer, UK

"Thank you to Sonia for completely changing my career direction and allowing me to fall in love with helping people in such an effective and rapid way. I would 100% recommend being trained by Sonia Richards. Thank you so much."

Leanne Jones, Life Coach, UK

"Sonia has a very straightforward and direct approach, which I love. I am using IEMT with my clients and continue to be amazed at the changes they make in such a short time. Thank you Sonia."

Kathleen Nusbaum, Michigan, USA

Dedication

This book is dedicated to all the clients and trainees I have worked with over many years since discovering this fabulous modality.

"If we could change ourselves,
the tendencies in the world would also change.
As a man changes his own nature,
so does the attitude of the world change towards him.

We need not wait to see what others do."

Mahatma Gandhi

INTEGRAL EYE MOVEMENT TECHNIQUES

The Definitive Guide

Sonia Richards

Creating Change in the Blink of an Eye

IEMT is the result of decades of development. This modality is now helping people all over the world to discover how to release emotional problems quickly, which in some cases, has trapped them in unhelpful patterns of thinking and action for many years.

This is a guide primarily for IEMT Practitioners, but also for anyone who is inspired by this amazing set of techniques and models. IEMT can enlighten us on the surprisingly similar ways that people from different cultures operate, plus how these patterns and ways of being can contribute to keeping problem scenarios in place often via a sense of 'stuck-ness'. For many, the calibrated eye movements can quickly release problematic emotions and feelings that are generated by declarative memory. Additionally it can help those with 'Who' they are being on an identity level, that is problematic for themselves and for those around them.

Once we understand these techniques and models of human behaviour, we can teach ourselves and others to use them. As many who have experienced these techniques have said, IEMT is a life-changing modality which can be used to create lasting change, for the better.

With this book you can consolidate your existing knowledge, learn to "Iron Out Life's Creases" and "Create Change in the Blink of an Eye".

About the Author

Sonia Richards was the first International Chair of the Association for IEMT Practitioners and one of the first IEMT Trainers appointed by Andrew T. Austin, the developer of IEMT. Sonia offers both online and in-person training, as well as trainee mentoring and client therapy sessions. She also runs the unique IEMTea Party sessions, where guest speakers in the field of change work are invited to talk about their work and share their experience.

Her teaching and training experience began as a trainer and university degree lecturer in her original profession of biomedical sciences. She holds a Master of Science with Distinction, and she is an award-winning scientist in the field of pathology.

She has worked as a trainer for several complementary therapies organisations in London and the South East of England, and has vast experience in delivering workshops in various therapies. She was an external lecturer in HypnoBirthing® for the University of Greenwich for almost 10 years and was a member of the UK HypnoBirthing® Advisory Board for many years, holding the post of board secretary.

Sonia leads Level 1 Practitioner and Level 2 Advanced Practitioner IEMT courses and provides post-course individual and group mentoring. She has spoken at the Goulding Institute International in Melbourne, Australia, as well as several HypnoBirthing® Conclaves in the USA. She leads Facebook groups which support practitioners in their use and understanding of all aspects of IEMT and is the editor of the Association newsletter, *The Eye*.

Sonia is also a Trainer in Metaphors of Movement (MOM), the newest therapeutic innovation from Andrew T. Austin. She gives talks and hosts introductory workshops on Metaphors of Movement, including at the Society for Mental Space Psychology (SOMSP) 2021 international online conference, Applications in Mental Space.

Something that you may not know about Sonia is that she has been a singer since she was a teenager and was a member of two bands from Liverpool in the early 1980s, namely Frankie Goes to Hollywood and Dead or Alive. Performing on stage in front of huge audiences over the years was great preparation for the trainings she delivers today. Her courses are extremely informative and interactive, and she believes in learning through hands-on experience, plenty of laughter, and of course some music.

You can contact Sonia directly via email:
sonia@soniarichards.com

Or via the contact form on her website:
https://www.integraleyemovement.com/Home/Contact

Contents

Acknowledgements

This book has been a long time coming. In fact, I have on occasion used my IEMT skills to help complete it when procrastination set in and it seemed like a metaphorical immersion!

There are many people to thank for keeping this project going and encouraging me (myself and I...!) to finish it, along with those who have contributed with advice and assistance.

First, my wonderful husband **Mike Richards**, who uses these skills day-to-day even more than I do. His achievements in changing things in his own life for the better are truly inspirational, and his metaphorical kicks up the backside to encourage this book's completion were much needed. Thank you for your continual support and belief in my abilities.

Next, thank you to my amazing students over the years. There are too many to mention here, but they have helped me to keep learning and adding to the work as I have honed my skills in teaching this modality. In turn, they have worked hard to achieve their own deeper understanding of using these tools and skills.

Thank you to my sister **Debbie Citrine** for her unconditional love and support. She is always someone who will listen and help to clarify issues.

And to **Steve Griffiths** for helping me to believe that I could transition from the world of biomedical science; first into complementary therapies, then into hypnobirthing, hypnotherapy and IEMT. The first meeting that we attended together opened my awareness to this amazing modality.

Also, my friend and fellow author **Anthony Asquith**, for being a beacon of light and encouragement and providing concrete information about book writing.

And to all those who have contributed their time and effort:

Charlie Lea, author and principal at Read Now Write Now, for practical advice on publishing.

Pete Linforth, for his eye accessing graphics.

Jane Pikett, “The Editor”, for getting this book over the line!

Lucy Rahman, for proof reading.

Ellie Richards, for various graphics for this book and for my many training materials, including the IEMTea Trees.

Rob Russell, for the front and back cover designs, formatting and layout, plus several other graphics including the wonderful 5 Patterns of Chronicity images.

And finally, **Andrew T. Austin** for the development of Integral Eye Movement Techniques and enabling me to write this book and contribute to the further development of IEMT.

Foreword

I am delighted to be able to write the foreword to this, the only definitive guide to Integral Eye Movement Techniques.

What started as a simple idea and exploration in brain change quickly developed into something I could never have anticipated. Today, we have IEMT Practitioners all over the world applying this work, creating improvements in mental and emotional health where previously there would have been little hope of a good outcome.

With more people learning and applying this work in the real world, the hive mind has been to work, making little tweaks here and there and bringing improvements to both the body of work and its application. Within this hive mind there are luminaries who have gone far above and beyond merely learning the work and applying it diligently. One such luminary is Sonia Richards, to whom I am grateful for producing this excellent review and explanation of the work known as IEMT.

I have known Sonia for some years, and she been witness to the development of IEMT along the way. She has been able to offer her own unique insights, and her contribution and guidance regarding the formation of the Association for IEMT Practitioners has been invaluable, greatly assisting in the creation of a support and information network for trainees of IEMT.

It is my hope that IEMT will continue to gain greater acceptance within the orthodoxy and that more people will be able to benefit from this work. This book is a significant step towards gaining that acceptance.

Andrew T. Austin
January 2021

Introduction

Welcome to the first ever book on the modality of Integral Eye Movement Techniques/Therapy (IEMT).

This is primarily a guide for practitioners to hone and develop their skills to become more effective, confident and competent in applying this modality.

It is also designed to give some understanding to those who are new to IEMT; either as clients who have experienced the techniques, others who would like to experience IEMT, or those looking to become practitioners.

First, this book will delve into some history, asking:

"How did IEMT get to be this way?"

We will start by looking at the person who developed IEMT, Andrew T. Austin, the unique set of circumstances that led to his evolvement of the work, the skills he gained and honed over the years, plus his 'eureka moment' and the early days of IEMT.

We will then get into **"What is IEMT anyway?"** and **"How does it work?"**

Needless to say, there has been much debate and head scratching over the years about what it is and how it works!

This then leads us to: **"How to we do it?"**

Here, we will look at using the process in its most basic form – a model that, while simple, can still lead to significant change. Indeed, many people become practitioners of IEMT and never progress beyond this most basic level, and that's okay. However, there is so much more to IEMT than just moving the eyes about and achieving a change in the intensity of a feeling. There are other modalities that can achieve this, and IEMT has far more to offer.

Those who have attended one of my trainings are aware of this, and those who have worked on case studies as part of the certification process are well-used to applying all the techniques and knowledge for themselves and with clients.

IEMT can go far beyond rectifying an emotional upset felt by a person when they think about a particular event. As experienced practitioners, we want to find out:

"How did this person learn to feel this way about this thing?"

Our techniques give us the skills to investigate the more complex interactions that form who we are and how we operate in numerous relationships, including our relationship with ourselves; hence the importance of the question that the identity work in IEMT is based on:

"How did this person learn to be this way?".

Very often, this is the thing that can help a person to achieve their desires or goals in life. Just as frequently, however, it may be the thing that prevents them functioning adequately to such an extent that they trap themselves in unsuccessful thought patterns detrimental to emotional, psychological, even physical health.

The foundation of the model is not just to ameliorate feelings, but to deal effectively with the behavioural patterns that can get in the way of life, sabotage change, keep people repeating mistakes or leave them stuck in a rut. So, this book looks at these patterns, which we term the Patterns of Chronicity, in addition to some cycling patterns of emotions, and explores effective means by which we can change them.

Now there are many tools and techniques available to therapists, change workers, coaches, practitioners, or whatever you choose to call yourself, and for those seeking self-help in order to create change. And some may well ask, *"What's so different about IEMT, then?"*

This isn't something that can be explained in a few sentences, paragraphs or even pages. Suffice to say, there are crucial differences from other modalities, and it is these differences which underpin the rapid, lasting changes we can achieve with IEMT.

As Andrew T. Austin, the developer of IEMT, says:

"*IEMT is not the grand unified theory of therapy and change work and is still a developing model, but it is a very useful adjunctive for trained therapists, and in the right hands can provide an excellent remedial tool for emotional change and a generative tool for identity change. Practitioners are reporting that IEMT enables excellent results where previously a good outcome might have appeared improbable*."

My own introduction to IEMT went like this…

It was a dark, foggy, damp November evening in Brighton. The smell of spent fireworks and bonfire embers filled the air. My companion and I trudged through the cold night towards an amber glow coming from a building in the distance. Finally, the outline of a pub emerged and we entered through the door into a brightly lit room with a welcoming fire and an even more welcoming bar. I had my usual Diet Coke, my companion ordered a beer, and we asked the staff about the meeting we had come to attend. This, we were told, was to be held upstairs, so we climbed a rickety staircase into a large, dimly lit, high-ceilinged room with several rows of chairs set out. Paying our attendance fee, we settled down as others began to join us.

At 7pm the host began her introductory spiel. As she explained that the speaker was running late due to the fog, she was interrupted by a tall figure who strode through the door dressed in black motorbike gear including a full-faced helmet. Removing the headgear, he declared: *"Hi I'm Andrew Austin, sorry I'm late."* As he removed his jacket, he asked if anyone had a vivid memory of something that, when they thought about it now, created a negative feeling. Something from the past, he said, which didn't have to be a huge thing - for example, the day when he was only very young he went to school and forgot his packed lunch - that at the time felt pretty traumatic. If we were to give it a score out of 10 it would be around a 6/10, that sort of thing. And we were off...

Suffice to say, I did have something. I went back to a memory when I was eight and had been summoned to the headmistress's office. I had a feeling it wasn't going to be good, and it wasn't. You see, I had found out the first name of one of my teachers, a Miss Young, and on seeing her one day at playtime I shouted her name across the playground - *"Hello, Susan!"* - much to her consternation and the amusement of my friends. For this transgression, I was sent to the headmistress, who was a tall, rather stern looking woman with tight lips who wore a scowl through her 1960s black cat-rimmed glasses.

Despite her being fairly austere, I was usually in her good books and would be offered a sweet if running errands for her. Not today, however. The intimidating headmistress gave me a severe dressing-down, told me how disappointed she was in me and said my parents would be informed. As someone who, even at a young age, had always tried to behave impeccably, was a bit of a girly swot and had been chosen for leading roles in school plays, the choir and so forth, this episode was mortifying, highly embarrassing and upsetting. And all these years later it still induced horrible feelings of embarrassment, shame, anxiousness and more.

The speaker asked us to pair up and think – *really* think – about our chosen memory, holding it as vividly as we could, while our partner led us in moving our eyes in three directions, six times each way. After we finished, the person acting as the 'therapist' was to ask: *"So now when you think about that memory, what do you notice about the memory and what do you notice about the feeling now?"* Brief answers were to be given and we were to then swap over.

What I now know as the 'usual question' soon came up:

"Erm, Andrew is this 6, or is this 6?" an audience member asked, demonstrating by waving a pointed finger horizontally in one direction and then backwards and forwards, i.e., in both directions. Andrew simply replied: *"That's right".*

My companion was a qualified hypnotherapist, so I knew he would know exactly what to do. So, holding on as strongly as I could to the memory, I began to move my eyes, keeping my head still as instructed. Andrew had told the person doing the finger waving that if the 'client' moved their head, to tell them to keep still. After about 30 seconds, the task completed, my partner asked some questions.

What did I now notice about the memory?
Blimey, I was finding it really difficult to visualise it, even though a few seconds ago it had been really vivid.

What did I notice about the feeling now?
Interestingly, those feelings of embarrassment and shame were no longer springing into my chest where they did before and had done for over 30 years if I had ever thought about that memory.

We were then told that if the memory and feelings seemed to have reduced or even disappeared, we were to *"try hard to get them back",* and if necessary, *"TRY ...HARDER..."*

So, I dug deep and, try as I might, I could not get this memory back as it was before, or the associated feelings. At this point, I burst out laughing. It couldn't really be that easy to remove a troubling memory could it? Well, it seemed that indeed it could.

From that huge 'Aha...' moment, I was fascinated to know more about this amazing process. I had experienced EMDR during my hypnotherapy training and it had never worked for me, but this process did work. I wanted to find out why and I wanted to train in this revelatory process in order that I could help my clients achieve these same changes. However, my NLP training was incomplete and I was under the misconception that I could not train in IEMT without being trained in NLP first, so I delayed for a while.

My companion was trained in NLP, so he enrolled onto one of the first IEMT Practitioner courses in Sussex. Due to my misconception about NLP, I had to wait a bit longer before the opportunity arose again. Luckily, Andrew did give my companion, who was a trainer and faculty member of the HypnoBirthing® Institute, a special licence to showcase IEMT with an introduction at the next HypnoBirthing® International Conclave in the USA, which we were both attending. So, I got to experience both the Basic Kinaesthetic and the more complex Identity models of IEMT before eventually completing my practitioner training.

This amazing set of techniques and models has been hugely instrumental in my personal development, as well as becoming the most-used modality in my professional change work repertoire. Having trained to Advanced Level, I have formed a deeper understanding of the importance of our sense of identity in all that we do and how we are being because of who we are. This work has given me a better understanding, not only of how people operate, but also of what can contribute towards them getting stuck in situations and keeping them there - plus of course how to release the 'stuckness'. I also teach clients many of these techniques so that they can help themselves ongoing to iron out any wrinkles or even larger challenges in their lives. After all, do they really want to see a therapist for any issue that may make them feel uncomfortable or is likely to drag them back into an unhelpful pattern or cycle?

In 2013, I was very fortunate to be among the first cohort of people trained by Andrew Austin to deliver IEMT training courses. Since that training, The Association for IEMT Practitioners has been formed and I was appointed the first International Chairperson by Andrew Austin. I have been fortunate to take IEMT trainings to several countries and in 2020, due to the Covid-19 crisis, was able to deliver the first-ever IEMT online training. This included delegates from the USA, Australia and Europe, and I have now successfully given many online trainings for both Level 1 and Level 2 (Advanced) IEMT.

My online resources are very comprehensive. They include full course recordings, downloadable resources, videos of techniques and exclusive video interviews with Andrew Austin. In addition, I have conducted online 'IEMTea Party' social learning events and practice sessions for new practitioners. Some of these events have raised money for charities such as Marie Curie.

We have now developed IEMT Certified Practitioner training from a 2-day course with a certificate and no further CPD, to a more professional qualification that includes case studies and coursework. Those who have attended my trainings know that, as a former university lecturer, I am a tough but fair assessor. My aim is to ensure that those who train in IEMT are using the comprehensive model and understand fully the patterns and cycles people run.

I teach people the need to listen carefully to clients, understand the giveaway core statements on intake questionnaires, and observe the physiological shifts which can reveal so much about a client's current emotional and identity issues.

So, I now hope you are now curious enough to read on, either to discover something new, or to reinforce your current knowledge and beliefs about this most amazing change work modality, where change really can be created in the blink - or more accurately the twitch - of an eyeball.

Chapter 1

How Did IEMT Get to Be This Way?

The What...

Now isn't that the 64million dollar question? Even its best-known pioneer Andrew Austin (AA), who further developed Integral Eye Movement Techniques (IEMT) from its fledgling steps via the influence of Connirae and Steve Andreas and their original EMI (Eye Movement Integration), has struggled over the years with this one.

There are several current methods widely in use today that involve the movement of the eyes in helping to reduce and remove emotional upset via the depotentiation of synapses in various areas of the brain (1-7). The term IEMT has changed over the years, the first incarnation being Eye Movement Integration (before AA realised that something of this name already existed). Eventually, it was his friend and Provocative Change Works developer and practitioner Nick Kemp who suggested the term Integral Eye Movement Technique in 2007. This has stuck and we have now added an 's' – Techniques – to signify that IEMT is far more than a single method. It is also far more than merely an eye movement modality.

Integral Eye Movement Techniques is a change work modality that can help to reduce and remove unwanted emotional dissonance, and recognise and resolve behavioural and identity issues.

The term 'rapid change work' is often used in conjunction with IEMT. However, although the techniques can indeed work rapidly to reduce unwanted feelings and even resolve identity issues, this is not a rapid one-session 'fix' in all cases.

When asked how often IEMT works, we say that it will work for most people, most of the time. If you like statistics, anecdotally this will be 90%-95%, according to observations from many hundreds of practitioners. Again however, it is not the 'cure-all' of modern neuro/psychological approaches to change work, though in my experience it definitely works most of the time.

It never ceases to amaze me, even now, by its simple elegance in creating change and the reactions of those for whom it works so quickly. We regularly receive emails from practitioners who say they now use IEMT with more than 95% of their clients, and rely on other more conventional modalities such as hypnosis less and less.

The Where...

IEMT as we now know it came about thanks to a unique set of circumstances. On discovering EMDR (Eye Movement Desensitisation and Reprocessing), Andrew Austin was curious to see it in action. After working in nursing for a number of years in various departments such as Accident and Emergency, Cardiology, and Neuromedicine, with an interest in psychiatry and psychology, the young Austin, by then an Ericksonian hypnotherapist and neurolinguist, was occasionally invited to observe various psychiatrists at work.

It was on one such occasion that his 'eureka moment' happened. He was invited to observe EMDR being used on a psychiatrist. This person had a long-standing issue that was traumatic and she was undergoing a course of EMDR sessions. She was on the eighth of 10 sessions and was sitting in front of a lightbox. The consultant psychiatrist in charge of the case set up the box and instructed the patient to think about the event while following the light that was moving horizontally backwards and forwards with her eyes, keeping her head still. The consultant then left the room, leaving the patient to it.

As chance would have it, Andrew knew the patient, having worked with her in the past. While moving her eyes she said nonchalantly: *"This isn't going to work, you know."* When Andrew asked why she thought this, the patient said: *"Well, I've already had seven sessions and it hasn't worked so far, so it's my assessment that it's also not going to work today.*"

At this, Andrew, having observed previous EMDR work, decided to change the parameters of the session. He took a pile of books from a shelf and asked the patient for permission to alter the position of the box. She told him to go ahead, and he propped the light box so that it was now on a diagonal instead of a horizontal axis, then asked the patient to follow the light.

Within seconds she let out a startled cry: *"Oh my God, what have you done?"*

She then exclaimed: *"It's gone; it's gone!"* Asked what had gone, she said: *"The memory that has been with me for all these years that was perpetuating this problem; it's gone!"*

The obvious relief for this lady was extremely noticeable and profound. Soon after this, the consultant in charge returned to the room and, seeing the box now propped up with books and his changed patient, became rather vexed. The consultant ordered our intrepid AA to get out and never darken his door again.

What Andrew had done was alter the trajectory of the axis of deviation for the patient. This allowed her for the first time during this process to reach the actual point of connection in her brain between the memory of the event and the associated emotion that had become neurologically entwined via the potentiation of various synapses, most likely in the limbic system.

Metaphorically, this acted like taking an axe and splitting the complex in two. This then allowed parts of her brain, such as the hippocampus and amygdala, to depotentiate and adjust the information for processing and consolidation to finally deal with the troublesome memory of the event and its associated emotions and feelings.

The How...

From this, a series of workshops was arranged. These were originally half-day sessions which, with the help of volunteers, looked at working on altering various eye movements in conjunction with troublesome memories. This developed into one-day workshops and eventually, with the addition of Identity plus the Patterns of Chronicity work, into a certification training programme.

The first Practitioner Certification Programme was in 2007 with just a handful of people. Now there are hundreds of practitioners worldwide and more are stepping up every year to train under a network of approved trainers in the UK and overseas. Practitioners are now working in places as diverse as Poland, Spain, the Caribbean, Israel and India. I have been privileged to train IEMT in the UK, USA and Singapore, I've lectured in Australia and have yet to visit many more countries to deliver this amazing training. My training is also now fully available online, allowing me to teach this modality to people globally.

IEMT has now developed beyond the desire to elicit rapid change for emotional issues. I have mentioned the Patterns of Chronicity and the ability to be able to work with identity issues - two areas which will be looked at in more depth in subsequent chapters. This book also explores the training that often delights and perplexes people the most - the application for working physiologically with people.

The Association for IEMT Practitioners was formed in 2013 after the first IEMT Trainer Training in Hampshire. The goal was to provide regulation of practitioners, to improve standards of practice and the professional standing of IEMT in the field of talking therapies and coaching. A regular newsletter, The Eye, is now available for practitioners and anyone interested in knowing more about IEMT. I also write a blog and host online meetings on many aspects of IEMT called the IEMTea Party, with guest speakers from other modalities invited to speak.

Andrew Austin is Director of the Association and at the time of writing I am its Chair. Between us, we have implemented a code of conduct and ethical guidelines for all practitioners. There is also a post-course case study requirement for assessed client sessions for those wishing to become certified practitioners. Thus, we can ensure those who wish to provide IEMT in a professional setting have fully understood the range of methods and models and are confident in applying all facets of the training, not just the eye movement techniques. Only members of the Association are entitled to use the title IEMT Practitioner, and there is a requirement for CPD on the annual renewal of their practitioner status.

We are looking forward to running preliminary trials using IEMT with the aim of gaining university funding for research into its efficacy in the clinical setting. Many practitioners who work within the NHS, social services, the armed forces, HM Prison Service and the police are convinced of the efficacy of IEMT and have reported the beneficial changes it can achieve quickly, even for those with issues such as severe trauma and PTSD.

On the subject of clinical use and clinical trials, it is pertinent at this early stage in the book to look at possible contraindications for the use of IEMT, for which guidelines have been produced for Association members.

It is Andrew Austin's opinion that IEMT is unlikely to cause any detrimental or long-term unwanted effects. EMDR has been widely used for some years now and there appear to be no absolute contraindications for physical conditions, but there are some red flags for those suffering dissociative disorders and psychiatric issues. I ask clients to complete a confidential pre-session questionnaire, which includes some medical information, in order to discern if IEMT is appropriate or whether a client's GP, consultant or psychologist should be contacted (with the client's permission). All client information is held in accordance with the Data Protection Act1998 and GDPR guidelines 2018.

Below is a list from my training manual and our pre-course case study guidance of issues that may contraindicate IEMT:

- Eye disease, injury or surgery, including laser eye surgery: If the client is not 12 months post-healing please check with their consultant/GP.

- Epilepsy if not medically controlled, or if there is a history of dizziness or eye movement initiating seizures: Please avoid.

- Epilepsy if medically controlled: Permission from neurological care team may be required.

- Other neurological disorders such as Parkinson's disease, MND, MS, and Alzheimer's disease.

- Head injury/trauma or surgery (length of recovery dependent and checks as above).

- Hyperemesis gravidarum (if current).

- Psychiatric disorders/psychosis – e.g. schizophrenia, bipolar disorder, drug-induced psychosis, schizoaffective disorder, post-partum psychosis, depression with psychotic symptoms – unless you are medically qualified to work with such disorders.

- Moderate to severe depression unless liaising with a medical practitioner.

- Stroke: Particularly if there is muscle and nerve damage to the eye(s) and the client is pre-12 months recovery, check with consultant.

- For my own practice, my policy is that clients MUST be completely free of alcohol and recreational drugs for a minimum of 96 HOURS before eye movement sessions. Those with dependency issues will require medical supervision for withdrawal before eye movement work.

- Vertigo/Ménière's disease/labyrinthitis: If current, check with GP/consultant.

You may also consider seeking a GP/doctor's consent for:

DVT, embolism, heart disease - depending how recently the client has experienced this and the severity. Also, a check with a GP or consultant is highly advisable for some of the effects of long Covid if included above.

For information regarding epileptic seizures, visit: www.epilepsy.org.uk/info/seizures/focal-seizures

The Association recommends that practitioners complete a first aid course and have the details of a trusted person who can be contacted in case of an emergency, especially if working remotely. There are shorter courses available for therapists, and also first-responder courses such as those available by the Red Cross. Access to local mental health services is also important. I keep leaflets from MIND UK and know where my local MIND UK service is, and where the NHS mental health unit is located. The free MIND leaflet entitled *Guide to Seeking Help for Mental Health Problems* is useful, as is the MIND website: www.mind.org.uk

If you are reading this book outside the UK, you will have your own services - please investigate and keep contacts up to date.

The Association's Practitioners' Handbook includes information in dealing with medical and psychiatric emergencies. Please find below some information from the handbook:

Common factors affecting suitability

Ocular disease:

Until there is sufficient medical evidence to suggest otherwise, eye movement work should not be used with any individual who has any active or current ocular disease process. **There are no exceptions to this.** Such conditions include conjunctivitis, glaucoma, history of detached retina and recent trauma such as a black eye. Problems such as a 'lazy eye' and poor focal vision are not necessarily a contraindication unless there is an active and concurrent disease process underlying it.

Psychiatric:

A client may be unsuitable on the grounds of mental health. Specifically, unless the practitioner is experienced and qualified in working with psychotic illnesses, or is operating with suitable direct supervision, then a history of psychotic illness must be considered a specific criterion for exclusion for IEMT work.

Legal:

If the client is a victim or witness of crime and is likely to be giving evidence in any legal process, then without exception, suitable and relevant legal advice must be sought prior to any IEMT treatment. IEMT is a process that directly affects memory recall and memory coding, and thus IEMT treatment may potentially be raised to question the validity of an IEMT recipient's testimony.

Avoidance and appointment substitution:

Occasionally, a client may seek IEMT treatment in substitution for their regular medical or psychiatric intervention, treatment and/or support. In all instances, the practitioner should request and liaise with the client's existing treatment services prior to treatment.

Other:

In a recent questionnaire to Association members, there were a few reports of headaches, dizziness and some nausea in response to IEMT. These numbers were small and, as you will see later in this book, there are often emotional and psychological reasons for such reactions, which are not necessarily medically related to a new or existing condition. Indeed, IEMT has been used by some, including myself, to deal with migraines and severe headaches in addition to other physical pain issues and conditions, so the response will depend on the person's emotional as well as physical state.

Chapter 2

Eye Movements, Memory and Change

The Eyes Have It!

Voluntary or involuntary movements of the eyes help to acquire, fixate and track visual stimuli. We will discuss this in terms of IEMT and what the observer may see in Chapter 6.

For NLP practitioners, the following may come as a surprise in regard to their knowledge and belief in eye accessing cues. NLP's co-founders Richard Bandler and John Grinder did not actually discover that eye movements are involved with memory formation and retention. However, the work they did has most certainly helped to advance the field of change work facilitation.

Eye movement and memory formation has been known for a long time, and eye movement measures have long been used to investigate various cognitive processes. In the 1950s, Alfred L. Yarbus did important eye tracking research and his 1967 book, *Eye Movements and Vision*, is often cited. He wrote: *"Eye movement reflects the human thought processes; so, the observer's thought may be followed to some extent from records of eye movement (the thought accompanying the examination of the particular object)"* [(1)].

I have recounted the story many times on trainings about the neurosurgeons who almost laughed AA out of the operating theatre when he recounted his theories on eye movements and what they really mean neurologically. What I didn't tell you is why. So, here goes...

If you have completed NLP Practitioner and Master Practitioner courses, you will know all about eye accessing cues. On day one, lesson one, we are shown a picture similar to the one you see here.

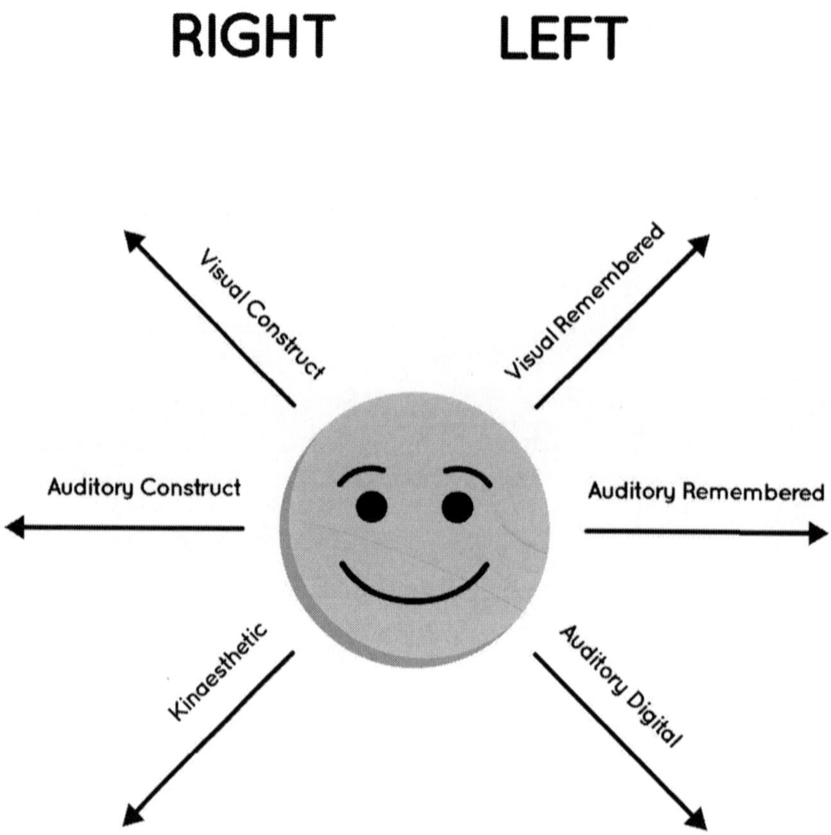

Then we complete an exercise in pairs, asking one another questions and looking to see where our partner's eyes move as they consider the answer. Now we know the picture above is a generalisation, because we aren't all wired in this way. It appears that the majority of us are, but some left-handed people may be the opposite way round. It is also only supposed to apply to the sound of mind!

Those new to IEMT or NLP may or may not have heard of eye accessing cues. Put simply, our eyes move when we access thoughts. However, these movements are so unconscious that many of us do not register them unless we have been made aware of them. If you are sceptical or unfamiliar with this, have a go now by asking yourself the simple questions below and notice the direction in which your eyes move. This is also a fun exercise to do with others, especially kids.

By yourself or in pairs ask the following questions and notice which direction your eyes move to in order to find the answer.

- What is the colour of your front door?
- How would a pink elephant look?
- How many pairs of socks do you own?
- The last time you had a headache - what was that like?
- What is the tune of your national anthem?
- What does your phone ring tone sound like?
- When soaking in a warm bath, what does that feel like?
- What is for dinner tonight or breakfast tomorrow?
- What would your voice sound like if you spoke like Donald Duck?
- What will you look like in 20 years?
- What does it feel like to lie in the sun?
- Can you recite the 12 times table in your head?

Rudimentary Eye Movements

These are the traditional names I prefer to call Auditory Digital, Internal Dialogue.

Visually Created

Visually Remembered

Auditory Created

Auditory Remembered

Kinaesthetic/Feeling

Auditory Digital/Inner Voice

Some attendees may be under the misapprehension that we use eye movements as some sort of diagnostic tool, that they are absolutes. This is not the case. One thing that is paramount about this work is that unless the practitioner is a registered medical doctor, they are not a diagnostician. If we as practitioners suspect physical or mental issues, we must refer out. The old adage, 'if in doubt, refer out' is key.

The developers of NLP proposed that the sensory systems were run by separate areas of the brain, and access was observed by cues given by a particular eye movement pattern. NLPers are trained in eye accessing cues and some may think they are almost diagnostic in their accuracy. They are not, but they are a good indicator as to how a person is remembering something or creating thoughts at that moment (2).

In fact, Bandler and Grinder (3) (4) were not the first to notice the phenomenon of eye movement and thought processes. It can be seen in writings from Qusta Ibn Luqa (864-923 AD), who was from Baalbek or Heliopolis in Lebanon, a Melkite Christian of Greek origin, living in Baghdad. He was a philosopher, physician, mathematician and astronomer. He combined Nemesius' ventricular localisation doctrine with the Roman physician Galen's account of a worm-like part of the brain which controls the flow of animal spirit between the middle and posterior ventricles. Ibn Luqa wrote that people who want to remember look upwards because this raises the worm-like particle, opens a passage and enables the retrieval of memories from the posterior ventricle of the brain. People who want to think, however, look down because this lowers the particle, closes the passage and protects the spirit in the middle ventricle from being disturbed by memories stored in the posterior ventricle (5).

A millennium later, in 1890, the psychologist William James defined four key types of 'thought' as follows:

> *"For some individuals the habitual 'thought stuff', is visual; in others it is auditory, articulatory [verbal], or motor [kinaesthetic]; in most, perhaps, it is evenly mixed."*

James repeatedly mentions the issue of the eye movements which accompany and can be used as cues for sensory accessing. Quoting Fechner's *Psychophysique*, 1860, Chapter XLIV he said:

> *"In imagining, the attention feels as if drawn backwards towards the brain."*

Describing his own experiences on visual images, James adds:

> *"All these images seem at first as if purely retinal. I think, however, that rapid eye movements accompany them, though these later give rise to such slight feelings that they are almost impossible of detection."* [6]

The classic NLP diagram of accessing cues is taken by some as gospel. It shows 'auditory digital' (AD) or self-talk on the left side, which suggests that all the accessing cues on that side may correspond to the dominant hemisphere, where verbal abilities are known to be processed. The NLP eye cues model places AD down and opposite kinaesthetic, rather than level and opposite auditory tonal. Howard Gardiner argues that verbal thought should not be termed 'auditory', as it is an entirely separate form of intelligence. He points out that the same area of the brain used by hearing people to generate verbal language is used by deaf people to generate sign language [7].

"She moved them to the right ear, she must be lying!"

There have been several studies undertaken in order to discredit or support eye accessing cues theories. In 2004, Susan Nate undertook a small study with children to decipher whether there was a difference between right or left handedness. There appeared to be no significant difference using chi square data analysis. The conclusions were also immediately obvious and confirmed the eye accessing cue model is not diagnostic. There was no difference in results by age, sex, ethnic group or handedness [(8)].

A study in 2015 discovered the precise neurological responses generating eye accessing cues, but not if this indicates activation of different areas of the brain. Rapid Eye Movement sleep studies during dream phases discovered that those blind from birth have eye movements. It had been thought that these movements were the scanning of dream images. The eye movements during sleep are similar to imagining a new image when awake.

Researchers from Tel Aviv University found that when scanning people's brains while asleep, a burst in the activity of neurons occurred just after the person's eyes flickered. This activity reflected a change of concept or scene (not image processing) during sleep. Dr. Yuval Nir, who co-authored the study published in Nature Communications, said that they demonstrated that this was the same brain activity that occurred when awake participants were shown pictures, especially those related to their memories. About 0.3 seconds after the picture appears, these neurons burst, i.e., they become vigorously active. He told New Scientist magazine:

> *"Every time you move your eyes, a new image forms in the mind's eye."* (Andrillon et alia, 2015) [(9)].

Further study is being undertaken by Dr Nir's team to identify which movements trigger which types of remembered or constructed experiences [(7)] [(9)]. I conjecture that it may be similar to the images above eye accessing images.

These basic movements are said to represent most of the population [(10)] who do not have any form of eye pathology, have suffered a stroke, or have any psychiatric disorder i.e. they have a 'normally wired' brain [(11)], whatever normal is . On the whole the above images are fairly accurate. I have had people tell me that they have noted discrepancies with left handed people and indeed have noted this on occasion also.

Memory and saccades movements now appear to have a robust amount of scientific evidence to substantiate the relationship. How change occurs at the cellular level, however, is still requiring much scientific investigation. However saccadic abnormalities also occur in varying neurological disorders and whilst the above is interesting it is not diagnostic of anything in an IEMT setting. Eye movements are however important in a clinical setting as Andrew Austin can attest to when he worked in Neurological Medicine. A paper from 2017 illustrates that saccade recording in the clinical setting can tell a neurologist a lot of information about normal movements and movement in neurological conditions. Terao et al, in 2017 state:

> *"Non-invasive and readily implemented in the clinical setting, eye movement studies, have been conducted extensively not only in healthy human subjects but also in patients with neurological disorders. The purpose of saccade studies is to "read out" the pathophysiology underlying neurological disorders from the saccade records.*
>
> *"We argue that it is important to understand the functional significance and behavioural correlate of saccade abnormalities in daily life, which could require eye tracking methodologies to be performed in settings similar to daily life."* [(12)]

Of course we have no way of knowing what thoughts or memories the patients were accessing when being studied, I am guessing however that this is irrelevant in such a setting [(13)].

For our purposes as IEMT Practitioners and scholars, one thing that is evident with many people who finally come to us having exhausted all other options is that resistance to change is one of the most fundamental and frustrating human traits there is. According to Sue Langley, research shows that even when faced with life-threatening situations many people resist change, despite the known repercussions:

> *"Studies reveal that when heart disease patients who had undergone traumatic bypass surgery were told that if they did not adjust their lifestyle, they would die or at best undergo the life-saving procedure again, only 9% modified their behaviour. The core of the challenge is changing behaviour - and our brains are extremely effective in tenaciously maintaining the status quo"* [14].

Anyhow, there is also one huge flaw in this model, which is the reason for the guffawing on behalf of the neurosurgeons: This is a 2-dimensional explanation of a 3-dimensional system.

Just to make the significance of this clearer, I repeat...

> **THIS IS A 2-DIMENSIONAL EXPLANATION OF A 3-DIMENSIONAL SYSTEM.**

So as far as it goes, the eye accessing cues model is very interesting, and it may in some circumstances even be very useful, but for neurologists it is not diagnostic of anything because it is not accurate enough.

For the purposes of IEMT, it is a good starting point for working with eye movements, but sticking rigidly to two dimensions means we miss a lot of information. In addition, not only does the eye accessing cues model limit itself to specific angles, it doesn't take distance into account. When a person is locating a memory, thought or feeling and the eyes are moving they have an almost 180-degree field of view. Interestingly, binocular vision, which is important for depth of perception, only covers 114 degrees (horizontally) of the field of vision in humans. There is no binocular vision in the peripheral 60-70 degrees because only one eye can see those parts of the field of view [15].

The distance the human eye can see depends on the particles of light, or photons, a distant object such as a star emits. The farthest visible object is the Andromeda galaxy 2.6 million light years from Earth and its 1 trillion stars emit enough light to excite our retinas on a dark night [16]. The naked eye can see the light of a flickering candle 30 miles (48km to you metric folks) on a dark night, and when a person is locating a thought, memory, sound, dialogue or feeling they have all this range to draw upon. Do you still think a 2D eye accessing cue map is accurate?

How the Eyes Move

There is often a misconception that IEMT and other eye movement-based modalities are entirely vision-based and that the optic nerve is crucial for the change that is experienced. Having discussed this with Andrew Austin, doctors and therapists, the consensus is that this is not the case. After all, this is eye **movement** therapy, not **eyesight** therapy. For those with impaired eye movement, this modality may not be as effective as it is for those with a full range of movement, but it still works.

Eye movements can be voluntary or involuntary, and primates plus many other vertebrates use three types of voluntary eye movement to track objects of interest: smooth pursuit, vergence shifts and saccades. These movements appear to be initiated by a small cortical region in the brain's frontal lobe (this is corroborated by removal of the frontal lobe). In this case, the reflexes (such as reflex shifting the eyes to a moving light) are intact, though the voluntary control is obliterated [17] [18] [19] [20].

Muscles

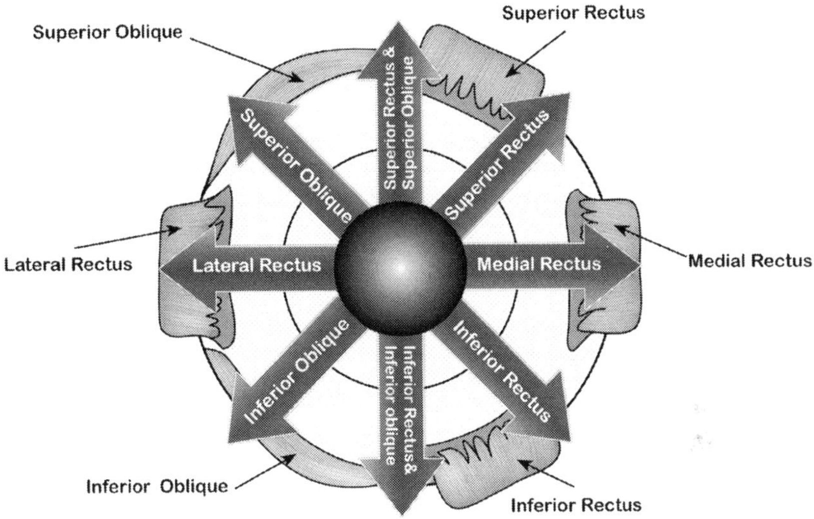

There are six extraocular (outside the eye) muscles present in the eye socket or orbit that attach to the eye to move it. These muscles work to move the eye up and down, side to side, and for rotation. Four of these - the inferior rectus, superior rectus, lateral rectus and medial rectus - are most frequently used.

- The *superior rectus* muscle attaches to the top of the eye. It moves the eye upward.
- The *inferior rectus* attaches to the bottom of the eye. It moves the eye downward.
- The *medial rectus* attaches to the side of the eye near the nose. It moves the eye inward toward the nose.
- The *lateral rectus* muscle attaches to the side of the eye near the temple. It moves the eye outward.

- The *superior oblique* comes from the back of the orbit. It travels through a small pulley, the trochlea, in the orbit near the nose and then attaches to the top of the eye. This muscle rotates the eye inward around the long axis of the eye front to back. It also moves the eye downward.

- The *inferior oblique* arises in the front of the orbit near the nose. It then travels outward and backward in the orbit before attaching to the bottom part of the eyeball. It rotates the eye outward along the long axis of the eye. This muscle also moves the eye upward. [20]

Nerves

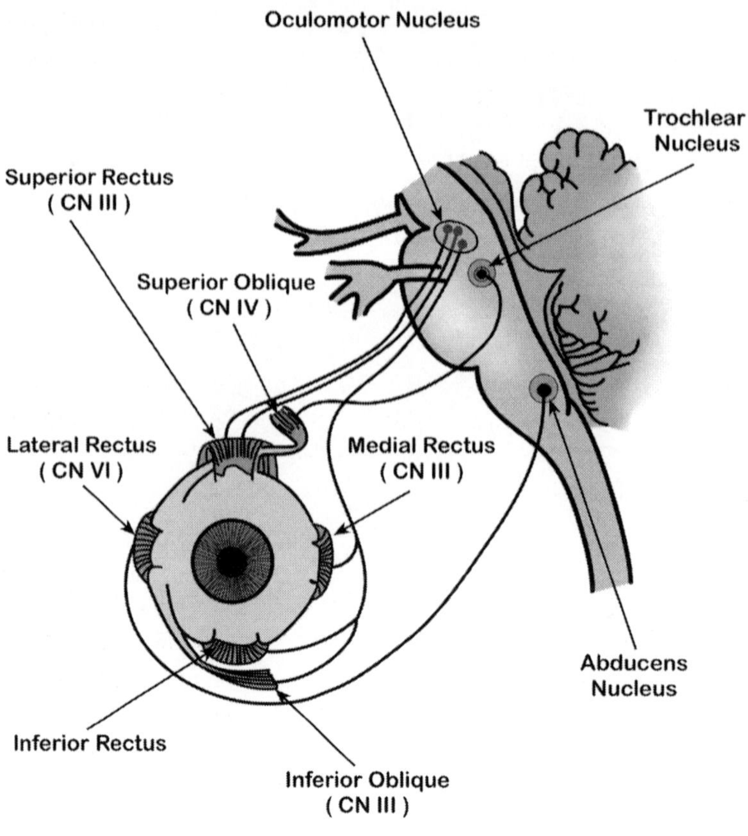

The brain exerts ultimate control over both voluntary and involuntary eye movements. Three cranial nerves carry signals from the brain to control the extraocular muscles. Three nerves control the eye muscles:

- The *oculomotor nerve,* which controls the majority of the muscles.

- The *trochlear nerve (CN IV)*, which controls the superior oblique muscle and moves the eye inward, down and laterally.

- The *abducens nerve (CN VI)*, which moves the eye laterally abducts towards the ear and which controls the lateral rectus muscle.

- In addition to the movement of muscles, numerous areas in the brain contribute to involuntary and voluntary eye movements. These include the areas providing the conscious perception of vision and those that facilitate tracking [(21) (22) (23)].

- Eye palsies involve paralysis of one or more of cranial nerves III, IV and VI that impair eye movement [(24)].

Eye Movement and Memory

There have been various attempts, with EMDR for example, to prove that eye movement has nothing to do with the resultant change that occurs.

These attempts have not been able to prove this. However, studies on PTSD have shown a link between the eye movements in REM sleep and eye movements during EMDR. The implication is that, like REM sleep, eye movements facilitate the transfer of episodic memory (this includes emotions, physical sensations and beliefs associated with an event) into semantic memory networks during which the meaning of the event is extracted and negative associations are no longer present [(25)].

What we do know, however, is that eyes move during sleep, even in people who are blind since birth. So, it is safe to assume that eye movements are integral to the formation and processing of memories and daily events during sleep, whether the person is sighted or visually impaired.

There has been a surge in the number of research papers written on the interaction between eye movement and various types of memory. The work is too exhaustive to discuss in this book, however a Google search will help the reader discover many such papers.

Memory, Sleep, Mood

There are several divisions of memory, both conscious and unconscious, and likewise there are several different areas involved with these types of memories. In IEMT we are primarily dealing with change in long-term episodic memory. Here is a diagram to simplify the divisions of memory (25):

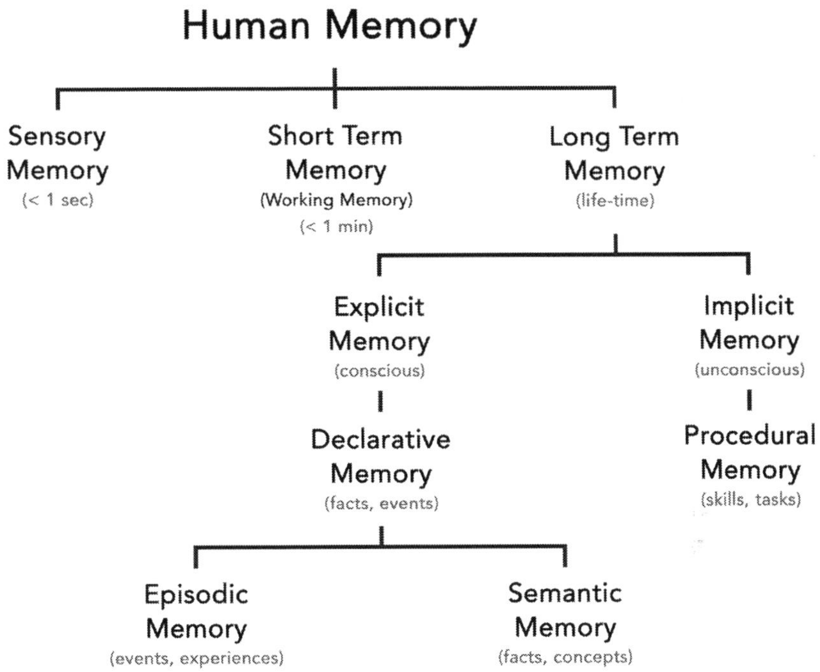
Human Memory
Sensory Memory
(< 1 sec)
Short Term Memory
(Working Memory)
(< 1 min)
Long Term Memory
(life-time)
Explicit Memory
(conscious)
Implicit Memory
(unconscious)
Declarative Memory
(facts, events)
Procedural Memory
(skills, tasks)
Episodic Memory
(events, experiences)
Semantic Memory
(facts, concepts)

This is a person's unique memory of a specific event in time in serial form. It enables a person to reconstruct an actual event at any given point in life. The emotional charge and the context surrounding the event is part of the memory.

Episodic and autobiographical memory are often confused. While autobiographical memory involves episodic memory, it also relies on semantic memory. Semantic memory is a more structured record of facts, meanings, knowledge and concepts about the external world that we have acquired. It includes, for example, place names, food types, vocabulary and mathematics. Much is abstract and relational and associated with the meaning of verbal symbols.

Encoding, the process of receiving and registering information, is required for episodic and semantic memories. Attention is a necessary component for effectively encoding events or information and the lower the attention on an event when encoding the memory, for example due to distraction, the lower the threshold is for recollection [(26)].

Semantic memory mainly activates the frontal and temporal cortexes. Episodic memory is concentrated in the hippocampus initially. Once processed in the hippocampus, episodes are consolidated and stored in the neocortex. Memories of different elements of an event are distributed through the brain – i.e., visual, auditory, olfactory – but rather than remain a collection of separate memories, all are connected by the hippocampus to form an episode [(25)].

Consolidation is another step in the process of forming an episodic memory. This is basically embedding the event into long-term memory. This helps the memory to become strengthened, stabilised and stored to facilitate later retrieval. It is ingrained, so it is not lost if the brain suffers an impairment. The neural pathways from the hippocampus to the cortex underlie the process of consolidation and storage. The number of neurons dedicated to a particular memory, as well as their joint firing frequency, help to strengthen the memory traces within the cortex. Episodic memory can be affected by hydrocephalus, metabolic conditions such as vitamin B1 deficiency, trauma, tumours and neurological conditions such as Alzheimer's disease [23] [24].

Retrieval is the last step in forming episodic memories. This is the conscious recollection of information that has been encoded. Retrieving information from episodic memory depends upon contextual information or cues, and whether the information was encoded and stored into memory. Sometimes a recollection from long-term memory is retrieved almost effortlessly, while at other times it may need something to trigger it, such as a word, image or smell [25] [26] [27].

So, we can now see that this process of the formation of episodic memories has many factors that can enhance the creation, storage and retrieval systems, and is therefore activated during the formation of traumatic memories that may be readily recalled. Hence, when working with IEMT, retrieving the memory that has the reciprocal emotion and feeling is of paramount importance.

Research into episodic memory has established that spontaneous eye movements occur to spaces associated with retrieved information even if those spaces are blank at the time of retrieval. Although it has been claimed that such looks to 'nothing' can function as facilitatory retrieval cues, there was no conclusive evidence for such an effect. In a study by Lund University, Sweden, this fundamental issue was addressed using four direct eye manipulations in the retrieval phase of an episodic memory task: (a) free viewing on a blank screen, (b) maintaining central fixation, (c) looking inside a square congruent with the location of the to-be recalled objects, and (d) looking inside a square incongruent with the location of the to-be recalled objects. The results provided novel evidence of an active and facilitatory role of gaze position during memory retrieval, and demonstrate that memory for the spatial relationship between objects is more readily affected than memory for intrinsic object features. Many IEMT Practitioners will have noticed these phenomena during client sessions and we can utilise this to create change [28].

Sleep and Eye Movements

We have seen that when dealing with memories that contain a negative emotional valency, whether classified as a trauma or not, the hippocampus is one of the key areas for episodic memory formation and is also active during rapid eye movement (REM) sleep. Also, those areas of the brain involved in a current dream are strongly active, but they don't appear to be active in communication. The emotions expressed in dreams can have a direct effect on mood the following day. In 1953, sleep was delineated into rapid eye movement sleep and non-rapid eye movement sleep, and studies focusing on the effect of specific sleep stages on memory were conducted (29).

Research has shown that even the pre-born, especially in the third trimester, and those without sight from birth, undergo REM sleep. New research from Tel Aviv University shows that during REM sleep the pattern of signalling in the brain is similar to that when we see or imagine a new image. The researchers found there was a burst in the activity of neurons that occurred just after a person's eyes flickered. This activity reflected a change of concept or scene (not image processing) during sleep. This was the same brain activity that occurred when awake patients were shown pictures, especially those related to memory (30).

The research was conducted with epilepsy sufferers over a period of four years. The subjects had already had electrodes implanted in their brains in a bid to help manage their seizures, and this allowed the team headed by Dr Nir the chance to measure the activity of around 40 individual neurons, mainly within the medial temporal lobe towards the bottom of the brain, while the volunteers slept.

Dr Nir stated that it was difficult to know what the patients were actually dreaming about and how the neuronal activity related to what they were 'seeing', because the team didn't wake them up to ask. *"But we are sure that the brain is alternating between different mental imagery,"* he told *New Scientist*. *"Every time you move your eyes, a new image forms in the mind's eye."* (30).

Dr Rosalind Cartwright has produced some compelling and influential work in sleep research, including that the sleep patterns in those with depression are very different to those without. In people who are clinically depressed, the first REM sleep period begins abnormally early in the night and is often abnormally long - up to double the usual 10 minutes. The eye movements too are abnormal - either abnormally sparse or abnormally dense. In fact, they are sometimes so frequent that they are termed *eye movement storms* (31). Cartwright says:

> "*Even if we often think of sleeping as 'switching off', it's a complex state during which a lot of important things occur in our bodies. In particular, dreams are vital for helping our brains to process emotions and encode new learning.*"

This continual research into memory, eye movements and dream formation will, I hope, continue to reinforce the importance of eye movement, not only in memory formation, but in intrusive memory reduction for those with overwhelming traumatic memories. The Association for IEMT Practitioners would welcome more research and would be delighted to participate in any way that it can.

Neurological Change

Since the publication of *The Brain that Changes Itself* by Norman Doige in 2007, there has been a plethora of new information published in journals, newspapers, magazines, online journals and books on the subject of neuroplasticity (32). Indeed, there hardly seems to be a week that goes by without our understanding of the function of the brain and/or the mind evolving with new research. However, this phenomenon is not a new discovery, and we can go back as far as 1890 for published literature, with the monumental text *The Principles of Psychology* by William James, the American philosopher, psychologist and physician. These writings covered a large number of topics, and some stand out even today as being more useful and applicable than others, particularly the sections on stream of consciousness, emotion, habit, and will (33).

William James was the first person to note that the brain could reorganise, while the first documented person known to use the term neuroplasticity was the Polish neuroscientist Jerzy Konorski, who in 1948 suggested that over time neurons that had coincidental activation due to the vicinity to the firing neuron would create plastic changes in the brain.

Other notable names in this growing field of research include Donald Hebb, a Canadian psychologist who put forth the following idea in the mid-1900s:

> *"When an axon of cell A is near enough to excite cell B and repeatedly or persistently takes part in firing it, some growth process or metabolic change takes place in one or both cells such that A's efficiency, as one of the cells firing B, is increased."* Today, this sentence is commonly summed up as: *"neurons that fire together wire together."* This statement illustrates simply that the brain can form fresh pathways by having new unique patterns of neural cells firing together.

Paul Bach-y-Rita produced work with stroke patients after his father suffered a stroke which resulted in balancing issues due to vestibular damage (the intricate system of the inner ear that controls balance). Bach-y-Rita believed from what he knew about the brain's ability to reorganise through neuroplasticity that his father's healthy brain areas could take over the functioning of the areas damaged by loss of blood flow due to the stroke. He developed exercises for his father that enabled him to make a near-full recovery of the language and physical impairments he had incurred.

Bach-y-Rita also helped to develop a treatment for people with the vestibular damage that causes severe balancing issues, developing a device called a brainport that when connected to the patient's tongue stimulates certain areas of it through vibration. The effects of the treatment happen incredibly quickly. He developed this research for the blind in order to help them to have some vision with the use of a camera [34].

Edward Taub is another very notable scientist who furthered the study of neuroplasticity and developed treatment for patients. He helped to create the most technologically advanced methods for treating people who have had strokes or other neurological disorders causing severe physical impairments or paralysis, and his clinic in Alabama, USA – the Taub Therapy Clinic – treats patients from all over the world [35].

Michael Merzenich is another modern-day neuroscientist who has left his footprint in the field of neuroplasticity. He has done a great deal of research and developed many practical applications for improving people's lives based upon what he has learned about neuro-tuning. Merzenich is the person behind BrainHQ and the author of Soft-Wired: How the New Science of Brain Plasticity Can Change Your Life. For nearly five decades, he has been a leading pioneer in brain plasticity research [36].

When working with IEMT we are aware that many people present with issues that they have been struggling to change, often for many years. There may be beliefs that *"I am stuck"* or *"I can't change this".* Some people can accept such conclusions and get on with life, however increasingly people refuse to accept such conclusions and go to therapists, coaches, counsellors, energy workers, psychologists and even psychiatrists looking for the magic wand that is going to miraculously change how they feel or even their way of life.

The work of Merzenich and others has demonstrated with tangible fMRI evidence that the brain can indeed change, and if the brain can change, so can the mind. The beauty of IEMT is that change can be experienced on several levels, sometimes within a few minutes. This may be not only emotional change, but in some cases physical change, including the effects of anxiety and pain. Sounds too good to be true? I thought so, until I experienced it for myself.

Chapter 3

IEMT and Neurophysiology

Brain or Mind?

Before I get into the process and techniques of IEMT and the Patterns of Chronicity, it is worth spending some time on relevant neurophysiology. As a former biomedical scientist, I have worked post-mortem with many human brains in the discipline of histopathology for pathological examination. Holding a person's brain can engender reflection about human mortality and whether the essence of a person's life really is the organ in your hands.

I like to teach some neurophysiology in client sessions, as I find that the more a person understands about emotions and feelings, how they think, are and how this is relevant to memories, the more they invest in their own transformation. With IEMT, they may well have experienced change almost from the start of a session and thus have experienced real change at a deep neurological level, which in turn, improves its longevity. If you have trained in IEMT with someone who did not teach any neurophysiology on the course, I hope this chapter will give you a better understanding of why we work in the way that we do.

There have been some interesting articles by neuroscientists and psychologists of late discussing whether the brain and the mind are the same or separate. Some believe in an identity theory of the brain and mind, where the feelings experienced in the mind and the electrical chemical activities of the brain are aspects of the same theory, though the process is not yet fully known. The theory is fascinating, though for our purposes we don't need to get into a deep philosophical exploration. If you want to explore this in more depth, there is a very interesting collection of video talks available from eminent neuroscientists, psychologists and philosophers on a website called *Closer to the Truth* [1]. Suffice to say, the jury is still out on whether the mind is just a function of the brain, but it would seem the most likely conclusion.

Interestingly however, the neuroscientist Christof Koch theorises that because experiences are so radically different - e.g., his experience of the colour blue is not the same as the brain state that gives rise to blue, or the conscious sensation of the pain of a toothache is not the same as some neurons firing on the brain - can this give rise to conscious sensation, i.e., the experience? He postulates that experience is in scientific terms 'fundamental' in nature, i.e., irreducible, as is matter and energy, space and time. This is quite radical thinking for a scientist. He cites the Integrated Information Theory (IIT) initially developed by the psychiatrist and neuroscientist Giulio Tononi, in which a mathematical model is intended to describe and quantify the nature of consciousness. This is based on the idea that the unconsciousness of a system may be measured by the amount of integrated information, denoted by the Greek letter Phi (Φ), which it generates.

When it comes to the work most people using IEMT will encounter, the machinations of the mind and experiences are usually behind people seeking our assistance. There is no need to educate people in how the brain creates memories and experiences, though in many years of working with people who want to create change, the consensus is that having a better understanding really can help to improve change and maintain it. This practice is followed in several fields including hypnobirthing.

For as education is empowerment, so awareness of how the mind and body work to create emotional and physical sensations, responses and beliefs, has a profound effect on the investment of time and thought for those wanting to achieve calm, relaxed and in some cases pain-free birthing. If people can do this, they are capable of many other changes.

A very interesting interview with neuroscientist Professor Murali Doraiswamy conducted by former neuroscientist Robert Lawrence Kuhn, saw the two agreeing on the subject of self-healing. What was thought of as alternative or peripheral medicine is now central to, and probably more important than, any pill exemplified when Murali says: *"If yoga were available as a medicine, it would probably be the world's best-selling drug"* (1).

So, the brain that changes itself can also be the brain that heals itself (a frightening concept to large financial corporations, no doubt!). And with IEMT we have seen that the brain can change itself and, indeed, heal emotional issues rapidly.

The Brain and IEMT

Let me be frank; at the time of writing this book no fMRI studies on the use of IEMT and brain function have been performed. However, if anyone reading this would like to fund some research, the Association would be extremely welcoming. As with any modality that professes to create change within the brain and mind, acceptance and uptake increases when there is scientific evidence published in a peer-reviewed journal.

What we do have access to is a vast range of work on eye movements, whether this be for more physiological studies or for those including an emotional element. There has been work using EMDR, for example. IEMT and EMDR do differ, and I have briefly outlined those differences in Chapter 2.

With IEMT we are more interested in specific calibrated axial deviations as opposed to simply moving the eyes in fixed angled straight lines. We also use non-linear movements which is explained later in the Identity Model work. Taking what we do know about how eye movements are instrumental in accessing thoughts and experiences, I explore below the parts of the brain that are most likely to be significantly involved with IEMT.

The Limbic System (history)

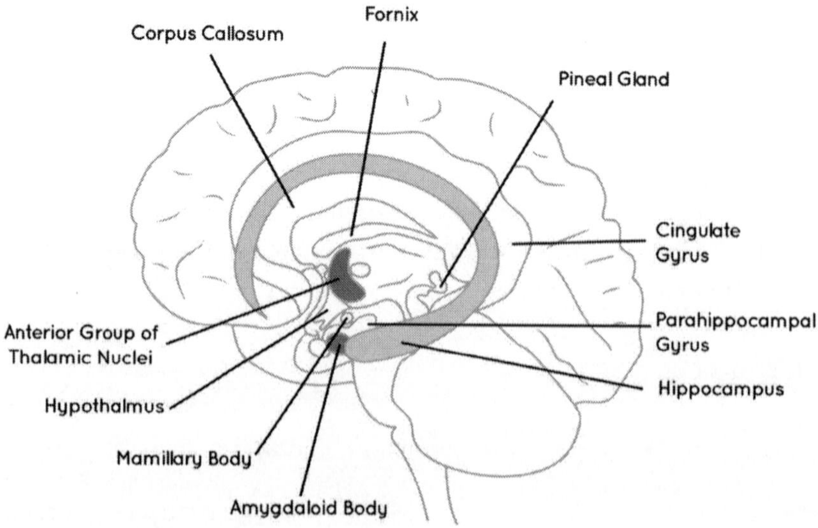

This is often referred to as the mid-brain or paleomammalian brain. Evidence for the existence of controlling centres of the emotions is thought to have begun with Aristotle (384 BC-322 BC) in Ancient Greece. He stated that the centre of intelligence and emotions was the heart, and that memory would generate learning based on emotions and feelings [(2)]. Galen (130 AD-200 AD), however, disagreed with Aristotle and developed theories on the somatic senses, having described the anatomy of the cranial nerves and the autonomic nervous system. Contrary to Aristotle, he believed that the brain, not the heart, was the centre of intelligence and that the 'animal spirits', although originating in the heart, were sent to the cerebral ventricles via the circulatory system [(3)].

Leonardo Da Vinci (1452-1519) contributed significantly to the development of neuroscience, particularly in neuroanatomy and neurophysiology. He directed his research regarding the development of human emotional processes towards a biological explanation of the brain processes responsible for visual perception as well as other sensorial modalities, trying to integrate these senses with an understanding of the mind [4]. Leonardo correlated cerebral structures to superior cerebral functions, and thus he can be considered the forerunner of the theory, developed centuries later by Franz J. Gall, called phrenology [2].

Fast-forward to the 19th Century, when important discoveries occurred and medical knowledge gained new impetus. The invention of the microscope and the development of histological staining (I had to get that in somewhere - once a histologist...!) enabled the identification of the neuron as the anatomical and functional unit of the nervous system by Ramón y Cajal. The discipline of neurology flourished as an independent field of research of the complex functions and dysfunctions of the nervous system [2].

Paul Broca established the Société d'Anthropologie (Society of Anthropology) to advance knowledge of the limbic system - 'le grand lobe limbique' or the great limbic lobe - and applied the term 'limbic' (from the Latin 'limbus', for border) as he named it, where debates about the origin of the family, human race, human intelligence, and the organisation of the human brain took place. He also studied eight cases of left frontal injuries and subsequently developed the concept of cerebral dominance. In addition, he coined the term great limbic lobe, which was later named 'Broca's great limbic lobe' [5].

IEMT Practitioners who use the Physiological State Accessing Cues techniques (surely that's all of you...) may find the following of interest. Charles Darwin's book The Expression of the Emotions in Man and Animals, became the precursor, together with the work of pioneering American psychologist William James 12 years later, of a research field currently called affective neuroscience. Darwin proposed that emotions in animals would be similar to human emotions (a logical extension of his work on the evolution of the species) and that humans expressed vestigial patterns of mammalian emotional behaviour by exposing the front teeth when expressing sadness through anger or crying. Darwin also stated that there is a set of basic, or fundamental emotions that are present throughout distinct species which are independent of cultural or societal norms. These emotions include anger, fear, surprise and sadness. This work was expanded on many years later by Paul Eckman [6].

In 1884, James' article entitled *What is an Emotion?,* began the quest for a reasonable explanation for the emotional processes. He proposed the innovative theory that various human emotions occurred in response to afferent feedback loops from sensory receptors in the skin, muscles, cartilage and other organs. This produced physical changes that were subsequently encoded into the cerebral cortex memory storage to determine the subjective quality of the stimuli being experienced as temperature change, pain, vibration and so on. James understood that different emotions were encoded by different corporal memory processes.

The Danish physician and psychologist Carl Lange had similar ideas and in 1885 the 'James-Lange Theory of Emotion' was formulated. The James-Lange theory states that the autonomic nervous system generates physiological events as a response to human experiential interaction with the world. This theory postulates that emotions are feelings that occur as a consequence of - rather than being the cause of - physiological changes.

In the 1920s, Walter Cannon contradicted the prevailing peripheral emotional theory of James. He also proposed a new emotional theory based on laboratory investigations by Phillip Bard. Experiments on the caudal half of the hypothalamus and the posteroventral thalamus revealed to both Cannon and Bard that those structures were essential for the emotional brain. This theory was later called the 'Cannon-Bard Theory of Emotion'. These theories, which contradicted the James-Lange hypothesis, were corroborated by the Swiss physiologist Walter Rudolf Hess at this time [7].

The first evidence was obtained by Heinrich Klüver and Paul Bucy in Chicago, 1939, that the limbic system was responsible for the cortical representation of emotions.

They demonstrated that the bilateral removal of the temporal lobes in monkeys - including the amygdala and the hippocampal formation, as well as the non-limbic temporal cortex - produced an extreme behavioural syndrome [2]. After temporal lobectomy, formerly aggressive monkeys exhibited reduced emotional threshold and became docile. They displayed a tendency towards oral compulsion, attempting to ingest inedible objects.

Ablated monkeys also demonstrated hypersexualised behaviour among the same and different species. These animals also demonstrated visual agnosia and were therefore unable to recognise hitherto familiar objects. At that time, this syndrome was designated by its proponents as the temporal lobe syndrome. Today, it is referred to as the Klüver-Bucy syndrome, resulting from bilateral lesions of the medial temporal lobe, including amygdaloid nucleus [8].

The limbic system's putative role in emotion was elaborated by the American physician James Papez in 1937, in a seminal paper entitled *A Proposed Mechanism of Emotion*. This anatomical model is known as the Papez Circuit [9]. The concept of the limbic system was later redefined and expanded by the American physician and neuroscientist Paul MacLean, who reintroduced the term limbic, at first as a descriptor of a complex system related to emotional functioning. In 1952, he coined the term 'limbic system' to describe Broca's limbic lobe and related subcortical nuclei as the collective neural substrate for emotion.

MacLean was also instrumental in proposing and defining the triune concept of the brain. His evolutionary Triune Brain Theory proposed that the human brain was in reality three brains in one: The R-complex (reptilian complex), the limbic system, and the neocortex [10]. The concept of the limbic system has since been further expanded and developed by Nauta, Heimer and others. Indeed, Walle Nauta was the first to describe the ganglions of the habenulas within the mesencephalon as the integrating part of the system responsible for the emotions [11].

The Thalamus

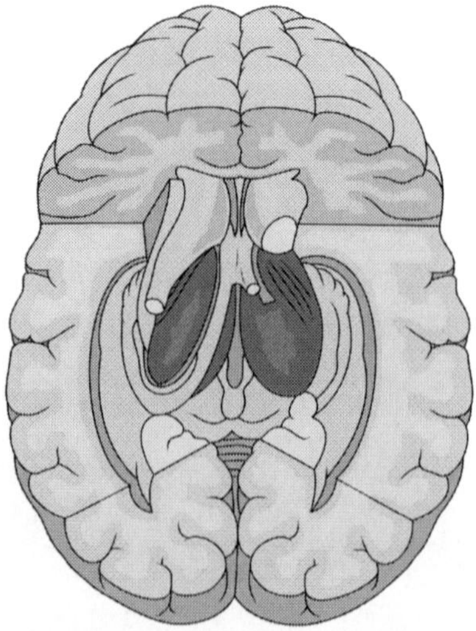

This image is not anatomically correct, but it is a good representation of the thalamus from a frontal perspective. This is a dual-lobed mass of grey matter (mainly nerve cell bodies and branching dendrites) deep in the cerebral cortex. It forms part of the limbic system and connects areas of the cerebral cortex involved in sensory perception and movement with other parts of the brain and spinal cord involved with these functions [(12)].

The thalamus is the largest component of the diencephalon; an area of the forebrain very deep inside the brain surrounded by the cerebral hemispheres surrounding the third ventricle. It is the primary site of relay for all the sensory pathways except olfaction on their journey to the cerebral cortex. Even olfactory signals reach the thalamus via indirect connections with the cortical regions initially receiving the olfactory signal [(13)].

The thalamus is a modulation site for sensory inputs and a relay site for cerebellar and basal ganglia inputs to the cerebral cortex. These are feedback pathways, since the cerebellum and basal ganglia respond to outputs from the cerebral cortex. Limbic pathways also make input to the dorsal thalamus. As a regulator of sensory information, the thalamus also controls sleep and awake states of consciousness. Made up from a number of discrete nuclei, the thalamus is more than a simple relay station, as it receives extensive connections from the cortex and brain stem structures and is critically involved in levels of arousal. The main nuclei are:

- *Anterior* - associated with the limbic system and prefrontal cortex.
- *Pulvinar* - associated with the posterior cortex.
- *Ventroanterior* and *ventrolateral* - associated with motor systems.
- *Ventroposterior* - associated with somatosensory systems.
- *Medial geniculate* - associated with auditory pathways.
- *Lateral geniculate* - associated with the visual system.
- *Intralaminar* - associated with pain pathways and basal ganglia.
- *Reticular* - associated with levels of arousal and some forms of epilepsy. [14]

The thalamus is pivotal to sensory experience and some motor functions. Tanaka and Kunimatsu (2013) describe thalamic roles in eye movements, asserting that serving as the gateway to the cerebral cortex all subcortical signals that ascend to the cortex are relayed by neurons in the thalamus. Different nuclei in the central thalamus receive inputs from the brainstem and send outputs to the eye movement-related areas in the cortex. Neurons in the central thalamus exhibit a variety of eye movement-related activities. Analyses of neural activity and eye movements in subjects with natural or experimentally induced thalamic lesions suggest that signals in the central thalamus are essential for the online monitoring of self-motions and in generating volitional saccades. In addition, the pathways through the central and the posterior thalamus appear to play a role in visuospatial attention that directly guides eye movements [15].

Hypothalamus

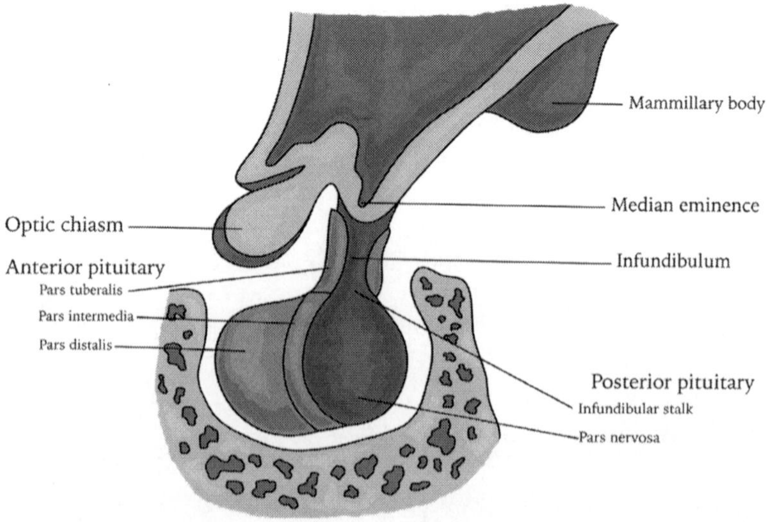

Residing either side of the third ventricle and weighing about 4 grams, the hypothalamus is a very small but extremely important part of the diencephalon involved in the mediation of endocrine, autonomic and behavioural functions. It receives significant input form the limbic system as well as the retina. The hypothalamus controls the release of eight major hormones by the hypophysis and is involved in temperature regulation, control of food and water intake, sexual behaviour and reproduction, control of daily cycles such as circadian rhythms in physiological state and behaviour, and mediation of emotional responses. It has a large number of neurons sensitive to hormonal levels, electrolytes and temperature changes and thus its involvement in homeostasis is essential for survival [14] [16].

It has an afferent output to the autonomic nervous system (ANS), along with a critical role in the control of pituitary function. While having an important role in the functioning of the ANS, its role in homeostasis is much greater, plus it has the ability to form retrograde memories in conjunction with the limbic system. The hypothalamus also helps to translate the response of emotional stimuli into endocrinological and autonomic responses.

In the supraoptic region of the hypothalamus there are two nuclei containing cells that secrete vasopressin (ADH, antidiuretic hormone), oxytocin, and CRH (corticotropin-releasing hormone). ADH and oxytocin, a nine-amino-acid peptide that is synthesised in the paraventricular and supraoptic nucleus of the hypothalamus, are transported down the axons from cells in the supraoptic and paraventricular nuclei through the infundibulum to the neurohypophysis (posterior pituitary), where they are released into the bloodstream.

Damage to the anterior hypothalamus blocks the production of ADH, resulting in diabetes insipidus. Oxytocin is incredibly important in socialising and is also known as 'the love hormone'. The structurally similar peptide arginine vasopressin (AVP) plays a key role in regulating affiliative behaviours, including sexual behaviour, mother-infant and adult-adult pair bond formation, and social memory/recognition. Oxytocin has been implicated in repetitive behaviours and stress reactivity. Given it is involved in the regulation of repetitive and affiliative behaviours and that these are key features of autism, it is believed that oxytocin may play a role in autism and that it may be an effective treatment for these two core symptom domains. It has been hypothesised there is a correlation between lower oxytocin production and the autism spectrum [17]. However, few studies have definitively linked autism to problems in oxytocin signalling. A study of 200 children on the spectrum failed to show a statistically significant difference in oxytocin production.

Sue Carter, a neuroscientist at Indiana University in Bloomington, USA, also advises caution in the use of self-administered oxytocin. Carter's group found that a single low dose of the hormone given to baby prairie voles improved their pair bonding as adults, but that higher doses interfered with that behaviour - possibly because oxytocin started to activate other receptors. And human studies have suggested that in certain contexts a puff of oxytocin can cause people to be more aggressive in defending themselves against outsiders or competitors. A single dose of oxytocin in patients with the psychiatric condition borderline personality disorder has been found to hinder trust and cooperation [18].

Neural connections: The most noteworthy (and complex) feature of the neural connections of the hypothalamus is that, except for a few exceptions, they are extensively bi-directional (afferent and efferent). The hypothalamus has a role within the limbic system in memory.

Limbic circuits: These pathways are essential for the normal expression and control of emotions, learning and reproductive behaviour. The bi-directional pathways include the medial forebrain bundle, the fornix, the stria terminalis and the ventral amygdalofugal pathway. The medial forebrain bundle interconnects basal forebrain structures and the fornix interconnects the hippocampal formation to the septal, pre-optic and medial mammillary nuclei.

In addition to these bi-directional pathways, there are also two unidirectional efferent limbic pathways from the hypothalamus. The mammillothalamic tract projects from the mammillary nuclei to the anterior nucleus of the thalamus. The anterior nucleus of the thalamus in turn projects to the cingulate cortex, which completes the Circuit of Papez by projecting back onto the subiculum of the hippocampus. The Circuit of Papez was the first circuit proposed to mediate emotions and still is considered one of the chief circuits of the limbic system. The mammillotegmental tract projects from the mammillary nuclei to the brainstem tegmentum and as far caudal as the lateral grey of the spinal cord.

The hypothalamus has a role within the limbic system in memory. Damage to the mammillary bodies which receive significant input from the hippocampal complex, for example that which is caused by chronic alcoholism with thiamine deficiency, produces profound amnesia or Korsakoff's syndrome (KS) of both anterograde (inability to form new memories) and retrograde (inability to recover old memories) forms. The latter distinguishes these patients from those with hippocampal damage and may explain the tendency of those with KS to confabulate information.

The hypothalamus may also have a role in sexual emotional behaviour independent of endocrinological influence [(19)].

The Papez Circuit

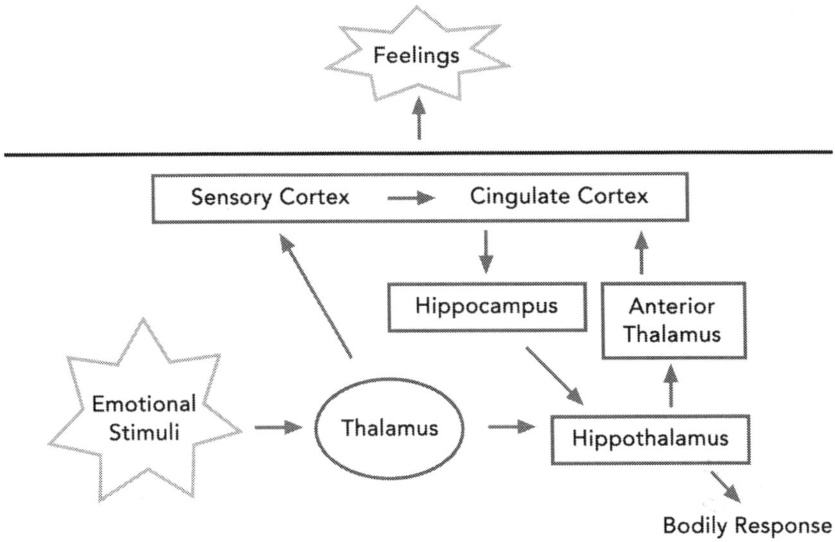

Cingulate Gyrus

The five-layered cingulate gyrus is situated in the medial aspect of the cerebral cortex and sits atop the corpus callosum. It can be broadly divided into two segments: the anterior cingulate, which is concerned with vocalising and emotional and motor functioning involving the hands and regulating autonomic and endocrine activities; and the posterior cingulate, which is involved in visual-spatial and tactile analysis as well as motor output and memory [20].

The posterior cingulate gyrus (PCG) is richly interconnected with the superior parietal lobe, the parahippocampal (inferior) temporal and superior temporal lobe, frontal lobe, caudate, putamen, substantia nigra, pulvinar of the thalamus, and dorsal hypothalamus. It may also be involved in visual-spatial and memory-cognitive activities particularly relating to the body and movement, hence the interconnections with the superior parietal lobe and the parahippocampal gyrus.

Functions of the PCG include: Episodic memory; speech comprehension and production (due to declarative memory functions during communication); strong interactions with the medial temporal cortex; Theory of Mind; pain; disgust; recognition of familiar objects and places; orientation in space; processing of information and objects relevant to self; introspection.

Disorders of the PCG: Early Alzheimer's disease; anxiety disorders; alexithymia; schizophrenia; anorexia nervosa; addiction (cocaine); autism.

The anterior cingulate is associated with processing and modulating the expression of emotional nuances, emotional learning and vocalisation, the formation of long-term attachments and maternal behaviour including the initiation of motivationally significant goal-directed behaviour, as well as influencing and in part regulating endocrine and autonomic activities. Among its many functions, the anterior cingulate is associated with processing and modulating the vocal expression of emotional, melodic, and prosodic nuances, emotional learning, identifying the affective attributes of noxious psychic stimuli, maternal behaviour, separation anxiety, and the formation of long-term attachments. As based on functional imaging, the anterior cingulate also becomes activated by hot, painful, and noxious stimuli and, as noted, has been considered by some to be the seat of pain and misery [(21)].

Functions of the anterior cingulate include: Error detection; error prediction; risk prediction; cognitive control; emotion regulation; conflict monitoring; minimisation of distractions; behavioural decision-making toward cognitively efficient tasks and strategies; information transfer to the auditory association cortices; brain stem vocalisation; autonomic structures in pathways that may mediate emotional communication and autonomic activation in emotional arousal; problem solving; fear (rostral anterior cingulate cortex/rACC, gating the efficiency of amygdala-dependent auditory fear conditioning learning); pain; dwelling on one's own thoughts and notions (inner life); motivation; important part of the reward system: anticipation of rewards; craving (nicotine); empathy (with pain).

Disorders of the anterior cingulate: Borderline personality disorder; ADHD; autism; depression; anorexia nervosa; bipolar disorder; addiction (cocaine, rostral); addiction (nicotine, dopamine) [22].

Abnormalities of the anterior cingulate cortex have been implicated in a number of psychiatric disorders including schizophrenia, obsessive-compulsive disorder, depression and post-traumatic stress disorder. However, it is still unclear how these abnormalities relate to the diversity of cognitive, emotional and behavioural disturbances seen in these disorders [23].

Hippocampus

Named, because of its shape, from the Greek words hippo for horse and kampos for sea or seahorse, the hippocampus' structure is divided into two halves which lie in the left and right sides of the brain in the medial temporal lobe underneath the cortical surface. The earliest description of the ridge running along the floor of the temporal horn of the lateral ventricle comes from the Venetian anatomist Julius Caesar Aranzi in 1587 [24]. The hippocampus is also called cornu ammonis. Ammon was an Egyptian god near whose temple ammonia, or the salt of Ammon, was prepared. The hippocampus is also called Ammon's Horn because the two hippocampi bend around in the form of the horns of a ram.

In terms of anatomy, the hippocampus is an elaboration of the edge of the cerebral cortex. The structures that line the edge of the cortex make up the so-called limbic system (Latin, limbus = border). In terms of anatomy, the hippocampus is an elaboration of the edge of the cerebral cortex [25].

The structures that line the edge of the cortex make up the so-called limbic system. These include the hippocampus, cingulate cortex, olfactory cortex, and amygdala. Paul MacLean once suggested, as part of his Triune Brain Theory, that the limbic structures comprise the neural basis of emotion. Some neuroscientists no longer believe that the concept of a unified 'limbic system' is valid, however. Yet the hippocampus is anatomically connected to parts of the brain that are involved with emotional behaviour - the septum, the hypothalamic mammillary body, and the anterior nuclear complex in the thalamus - therefore its role as a limbic structure cannot be completely dismissed.

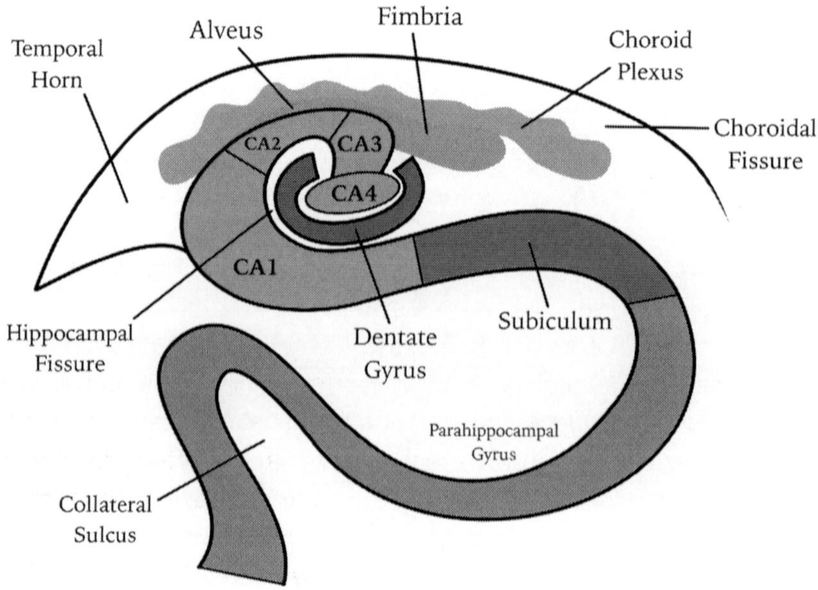

The hippocampus is found deep in the temporal lobe and straddles both the left and right hemispheres of the brain. It is a curved tube and is divided into the *Cornu Ammonis (CA)*, with the subdivisions CA1 to CA4. The main cells are pyramidal: *Dentate Gyrus (DG)* (tooth-shaped) formed of granule cells with tiny cell bodies; *Subiculum (S)*, continuous with the CA also composed of pyramidal neurons; *Entorhinal Cortex (EC)*, adjacent to the hippocampus.

Functions: The function of the hippocampus is defined by the connections within and between the different areas. All input enters through the EC. The axons from the EC project mostly to cells in the DG but also to CA3 and CA1.

This fibre track is known as the perforant pathway as it perforates the subiculum. The hippocampus is involved in memory formation, specifically long-term memory by encoding, retention and retrieval of spatial and episodic experiences. It is also involved in episodic and autobiographic memory, but not procedural and only in part semantic. It has a role in learning; recognition; encoding and retrieval of relational information in visual short-term memory; spatial (CA3 subregion) and contextual learning and memory; continuous encoding of ongoing experience; categorisation; pattern separation and pattern completion; behavioural regulation and inhibition (e.g., of food intake for body weight regulation); speech comprehension through mnemonic encoding of narrative information.

In an interesting paper by Moscovitch et al (2005) J Anat concluded that:

> *"The evidence reviewed suggests strongly that the function of the hippocampus (and possibly that of related limbic structures) is to help encode, retain, and retrieve experiences, no matter how long ago the events comprising the experience occurred, and no matter whether the memories are episodic or spatial. We conclude that the evidence favours a multiple trace theory (MTT) of memory over two other models: (1) traditional consolidation models which posit that the hippocampus is a time-limited memory structure for all forms of memory; and (2) versions of cognitive map theory which posit that the hippocampus is needed for representing all forms of allocentric space in memory"* [26].

It has also been concluded that early memory must show properties associated with full function of the trisynaptic circuit to reflect 'adult-like' memory function, i.e., [1] rapid encoding of contextual details of overlapping patterns, and [2] retention of these details over sleep-dependent delays. Much scientific evidence suggests that these functions are not apparent until 18-24 months of age in humans.

Hippocampal Indexing Theory and Episodic Memory

The role of the hippocampus in memory function has been characterised in a variety of ways, one common thread being that it binds together the sensory features of a situation or 'episode' to create a unitary experience. There is still no absolute theory of episodic memory, but in 1986 Teyler and DiScenna published their theory of memory indexing [27].

The indexing theory of the hippocampus gave a set of principles demonstrating how the intrinsic organisation of the hippocampus, its anatomical relationships to other brain regions, and its synaptic physiology could offer support for the acquisition, storage and retrieval of episodic memories.

This was updated in 2007. The essence of their idea was that the hippocampus was functionally designed and anatomically situated to capture information about neocortical activity generated by the individual features of a behavioural episode. Moreover, because the hippocampus projects back to these neocortical regions, the information it stored could serve as an index to the pattern of neocortical activity produced by the episode. Consequently, a partial cue that activated the index could activate the neocortical patterns and thus retrieve the memory of the episode. The conclusion in the latter paper is that this theory is still very accurate. Its core ideas can be seen in many contemporary theories and there is a wealth of data that support this conceptual framework [28].

Updating Theories on Memory

Since the neuroplasticity theory revolution, much interest in the neuroscience and psychology communities has focused on memory formation, storage and retrieval, and altered memory from damage through disease or trauma. This book can only offer a snapshot of current theories and will not endeavour to take the reader into an in-depth study of neuroscience. However, those of us working in the field of memory change therapeutics may find some of the more recent theories interesting. I suggest that you join organisations such as Research Gate and subscribe to *Scientific American*, *New Scientist* and *Nature* if you wish to read regularly updated information.

An interesting article in *New Scientist* entitled *Where old Memories Go* said there remain many divisions among neuroscientists. Some of the best information about how the brain processes memories has come from patients who can't remember. If damage to a particular brain area results in such memory loss, researchers can be confident that the region is important for making or recalling memories, as seen in patient HM (Henry Molaison), after the surgical removal of a large part the medial temporal lobe including the hippocampus. He could recall some very old memories, but could no longer make new memories or remember the years leading up to his surgery [29].

Some researchers have seen patients with hippocampal damage who have memory deficits extending back through most of their lives. An alternative theory accounts for these discrepancies by proposing that the hippocampus selectively stores one type of memory – 'episodic' – while the surrounding cortex stores another – 'semantic'. Episodic memories are rich in detail about past experiences, whereas semantic memories are based on impersonal, factual knowledge. The model proposes that over time memories are copied many times in both the hippocampus and the cortex. All cortical copies generate a new semantic memory, representing only the key facts or gist of an experience without the elaborate episodic details. Interestingly, this theory is backed by patients who exhibit memory problems depending on the type of memory rather than its age. For example, without a hippocampus, such patients couldn't remember the details of the experience of a childhood trip, e.g., to Disneyland (an episodic memory) but remembered the fact that they had visited Disneyland (a semantic memory).

Some of the controversy may be settled by research from Johns Hopkins University with the theory that memories are transformed each time we revisit them. The neurons activated on subsequent recall of the memory are similar but not an identical set, and those activated frequently become part of the memory trace in the cortex. Each reactivation re-encodes the memory and, depending on the cortical neurons engaged, can strengthen, weaken or update particular memory features. This theory breaks the longstanding stalemate by proposing that what we do with a memory, rather than its age or type, determines where it is stored in the brain. While the competing theories debated whether the hippocampus is only needed for recent or episodic memories, the new model suggests that what really matters is how often the memory is revisited [30].

Amygdala

Normally referred to as the amygdala, there are actually two bilateral amygdalas, or amygdalae, and each has partly different functions. These two almond-shaped groups of nuclei are located deep and medially within the temporal lobes of the brain in complex vertebrates including humans. It is a complex structure involved in a wide range of normal behavioural functions and psychiatric conditions.

The existence of the amygdala was first formally recognised in the early 19th Century and not so long ago it was an obscure region of the brain that attracted relatively little scientific interest. Today, it is one of the most heavily studied brain areas. Research shows that the complex performs a primary role in the processing of memory, decision-making, and emotional reactions, which are all considered part of the limbic system [31]. Much debate continues about how the amygdala should be subdivided, and there is controversy as to how these subdivisions relate to other major regions of the brain.

Structure: If the brain is turned upside down, the end of the structure continuous with the hippocampus is called the uncus. Peeling away the uncus will expose the amygdala, which abuts the anterior of the hippocampus. As with the hippocampus, major pathways communicate bidirectionally and contain both efferent and afferent fibres [32].

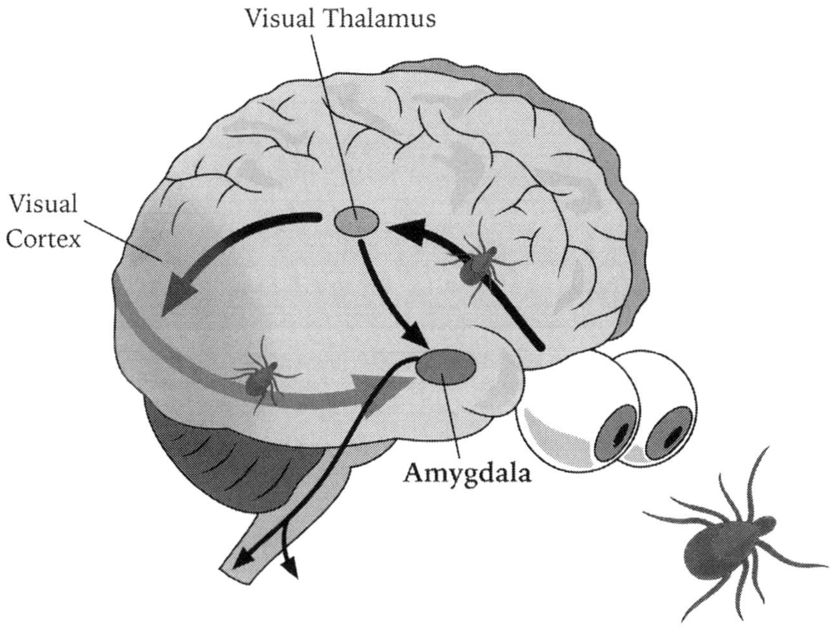

The amygdala nuclei encompass several structures with distinct connectional and functional characteristics in humans and other animals. Among these are the basolateral complex, the cortical nucleus, the medial nucleus, the central nucleus, and the intercalated cell clusters (ITCs). The basolateral complex can be further subdivided into the lateral, the basal, and the accessory basal nuclei.

The intercalated (ITC) cells of the amygdala are a group of GABAergic (γ-aminobutyric acid) neurons situated between the basolateral and central nuclei of the amygdala that are important for inhibitory control over the amygdala. ITC cells are thought to play a role as the off-switch for the amygdala, inhibiting the its central nucleus output neurons and its basolateral nucleus neurons. Some researchers speculate that ITC cells, via their extensive local inhibition within the amygdala, could serve as a substrate for expression and storage of extinction memory. Extinction memory is a process in which a conditioned response gradually diminishes over time as an animal learns to uncouple a response from a stimulus. With contextual fear, extinction occurs when a mouse for example is placed into the context of the environment without the shock, after training [33] [34].

Cell groups within it appear to be differentiated parts of the traditional cortex, the claustrum, or the striatum, and these parts belong to four obvious functional systems; accessory olfactory, main olfactory, autonomic and frontotemporal cortical.

Projections are sent from the amygdala to the hypothalamus, dorsomedial thalamus, thalamic reticular nerves, trigeminal nerve nuclei and facial nerve, ventral tegmental area, the locus coeruleus, and the laterodorsal tegmental nucleus. The medial nucleus receives input from the olfactory bulb and olfactory cortex and is involved in the sense of smell and pheromone-processing.

There are functional differences between the right and left amygdala. In one study, electrical stimulations of the right amygdala induced negative emotions, especially fear and sadness. In contrast, stimulation of the left amygdala was able to induce either pleasant (happiness) or unpleasant (fear, anxiety, sadness) emotions. Other evidence suggests that the left amygdala plays a role in the brain's reward system. The right and left portions of the amygdala have independent memory systems, but work together to store, encode, and interpret emotion [35].

As above, the right hemisphere is associated with negative emotion. It is involved in the expression of fear and in the processing of fear-inducing stimuli. Fear conditioning, when a neutral stimulus acquires aversive properties, occurs within the right hemisphere.

Presented with a conditioned aversive stimulus, a person processes this within the right amygdala, producing an unpleasant or fearful response. This emotional response conditions the individual to avoid fear-inducing stimuli.

The right hemisphere is also linked to declarative memory, consisting of facts and information from previously experienced events, and must be consciously recalled. It also plays a significant role in the retention of episodic memory, which does not require conscious recall. The right amygdala plays a role in the association of time and places with emotional properties [36].

Development and gender distinction: The amygdala is thought to be the most sexually dimorphic structure of the brain in humans. One major difference between the sexes is the size of the amygdala. The male amygdala is significantly larger than the female amygdala in the adult human brain, even when total brain size is taken into account. Neuroimaging studies have found that amygdala develops structurally at different rates in human males and females and contains fairly high concentrations of sex hormone receptors.

Considerable growth occurs earlier in females and makes the female amygdala develop more rapidly, ceasing its development approximately 1.5 years earlier than in males. Hence, the larger size in men may be due to this longer development. Other neurological and hormonal factors may contribute to the differences in development. Rich in androgen receptors that are required in DNA binding that regulate gene expression, far more testosterone is present in males, which may contribute to its larger mass. The amygdala shrinks by more than 30% in males upon castration.

The left amygdala in both genders develops more rapidly, reaching its peak at about 1.5 to 2 years, and is thought to enable an infant to recognise danger. The right develops over a longer period and is associated with the fear response and facial recognition. During childhood, the amygdala is found to react differently to same-sex versus opposite-sex individuals. This decreases until a person enters adolescence, where it increases dramatically at puberty [37].

Emotions, memory and socialisation: Amygdalae are implicit in the formation and storage of emotion-based memories. During fear conditioning, sensory stimuli reach the amygdalae to form associations with the memory of the stimuli. Damage to the structure can interfere with memory that is strengthened via emotion.

The central nuclei are involved in the generation of many fear responses, such as neuroendocrine responses (stress-hormone release), defensive behaviour (freezing or escape responses), autonomic nervous system responses (changes in blood pressure and heart rate/tachycardia) and similar. Damage to the amygdalae impairs both the acquisition and expression of Pavlovian fear conditioning, a form of classical conditioning of emotional responses [38].

The amygdalae are also involved in appetitive (positive) conditioning and distinct neurons respond to positive and negative stimuli, but there is no clustering of these distinct neurons into clear anatomical nuclei. Research into lesions of different regions of the amygdalae indicate that different nuclei have different functions in appetitive conditioning.

Memory consolidation is the process of stabilising a memory after initial acquisition, while the long-term memory for an event is not initiated immediately. This is a slow process involving long-term potentiation for possible lifelong storage. It has been seen that the amygdala regulates memory consolidation elsewhere in the brain. During consolidation, the greater the emotional arousal of the learning event, the stronger the retention [39].

fMRI studies into loving kindness meditation and compassion meditation as practised by Buddhist monks have shown that the amygdala modulates during such meditation along with the temporoparietal junction and insula, and more intensive insula activity was found in expert meditators than in novices. It is suggested that increased amygdala activity following such meditations increased feelings of social connection and positivity toward novice individuals on both explicit and implicit levels, and may help to increase positive social emotions and decrease social isolation [40].

The amygdala is thought to contribute towards the level of a person's emotional intelligence. It has been hypothesised that larger amygdalae allow for greater emotional intelligence, enabling greater societal integration and cooperation with others. Its volume correlates positively with both the number of contacts a person has and the complexity of social networks. According to some studies in adult humans ranging in age from 19 to 83 years, those with larger amygdalae had larger and more complex social networks [41]. They were also better able to make accurate social judgments about other people's faces. The analysis of social situations show that the amygdala has the ability to identify and process changes in facial features, but it does not process the direction of the gaze of the person being perceived. Processing of gaze direction may rely on a predominantly cortical network rather than the amygdala [42].

Neuropathology and neuropsychology involving the amygdalae: The full extent of amygdala involvement in many disorders cannot be covered here. Some of the more well-known and those that the IEMT Practitioner may encounter are noted, however. As we know, the amygdalae are involved with certain types of emotional response and behaviours, and amygdalae are highly sexually dimorphic.

Damage and changes in neuroplasticity via trauma or disease in the amygdalae can contribute to changes in emotional states and behaviours. One such disease, Klüver-Bucy syndrome, is discussed earlier in this chapter. The urban myth about the man who made love to a pavement in New York is not as unusual as one may believe. In 2007 in Ayr, south west Scotland, a man was arrested and put on the Sex Offenders Register for such an act, as was a man in Redditch, England in 1993. There are also stories of men having sex with lamp posts, UK 2008, and with bicycles - and not just as a result of a stag night [43]. I am making an educated guess that if they had been investigated further, these men would likely have had amygdala-related tumours or diseases.

Klüver-Bucy syndrome was described in the 1950s as a group of neuropsychological symptoms such as changes in behaviour and emotions; hypersexuality of all kinds; hyperorality (a compulsion to examine objects by mouth); hyperphagia characterised by eating inappropriate objects and/or overeating; visual agnosia or an inability to recognise familiar objects or people; hypermetamorphosis, which can develop in human beings after bilateral damage or dysfunction of the medial part of temporal lobes.

It has been established that the key role in the genesis of the above symptoms is fulfilled by changes in neurotransmission resulting from destruction of the amygdala and its connections with other structures of the limbic system. When the excretory fibres extending from the temporal lobe to the amygdale are disrupted, the level of dopamine and serotonin drops, while the level of norepinephrine increases in the amygdala.

The most common cause of bilateral damage of the amygdalae and in consequence of Klüver-Bucy syndrome is herpetic encephalitis, frontotemporal dementia, late-stage Alzheimer's disease, paraneoplastic limbic encephalitis, bilateral temporal lobe stroke, as well as disturbances associated with epileptic seizures [(44)].

The vast improvement in brain imaging in recent times with fMRI has improved the success of studies involving the amygdalae and other areas of the brain. A small study by Blumberg et al in 2003 into the pathophysiology of bipolar disorder demonstrated statistically significant decreased volumes of medial temporal lobe structures, with greater effects on size in the amygdala than in the hippocampus. It stated that the abnormalities are likely manifested early in the course of illness, as they affected adolescent and adult subjects similarly in the sample [(45)]. There has been significant research into anxiety disorders and the involvement of the amygdalae.

Impacts of Dementia on Emotions & Memory

The following anecdote is from Andrew Austin during the time he was nursing and before he began investigating eye movement work with regard to memory and emotion. It demonstrates the huge impact on individuals when memory degenerates, and when emotional memory remains but the episodic information of a situation is lost.

The lady who cried herself to death

> *"I was working an agency shift in a nursing home. It was an excellent care environment where the staff worked hard to*

maintain the dignity and good humour of their residents, most of whom had a range of cognitive impairment.

"We heard screaming coming from upstairs and I and two other nurses raced to the scene to find two elderly patients rolling on the floor fighting. One appeared to be trying to stab the other with a toothbrush, while the other was flailing with a stiff hairbrush. We separated the two and proceeded to try to repair the physical damage. The paper-like skin of the elderly meant that the superficial wounds were numerous and required quite some time to repair and bandage up.

"The physical damage was easy to fix, but the mental damage was a different matter. One of the two had a generalised dementia; she could be reasonably described as 'happily confused' - a common nursing term when defining the form of dementia for the purposes of patient management. This resident quickly settled back into her normal happy self as though nothing untoward had happened.

"The other lady was less fortunate. With an aggressive Alzheimer's disease, she had lost much of her hippocampal regions. The rest of her brain, including that of her amygdalae, was still working well, and this proved to be catastrophic. Without the ability to encode a visual representation of the recent events in order to contextualise how she felt, her amygdalae continued to fire off a mixture of anger, despair and distress. She cried and cried, but of course she did not know or understand what she was crying about.

"An hour passed and no matter what we tried to do to console her, her distress continued unabated. As the second hour passed without sign of change the situation was passed to the doctors for management and sedation was given, but without benefit. Within three days, where this poor soul did not find relief from her tears and distress, she died."

This sad story highlights the issues that can arise when the connections between memory and emotion deteriorate via dementia and other neurological conditions. Losing the ability to understand why a sudden feeling arises can be very disconcerting as normally our emotional memory will provide a quick flash or an event memory. Emotional memory may not evoke as intense a feeling as felt at the time of the event response such as happiness, joy or even pain can still be experienced.

Emotional memory uses the hippocampus and amygdala to cue the memory as opposed to event memory that uses the hippocampus and sensory cues [(46)]. Also something that can be extremely disconcerting for the person is when they lose the ability to locate certain words or a certain memory of an event that they know they have lived. The feeling of fear and panic can manifest as a result and this can feel as though a person is going mad.

Having experienced the menopause myself, the sudden drop in oestrogen/oestradiol can have a huge impact on the hippocampus hence the tendency for women to experience dementia disorders earlier than men. I can say with experience how very frightening this loss of memory can feel, even if it is only transient. The ability of oestradiol to improve cognition declines with advanced age along with decreased expression of oestrogen receptors. Hopefully future research will be able to determine the mechanisms that regulate oestrogen receptor expression during menopause and ageing to help create better ways of managing what can be a sudden onset of memory dysfunction [(47)]. In the meantime, thank goodness for HRT!

Chapter 4

The Foundations of IEMT

Patterns of Chronicity

People often seek the help of therapists because of how a certain issue or situation is making them feel. For many, the outcome of a session will be to leave feeling differently or better about the issue or situation. This is not an unrealistic expectation and there are many modalities available that can assist with ameliorating feelings either in the short or long-term.

Practitioners involved in the field of change work can often be lulled into thinking that when a person feels differently the work is complete. This may not be the case however, and for some the change will be transitory, possibly due to conscious or unconscious sabotage. Many describe IEMT as *Creating Change in the Blink of an Eye*. Anyone reading this book who is already a practitioner or a recipient of IEMT will know that long-lasting change can indeed take only a few minutes in some cases. Trainee practitioners from a more conventional counselling, psychology or psychiatry background can find this concept extremely difficult to accept. Some can feel as though we are taking their many years of study and somehow negating it, as if we are saying forget everything you have learned thus far and have trust in this process.

Well, that is pretty much what we *are* saying, but only when using IEMT, not for the overall care of clients. Don't over-think, over-theorise or try to fit this into your model of the world by attempting to reshape it into something you find more palatable. On our training courses, the people who are more likely to exhibit something called a Three Stage Abreaction (thankfully this is rare...) are often the trainers of various other modalities - clinical psychologists or people who have appeared in the media as an expert in their field. Often, their own ego is put before the learning.

To reiterate: *"IEMT is not the grand unified theory of therapy and change work and is still a developing model, but has proven to be a very useful adjunctive for trained therapists and in the right hands can provide an excellent remedial tool for emotional change and a generative tool for identity change. Practitioners are reporting that IEMT enables excellent results where previously a good outcome might have appeared improbable."*

Now that we have established that IEMT is a very useful modality for emotional change and a generative tool for identity change, let's explore this in more depth, beginning with the foundations of IEMT (without this, full understanding and use of the modality is not possible).

The Five Primary Patterns of Chronicity (5 POC)

At the core of the IEMT model is what has come to be known as the Five Patterns of Chronicity. It is these patterns that primarily set IEMT apart from other eye movement-based models. IEMT practitioners are taught the significance of these patterns and how to familiarise themselves with them. Thus, they can closely observe the verbal, visual and written indications from clients that often defeat the most competent of therapists unaware of the existence of these patterns.

Often, therapists of other modalities will ask: *"So how does IEMT differ from EMDR?"*

There are many ways of answering such a question – a question which can have different meanings depending on the intonation of the questioner. I may answer (annoyingly for some) with a question: *"What do you know about EMDR?"* The answer is usually "*nothing*", to which I will often reply: *"So what is the purpose of me describing the differences if you have 'nothing' to compare it with?"* This may provoke stage 1 of an abreaction POC.

Occasionally, the question is asked by an EMDR practitioner who is either truly curious or perhaps wanting to provoke me into saying something they can challenge. People can become defensive of something they are qualified in, identify with, and in which they have a strong belief. I try my best to stay out of other people's beliefs as this can lead to a whole lot of trouble...!

As I am not an EMDR practitioner (although I did a short training course – not the full medical practitioner training – some years ago) I am not fully qualified to make the direct comparison. If people truly want to know, the best way is to take both trainings; then they will be able to ascertain how the two modalities differ.

For those who genuinely have this question, IEMT really began with the Basic Kinaesthetic model, which in itself differs quite markedly from EMDR as I was taught it. However, as IEMT evolved, Andrew began noticing certain commonalities in clients who had long-standing chronic issues, had perhaps tried every other 'therapy' and had come to him and IEMT as a last resort. Many were referred by GPs who sent him what they termed their 'heart-sink patient', i.e., these doctors had tried everything they knew and there was still no change for the patient, hence their heart would sink when the client booked yet another appointment.

After cataloguing these cases and reviewing them, it became apparent that all were running the following five behavioural patterns (and perhaps a few more), which appeared to keep the person in a stuck state, incapable of undergoing long-term change. Some may have achieved short periods of change, but eventually they would go back to repeating the behaviours and experiencing the same problems.

For practitioners and clients, being able to spot these patterns and deal with them is often the key to the start of neurological change, and I believe this set of skills should be taught at a young age as basic emotional life skills. There is no particular order in which these patterns are exhibited, but I will begin with the one I see most frequently.

1. Being 'at Effect' rather than 'at Cause'

By being 'at effect', the person experiences emotional problems happening *to* them, rather than *by* them. A person 'at effect' will seek 'treatment' rather than 'change'; in other words, they seek the magic wand.

The person exhibiting this pattern will use statements such as:

> *"I'm so fat, can't you just hypnotise me to lose weight?"*

> *"I'm depressed, I need some medication for my chemical imbalance."*

Or when explaining self-behaviours:

> *"It's not fair...it always happens to me."*

> *"I can't help myself."*

> *"It just seems to happen by itself."*

> *"Life has it in for me."*

Such statements can be demonstrations of learned helplessness, passivity and inactivity. For example, the client doesn't follow up as required, or fails to complete tasks set by the therapist, no matter how simple. Also, the client may ignore the suggestion that this issue is a conversation that is best had with a medical doctor, and insists on discussing whether or not the practitioner thinks medication is a good idea.

This pattern of chronicity is one of the easiest to spot, and one of the easiest to over-empathise with. It could be called the 'woe is **me'** pattern, and as we will see in the chapter on Identity, it is often **me** who is 'at effect'. In terms of therapy or coaching, we know that rapport with a client is important in order that they want to work with us, and we want to work with them. Empathy, on the other hand, is not always required in order to effect a change. Empathy can sometimes give way to sympathy, and this may lead the client to using the session to tell their 'story'; resulting in the session becoming about the story rather than the issue. Getting the client to focus and work on the cause and not the effect, and demonstrating this to them, is a crucial step in breaking this chronic pattern and others.

Start tuning in from the moment of first contact with a client, pupil, patient, friend, family member, and in your own self-talk. These patterns are often seen in emails, social media chat and conversation. However, don't be tempted to 'fix' people, especially if they haven't sought your professional opinion. People might start shunning you at parties!

The next pattern is one that you may hear very early in the IEMT Kinaesthetic pattern process, and you may note it in the client pre-session questionnaires you receive if you are an IEMT Practitioner, as well as in others' general speech. This can slip by so quickly that it can be easily overlooked, especially if the person is a friend or family member and you have a high level of familiarity with them.

2. The Maybe Man

The Maybe Man/Person is uncertain of their own experience and this leaks out into their language. By remaining uncertain and without precision, they do not commit to their genuine experience or to their identity, and thus inadvertently sabotage effective therapy. I call him/her the 50 shades of grey person, i.e., they are analogue in nature and are unable to be specific about their own experience. A Maybe Person often exhibits anxiety which can become chronic and which in turn can lead to other Patterns of Chronicity and the linking and cycling of sets of unhelpful emotions.

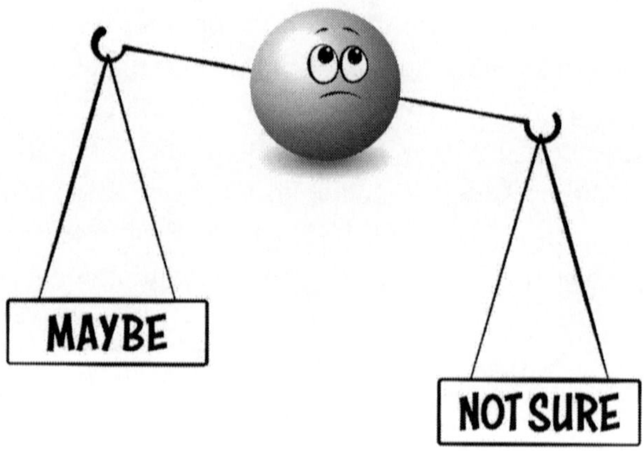

Examples:

"I don't know", "I'm not sure", "sort of", "kind of", "perhaps", "well, it could be this or that..."

They often answer a question with a question, as below:

Q: Practitioner asks for example:
"On a scale of 1 to 10 how strong is this feeling?"

A: Client hedges their bets,
"Maybe a 7 or 8?"

And we also will hear replies like these:
"It's probably that, perhaps";
"Not sure really, what do you think?";
"Could be a 6 or 7..."
"Part of me wants to say that, but part of me doesn't."

Other traits:

- The client is late or inappropriately early.
- The client turns up on the wrong day or not at all.
- They use the word 'try' a lot in their vocabulary, e.g., *"I'll try to remember what you told me", "I'll try to do that at home".*
- When taking medication, the client only takes it when he or she "remembers" and reports that s/he isn't sure if the medication is helping.
- The client doesn't follow instructions very well, but 'goes through the motions' of following them.
- With just a few minutes left to the session end or even on the way out of the door, the client says, *"oh, do you think this will be effective for..."* and reveals the key problem or piece of information that had, until this point, been withheld. The client is then never heard from again.

Everyone will exhibit this pattern at some time. However, it becomes a problem when a person finds it difficult most of the time to give an exact answer to a question, to make a choice over something, or would like to hand over responsibility to others. Of course, what can happen is that in handing over that responsibility, if all doesn't go to plan, they are often the first to blame the decision maker. This person is likely to procrastinate over decisions and with this anxiety can result.

During my Sleep Talk for Children sessions, I ask parents to listen out for this pattern in their children, because if left unaddressed, it can become a lifelong pattern and hold a person back from all sorts of opportunities. It can also lead to low self-esteem and issues with self-confidence and self-worth. It can even become a flag to other kids to bully a child. Far easier to correct this in a firm but fair way, encourage them to make a decision for themselves and not to be fearful of an outcome, than to try to tackle this ingrained issue as an adult. Not all decisions in life can be correct, but far better to learn to make a decision than to sit on the fence and become ineffectual as an adult.

It is a key component of the IEMT training that practitioners ensure their emotional state is stronger than the client's problem, and as such challenging these Patterns of Chronicity is of paramount importance. After all, if a person doesn't know they are running this pattern even though they are, e.g., a procrastinator, how are they going to change it? I feed this information back to them as soon I hear an example, with dialogue such as:

"So is this a 7 or an 8? I like people to be specific".

I won't accept a 7.5 either! Also a *probably, maybe, sort of*... language. I will say again:

> *"Now I like people to be specific, so is it or isn't it X?".*

It is highly unlikely that a person will only do this once. In all likelihood, I will also have seen this in the answers they have written in their pre-session questionnaire. In a session, this pattern soon emerges, so after two or three corrections I will stop and explain why I am asking them to self-correct and what this pattern is called. This is a major 'Aha...' moment for many people and they start to self-correct in the session, by themselves or with the encouragement of the bell that I sometimes ding every time they do it. Often, great humour ensues, with the client saying, *"Nooo, I've noticed, don't ding the bell!"* or, *"Oh, I've done it again!"* By bringing this unconscious pattern to the attention of their frontal lobe they now have the opportunity to learn a new and better way of behaving by structuring their own language differently. Over the years, this has produced some of the most profound changes in behaviour I've seen. We all speak this way on occasion, even IEMT Trainers, however I immediately self-correct and this stops me - becoming that person who can't make a decision, sits on the fence, and as a result starts to lack self-confidence and self-trust in myself and my decision-making.

Next is another pattern which people with anxiety-based issues are likely to exhibit. I often say the Maybe Man and the following pattern are two sides of the same coin because they so often go hand in hand.

3. The Great Big 'What if...?' Question

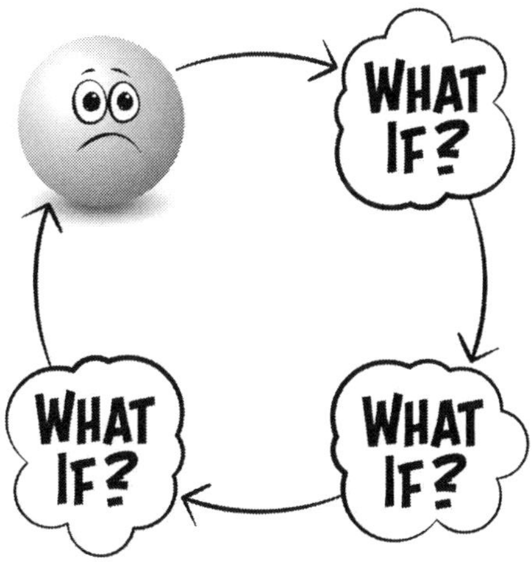

The Great Big 'What if...?' is often the major realm of the 'great big' anxious person. I have seen this so many times over the years in others, and indeed have exhibited it myself in the past. Of course, my justification is that as a scientist the 'what if' question is perfectly plausible in research and in designing new experimental hypotheses, which it is. However, it is also a sure sign that a person is running some anxiety-based issue - as I have myself over the years.

On a secondary level, this question is also designed to disarm any generalisation from, for example, a therapist or coach, with a single counter-example. This counter- example is usually generated spontaneously, and although it does not always have any basis in the real world, is suddenly of the highest importance to the client or course attendee.

Some of the most common questions are: *"What if this doesn't work?"*, and *"What if this doesn't last?"* These questions and the answers demanded usually take the place of actually doing the intervention that will provide relief from the psychological suffering. In other words, it is a form of psychological sabotage. It typically arises *prior to* the intervention and not *because of* it.

Having taught hypnobirthing for many years now, I can honestly say this is one of the most frequently asked questions during classes. My response is always to use the IEMT model to demonstrate how the first question can lead to a cascade of questions that end up with the question that is really the issue; fear-based questions like:

> ***"What if the baby dies?"***
>
> ***"What if my wife/partner dies?"***

Hypnobirthing's generalised techniques are often not sufficient to deal with this current and anticipatory fear, but IEMT frequently can be. Also, teaching the client resources inside the problem state is hugely effective. This can enable them to start to create real change by becoming informed of their birthing rights and preparing for many eventualities in a calm and educated way. They will formulate a stack of resources with which to deal with their own 'what if' scenarios, should they arise.

This pattern and the use of a single counter example that sabotages and counteracts any therapeutic generalisation can be demonstrated by the following looping cycle. These future-paced questions indicate anxiety loop around and are indications of beliefs.

Example 1:

'What if' logic is one of the ways in which negative beliefs are structured with three steps in the logic:

What if [**A**] is true/or happens, then [**B**] will be true/will happen, which means [**C**] will be true/or happen, e.g., then I/you/we/they will fail, etc...

Example 2:

Or where there is anxiety:

What if [condition **A** is true] then [condition **B** will be true
and
What if [condition **B** is true] then [condition **C** will be true]
and
What if [condition **C** is true] then [condition **D** will be true]
and
What if [condition **D** is true] then [condition **A** will be true]

Those who have taken one of my courses will remember that at the start I present my course rules. One of these rules is: "I don't answer 'what if' questions". This often gets a few funny looks, which is good as it gets people thinking. It is almost always forgotten by some part way through the first session and somebody will ask a "what if?" question. My retort is, *"I don't answer 'what if' questions"*, and I carry on. The great thing about being aware of this pattern is that it hones the mind into 'what if' questions that come cleverly disguised such as *"yes, but how about..."*, or *"well, I've read..."*, or *"in my experience X, Y & Z can happen, how would you deal with that situation?"* and so on.

The reason I am good at spotting these questions is because I had the same response levelled at me during my first training with Andrew Austin. I was 'that person' who wants everything explaining in terms of my own references and the one who liked to offer challenges based on my own experience/beliefs.

As stated, having been a biomedical scientist, 'what if' questions are very plausible, because in genetics and pathology our investigations are often like detective work. Hence, this is my default setting, along with a default towards anxiety. Yes, I also tend to be that person who is always at least half an hour early for any appointment - be it the doctor, hairdresser or a training course. I've even been known to turn up the day before to make sure I know where the venue is! I've had a few delegates like this on courses over the years, so I tend to know what to expect in terms of temperament and questions during the training.

To elaborate on the previous two examples:

Example 1 a:

> "What if the person is always in pain" *then* "they can't move their eyes as directed" Which means? "That IEMT won't work for them, will it?"
>
> **1 b):**
>
> "What if the person's been depressed their entire life" *then* "it will be impossible for them to see the point of this". Which means? "This is a waste of time".

Example 2:

> "What if I'm in pain" And what if you're in pain? *Then* "I won't be able to relax",
>
> ....and "What if I can't relax", *then* "I won't be able to breathe properly in labour",
>
> ....and "What if I can't breathe properly in labour", *then* "I may begin to panic",
>
> ....and "If I begin to panic", *then* "I will be in more pain"...

Sometimes they may skip from [A] straight to DEATH - in one move!

In the previous examples we see that the person often already has the answer to the previous question. As I have stated in many scenarios, the questions loop around or the person leaps to the worst conclusion, i.e., death. I see this pattern a lot in hypnobirthing work with anxious clients when we go through the concerns audit exercise, and also with non-birthing anxiety-based clients.

With such clients I will get out the board and pens and work through the process with their 'what if?'s. Some get a huge 'Aha...' moment very quickly.

> I recently had a great example of a lady who asked:
> *"What if I can't manage financially on my own?"*
>
> So, I asked: *"And **what if** you can't manage financially on your own and then what?"*
>
> Client: *"Well then I will fill my pockets with rocks and jump off the pier into the sea."*
>
> Me: *"Wow, that's really impressive. You've gone from 'what if' to death in one move! You get this week's prize."*

The lady roared with laughter, realising this really was a massive over-catastrophisation.

Being equipped with knowledge of this pattern and the solution to it is empowering. Hypnobirthing is all about parents empowering themselves to be in control of their experience as much as possible in order to achieve a great experience, no matter how their baby is birthed.

'And what is the solution?' I hear you ask...

THEN, DEAL WITH IT! - My emphasis is always on **THEN.**

These people are living very much in the future and often in the land of make-believe. They are over-thinking, over-worrying and catastrophising. Later in the book, we will look at such future-based thinking in a model called the Three Pillars. These people require a reality check and resources for learning to live in the here and now instead of the anticipatory future. This is why I emphasise the word **THEN** and explain the reason *why*. We will also look at putting useful resources in place if those anticipatory events are based in reality or past experience, as in childbirth.

For some people, working with the Pattens of Chronicity is as much a matter of education and training as it is therapy. Thus, along with eye movements to help them with their feelings, behaviours and identity, I will explain the Autonomic Nervous System and why people experience anxiety, and how learning new skills, strategies and resources is a powerful way of creating tangible relief and change.

4. The Three Stage Abreaction

Like each of these patterns, the Three Stage Abreaction can be seen outside a therapeutic session. However, in a session we will find a client's negative problematic emotions may inadvertently sabotage therapeutic manoeuvres by the therapist. What can be observed is that the emotion is often a diversion tactic (conscious or unconscious) to divert the session's course, or a specific behaviour. This can be seen to follow this pattern:

Stage 1. A signal or communication that is a **warning**.

Stage 2. An increased amplitude of this signal that takes the form of a **threat**.

Stage 3. An abreaction or release of emotion that serves as a **punishment**.

The above pattern of escalating emotional behaviour is enacted in order to create or force a change in the external environment. The perpetrator wants others to change because they don't want to, so change in others makes them feel better. Parents will no doubt have experienced this pattern many times with their children. This type of person trains others to respond to their needs and demands. A mere look can do the trick and have others running around placating the abreactor in a bid to keep them from exploding.

Example:

A: *"Let's go out to eat tonight."*
B (**Stage 1** - signal):
"No, I don't feel like it."

A: *"Oh come on, we haven't been out in ages."*
B (**Stage 2** - threat):
"Look I told you, no. I don't feel like it, okay!"

A: *"My treat, you can choose the restaurant."*
B (**Stage 3** - punishment):
"I DON'T WANT TO 'F*in' GO OUT, END OF..."

Stage 3 doesn't always result in verbal anger; it could be throwing something, walking out, becoming tearful, fainting, convulsions - anything to make the other person feel responsible for B's emotional or physical state.

Some stage 1 and even stage 2 behaviours can be quite subtle, and therapists trained in maintaining rapport and empathy can find themselves ensnared in this pattern because they don't want to do anything to make the client, who has come for help after all, feel any worse than they already do. This can be a mistake, as the dynamic and locus of control of the session may shift. One mantra that I use when seeing clients with such behaviours is that **my emotional state must always be stronger the client's problem state.** This is something I learned after training with Andrew Austin and it is rarely taught elsewhere other than in IEMT.

A good example of a more subtle stage1 is being late to a session. This permits the client to launch into a series of emotive explanations about why they are late, why they are so grateful for the appointment, why they are so sorry and so on. This behaviour is designed to control the emotive reaction set of the therapist and the therapist is expected to accept these explanations without negative judgement.

Statements such as, *"I might get quite emotional, so please forgive me if I cry"*, and *"I've brought lots of tissues with me, just in case"*, set the scene for a later abreaction.

Another stage 1 indicator may be flamboyance – when a client arrives over-dressed for the occasion, with too much make-up and perfume (or male equivalent), and a jubilant and flamboyant manner as though they're attending a great social occasion. The client may arrive bearing gifts for which they require a sufficient display of gratitude from the therapist (this has rarely happened in my sessions!).

Although I stated earlier that these patterns will not occur in any set order, I do often find that the 3 Stage Abreaction can follow the Great Big 'What If?' pattern. We will go into more detail when looking at anxiety with the Three Pillars later in this book. Suffice to say that the first example of the 'What if' pattern is often in itself a 3 Stage Abreaction pattern.

> **What if [A], then [B], which means [C] e.g., then I/you/we/ they will fail, etc...**

Again, I have seen this in training; when I won't answer a 'what if' question the 3 Stage Abreaction may not be far behind. In some extreme cases where people do have anger issues, stages 1 and 2 are bypassed and a full punishment stage 3 will result. In general though, most people will accelerate the emotional state via the **Signal, Threat** and **Punishment** algorithm. I am reminded of an episode years ago at a friend's house. He was a single parent and his 12-year-old daughter was asking to go to see one of her favourite bands. Her friends were going and she wanted to go too. The ticket cost £50 and dad couldn't afford it. The 3 stages were as follows.:

> A: *"Dad can I go to see X band in London? All my friends are going. Tickets are only £50."*
> Dad: *"Sorry love, I don't have the money to spare at the moment."*.
>
> A: *"Oh! All my friends are going."* **(Signal)**
> Dad: *"I know, but things are really tight at the moment, perhaps next year."*
>
> A: *"It's not fair, don't you want me to be happy?"* **(Threat)**
> Dad: *"Yes of course I do, but as I said I can't afford it at the moment."*
>
> A: *"You said you loved me and would always do your best for me! Well, your best isn't good enough!"* Tears, runs out, slams door **(Punishment)**

Had I known about the 3SAR back then, the dad may have been able to handle the situation differently and begun breaking the escalation that ended up becoming a habit.

The counter action to the Three Stage Abreaction

Your emotional state needs to be consistent and stronger than the abreactor's problem state, so do not accept this behaviour. The client is giving the signal that they don't want to change or put in any effort, the practitioner is supposed to do all the work so that the client can feel better. Give no reaction to behaviour that will provoke larger behaviours.

If, as sometimes does happen, your lack of response still ignites the blue touch paper, stand back and let the firework go off and fizzle out, then calmly ask if they have finished and are ready to do some work. Let them keep their own emotions and not transfer the responsibility to you. A well-constructed IEMT session will move a person from zero sum to non-zero sum reasoning (a little exercise we do on the Advanced/Level 2 Course).

Zero sum game - a zero sum game is a mathematical representation of a situation where each participant's gain or loss of utility is exactly balanced by the loss or gains of the utility of the other participants. If the total gains of the participants are added up and the total losses are subtracted, they will equal zero. Draughts (American checkers), backgammon, the card game snap are all examples of zero sum game. Basically it's winner takes all.

Non-zero sum game - non-zero-sum describes a situation in which the interacting parties' gains and losses can be less than or more than zero. A zero-sum game is also called a strictly competitive game while non-zero-sum games can be either competitive or non-competitive.

A consequence of not challenging this behaviour, which is like a zero sum game, ends when the abreactor gains victory in a situation, as follows:

The abreactor has trained you to respond in a placatory way by their 3SAR!

• **Stage 1: *"That's Right"*** - The person having the emotional issue can be described as an off-loader or dumper. They dump their issues and problems on to you and expect you to either deal with them or change your emotional response to make them feel better.

Once everyone in the social system of the abreactor is adequately trained in the meaning of the stage 1 symptoms and they start responding appropriately to what the abreactor wants, stage 2 and 3 often won't be required. However, when a new person enters the system, they will require training, and if an existing trainee dares to ignore or challenge the first signal, escalation to stage 2 occurs.

Dealing with stage 1:

> An example of how to deal with this stage 1 could be:
> Abreactor: *"I'm very disappointed in you."*
> Responder: *"That's right..."*

i.e., agree with them, and don't take ownership of their emotional state. They have often trained those around them with the threat of anger/tears etc. to get what they want. Time to break the pattern of the dumper and the dumpee!

When they give the signal, you just need to reply ***"that's right"*** - don't let them drag you into their stuff. It can cause confusion and often can stop the situation.

Dealing with stage 2 - *"That's right"* and feedback:

> If they amplify the situation, e.g., *"Listen, I said I was angry with you..."*
> Your reply: *"That's right you're angry..."*

You're feeding the response back to them while still agreeing with them, with the emphasis that they are angry; it is their anger, i.e., their issue

Dealing with stage 3

If it gets this far, do as in stage 2 and the above statement. Let them have their abreaction. The difference with this type of AR is there is generally no true emotional release or learning from it. They will repeat the pattern again and again if left unchallenged.

> Your response can be: *"Your emotional state does not dictate my response"*, or "*your emotional state is not my responsibility"*, or *"your emotional state/behaviour does not influence my actions."*

For a masterclass in subtle Three Stage Abreactions this interview with David Bowie is very enlightening. There is no shouting and very little swearing: **https://www.youtube.com/watch?v=XPi0mkWkTco**

5. Testing for Existence of the Problem Rather Than Testing for Change

This can often be the most problematic of all of the patterns to change, as often it is exhibited in people with long-term physical or psychological issues or conditions.

Despite evidence to the contrary, this client will typically disregard any improvement and instead focus attention on aspects of the problem that remain unchanged.

Even though 99% improvement might be made, if the person with this chronicity is able to locate just 1% of the problem existing, this will generally be seen as representative of 100% of the problem existing.

Examples:

i. The weight loss client who, despite losing weight and looking fabulous, says: *"I won't feel happy until I lose the last few pounds of my target."*

ii. The parent who, on hearing that their child has achieved an A, wants to know why they didn't get an A+.

iii. The client who has a great hypnobirth, but focuses and sometimes obsesses on the fact, for example, that just before transition they briefly felt like they couldn't do it and asked for a Caesarian section or anaesthesia. For the person with this pattern, this can totally mar their memory of the experience and interfere with post-birth bonding and parenting. Hence this pattern, if not changed, can cause deep unhappiness. In some extreme cases it could even manifest as PTSD.

There are many examples to choose from. People who strive for perfectionism will often exhibit this pattern. Interestingly, this is also often a pattern for people who are prone to procrastination. If they focus on the fact that something isn't perfect, it stops them committing fully. This person is filtering for evidence of the problem, working from a position of belief. They are allowing themselves to not only interpret/distort the experience to support the continued existence of the problem and their current beliefs, but also to allow themselves to ignore or dismiss any evidence of change.

It is a digital, black and white, all or nothing (the problem is either 'fixed' or it's not) way of being and there are no shades of grey (or analogue gradient) between these two positions for this person. Labels are a common contributory factor in this way of thinking as these people are digital in nature, so a person is either 'X' or they are not. They will often identify themselves as 'a perfectionist', hence the Identity model is of great use to the practitioner when dealing with this pattern, which is illustrated in phrases such as:

> *"I am a perfectionist, and I won't allow myself anything but 100%."*
>
> *"Every ounce of me needs to feel this."*
>
> *"She's perfect, I need to be exactly like her."*

Listen for the following warning words:

> **Always, Never, Impossible, Awful, Perfect, Terrible, Ruined, Disastrous, Intolerable, Furious**

A person exhibiting this pattern may also be short on patience and prone to a loss of temper, hence the Three Stage Abreaction may be another of their patterns. Also, their perceived lack of perfection may make them prone to anxiety, and black and white thinkers may also be prone to depression.

We will look at the 3 Pillars of Depression model in another chapter; suffice to say, a major reason people become depressed is because of the way they perceive reality. Depression can centre around one recurring belief, such as, *"I am not good enough",* as per this pattern of chronicity, or *"I'm not the sort of person other people like"*. Thinking and talking in this 'all or nothing' pattern is more emotionally exciting to these people, and they may find it difficult to want to give it up. Indeed, most people will talk this way at times, particularly when they're excited or angry.

Self-Use

Now that you have conscious awareness of these patterns as practitioners, do practise improving your IEMT listening and reading skills, tuning in your IEMT antennae to be able to pick up on them quickly and easily. By doing this, you can start to help your clients to become consciously aware of their patterns and thereby able to challenge themselves and make changes. I'd like to say that as IEMT Practitioners we will never be running these patters ourselves, but of course this is untrue. At some time, all of us will run one or even all of these patterns, however, hopefully the difference is that as soon as we think the statement, even if it does leave our mouths, we know how to change this ourselves in order to make better decisions and take better actions.

Chapter 5

Taking the First Steps to Create Change

> **“Memory is never a precise duplicate of the original; instead, it is a continuing act of creation.”**
>
> **Dr Rosalind Cartwright**

Most people reading this book are likely to want to use IEMT with other people, whether clients or friends and family members. As with any new technique, when learning IEMT, practice is key to becoming skilled in its use.

On Practitioner (Level 1) training courses and with most clients, the exercise that follows is the first we utilise in illustrating the use of eye movements to create change. This is the exercise briefly described in the introduction, when I first encountered IEMT upstairs in that Brighton pub. It is paramount to remember with this exercise that there is **no requirement for any disclosure** by the person you are working with in order for tangible change to occur. IEMT is often labelled a ‘brief change therapy’, which can be a tad ambiguous. The process in many cases is brief, while the effects can last a lifetime.

This ‘no disclosure’ rule may be unfamiliar to those from a counselling or psychotherapy background, as many of their clients are looking for care and support as opposed to rapid change. I ensure that prior to this exercise everybody on a training course is absolutely clear that ‘no disclosure’ means exactly that; neither the ‘client’ nor the ‘therapist’ is permitted to disclose details of the issue being worked on. I have on occasion walked around training rooms with a comedy prop such as a ruler or rolled-up newspaper in case anyone strays from the instructions. I’ve never had to use it…yet!

Also, at the beginning of a course I produce a set of course rules. They are a tad provocative, and I invite attendees to add more if they wish. I learned this from training with Andrew Austin, and the reasons are as follows:

- The questions and processes in IEMT have been researched and fine-tuned so that the most appropriate language is used in order to elicit the most appropriate responses from clients. Hence, I ask people to stick to what is written on the sheet; i.e., to follow the instructions.
- IEMT does not require in-depth historical or archaeological digs into what has happened, what their philosophical ideas are regarding an issue, or even how a person feels. Stories are exactly that. They are often peppered with generalisations, distortions and deletions because a huge amount of neural processing is required in order to recreate a memory, the component parts of which are retrieved from different parts of the brain. Keep out of the story, otherwise you can end up working with the story, rather than the actual issue. Many people are grateful for this aspect of the work because they dread having to dredge through stuff yet again. It also enables them to keep aspects of the issue private if they wish.
- At the start of the training I make large generalisations with some of my statements. This is in order to elicit certain responses from delegates for the purpose of demonstrating the Five Primary Patterns of Chronicity. I find that understanding these patterns can be confusing for people at first, so actual examples work best. Having had the 'Great Big 'What If?' response used against me by Andrew Austin at my original training, I am unlikely to ever forget this POC and can therefore easily spot it, even with some language alterations.
- It is always good to start the course with the mindset of what is and what isn't acceptable within the training environment, and to look for any unconscious responses that may indicate a person who has status issues or a penchant for 'what-iffing' or Three Stage Abreacting.

I have had one or two such people on courses over the years, and I've been able to glean prior warning of possible outbursts or status issues by stating the rules. I also ask delegates to complete an ice-breaker exercise, and this often reveals further insights. It has to be said that most attendees are a delight to work with, as they have come with the purpose of learning something new for their own benefit or that of the clients they work with.

One of the reasons for what is now a three-stage qualification process is to create practitioners who are not just ticking off this modality for another certificate and set of logos to put on their website after a two-day course, without having actually understood it or used it in a client setting. Some overseas trainers use a third day of training for assessments, which is a perfectly viable option towards IEMT certification, and during the coronavirus lockdowns I have spread some courses over four shorter sessions across two weekends.

The process for anyone wanting to become an IEMT Practitioner is:

- Attend the course.
- Complete the post-course case studies and written work satisfactorily.
- Join the Association for IEMT Practitioners to become a recognised Practitioner on the members' directory.

The Consultation/Training Process

In a therapy setting, clients are asked to complete a fairly comprehensive questionnaire prior to a session. Those who have trained with me for certification purposes will have a copy of the form in the Case Study Guidance or available to download on the training website, and it is free to adapt as you see fit. This use of a pre-session questionnaire is also a requirement of the Association for all IEMT Practitioners.

There is also a consent form, signed and dated at every session, with the appropriate information on GDPR for those in Europe. Most professional bodies have a requirement for data and client notes to be kept for specific time periods and anyone working with clients in the UK and Europe who keeps information online is advised to obtain a licence for this. It is a very simple procedure and costs £40 annually. The following is a link for the UK licence: https://www.gov.uk/notification-to-process-personal-data

Once the completed client questionnaire is received, the medical information given must be checked for contraindications or for the need for further information or clarification. For example, in the case of a client who has had an eye or head injury, we need to know how recently it occurred and if they are fully recovered. If a person has been previously admitted to a psychiatric in-patient unit and are still receiving outpatient treatment, then IEMT is contraindicated. I ask about current medication, plus recreational drug and alcohol use. This may seem invasive; however, I need to ensure that clients are fully aware that they are responsible for attending a session in a clean and sober state. If they are not clean and sober, the session will not proceed.

One thing I have added to my requirements for information is whether a person is involved in any legal case where they are required to give a witness statement or testimony. In recent months, I have received several requests for sessions in such cases. Having clarified this with the Association, it has been decided that, as eye movements in IEMT can alter memory, it could cause issues with legal cases. Andrew Austin writes:

> *"Memory is definitely being changed, both in terms of content (it usually fragments, some of these fragments then re-order in their time sequence, so that sometimes they will be out of sequence) and also structure (i.e., distance, focus, etc.). The result of this is that the subsequent kinaesthetic loading is altered."*

Terms & Conditions are issued to all clients and course delegates as part of my pre-session preparation. Again, this enables clients/delegates to understand my commitment to them and their commitment to the session or training in return. If anyone was to abreact and not agree to sign the Ts&Cs, they would not be seen or be able to attend a course (this has only happened once). I find that as long as everyone knows where they stand with regards to the Ts&Cs prior to a session, there can be no surprises and we are then both free to enter the process.

Beginning a Session with the Introductory Exercise (the Discovery Frame)

So, having tempted you once or twice with mention of this, here is the Introductory Eye Movement Exercise - 'The Tester', as I like to call it. Those from an NLP or hypnotherapy background will be familiar with the concept of 'the convincer'. For example, the convincer whereby we chat to people and get them to feel as though they are holding onto a set of helium balloons or a bucket of wet sand, sending arms flying in all directions while the person is seemingly perfectly awake and alert. It may seem a bit showy, and in fact it is – the therapist demonstrating their ability to influence another into an unconscious response.

The Introductory Exercise is not a demonstration of how brilliant the practitioner is, but in fact how brilliant the client/trainee's brain is and the robustness of the IEMT process in enabling their brain to create change, rapidly. This is how I frame this exercise after it has taken place. Prior to the exercise, I say that I'm going to *"just test your* [client/trainee's] *eyes' ability to follow my fingers while you think of something, just to make sure IEMT is a suitable modality in this case."*

One other thing to note is that I make an audio or video recording of each session (with the client's permission). This means I'm not taking copious notes and therefore missing out on the verbal and visual cues and clues which are crucial to the IEMT process. I have never been refused consent and clients are provided with a copy of the recording if they wish. I also run through any points from their questionnaire that need clarifying or that I find interesting. There may be some interesting metaphors and idioms used by the client, for example, and I'm always looking for identity-based statements such as: "*I just can't help myself*"; "*Things always seem to happen to me*"; "*You just have to get on with it don't you*", and so forth.

The Introductory Exercise in Brief

The following is the basic exercise that I carry out on the course, and follow with a more detailed set-up and explanation of the process when working with clients. If you are working online, this can be done easily via Zoom, Teams etc., and it achieves the same effects:

Introductory Exercise on Trainings

1. Partner up, preferably with somebody that you don't know, or out into break-out rooms randomly assigned on Zoom.

   One is to act 'the client' the other 'the therapist' (you will swap over after you've been through the exercise once).

2. The person acting in the role of 'client' is to:

   "Think of something that stands out in your memory, something as troublesome, bothersome or negative. It can be from a long time ago and it stands out in the memory as vivid. It doesn't have to be major, traumas aren't always huge (e.g., losing your lunch money or keys on the way to school, argument with a sibling when young etc.)"

   This should be a maximum of 6/10 on an SUD scale.

   NO DISCLOSURE & NO SHOWING OFF YOUR "THERAPY" SKILLS

3. *Concentrate on the vivid memory that has the negative feeling.*

4. Person acting as the 'therapist' asks the 'client' to move their eyes 6 times each way while the 'client' thinks of the memory a vividly as possible.

   Reminder: "*You don't need to talk about it.*"

5. Start with the horizontal axis and cover the visual field to the peripheries.

   Remind the client to keep their head still and keep thinking of this memory.

   This should only take 30-40 seconds.

6. Feedback – briefly:

   i. *What do you notice about that memory now?*

   ii. *What did you notice about that feeling now?*

3. Swap over and repeat.

4. Group discussion regarding observations and experiences.

The Set-up With Clients

The use of eye movements can be suitable at the beginning of a session, or it may not be appropriate until partway through. If there are, for example, issues with anxiety, exploring the Patterns of Chronicity or the 3 Pillars Model (see later in this book) would be a good way to start in order to shift ways of thinking, beliefs or behaviours first.

I like to work in an informal conversational way with clients. At the start of an in-person session, I often ask if they would like a drink before we start, and then digress - as follows:

1. But before I get your drink and before we go into the issue that brought you here today, let's check that the eye movement process is suitable for you.

2. Do you have something, some memory from the past, that when you think about it now is vivid and the feeling is troublesome or bothersome?

3. Now I'm not talking about the worst thing that has ever happened, not even the thing that may have brought you here today, but something that if you gave it a score of 1 to 10, where 10 is the worst feeling and 1 being nothing of any significance, you would score say a 6/10.

4. I always offer an example, such as:

   "For example, when I was five I got stuck in an elevator between floors. I was with my mum and older sister and my mum was 6 months pregnant at the time. We were stuck for what seemed like hours and hours (time for a 5-year-old seems to stretch on forever), but it was in fact only about an hour. The fire brigade quickly came and rescued us, lifting us safely up onto the next floor. Now, for years after that I would not go into an elevator, even though we lived in high-rise flats on the fifth floor, so I would walk alone up the big stairs to the flat. Now, even though that was such long time ago and I now do use elevators, whenever I think of that incident it gives me a certain set of bothersome feelings and physical reactions such as butterflies in my stomach... Do you have something like that from the past? It may be from years ago or even the recent past. As I say, nothing too huge in the great scheme of things, but something that you can remember vividly when you think about it right now? Incidentally, you also don't have to tell me anything about the incident at all; in fact, I insist that you don't."

5. Now wait for them to search their memory and come up with a suitable response. They may wish to delve into the story, so just remind them that they do not need to disclose any details about the incident. If they want to tell you how it makes them feel, that's fine.

6. Next, I will ask: *"Great, so you have a memory and is it vivid?"* If the memory is not clear, get them to find another memory that is vivid.

7. Then I say:

   "And I want you to bring this memory up as vividly as you can in your mind's eye. That's it, and now, keeping your head really still, I want you to follow my fingers with your eyes."

   This is **eye movement** work, not **head movement** work - so keeping the head still is important.

8. The eyes are moved approximately six times in three directions, the practitioner ensuring that they direct the eyes to the peripheries. The movements are neither too fast nor too slow. I use my index and middle fingers to direct the eyes, while some people will use their index finger only, and others use a pen or light pen.

   Light pens can be useful for those with limited eyesight. With children I often use a magic wand or pen with character on the end, such as a Disney favourite or a superhero.

9. The three axis we use to move eyes for this 'tester' are:

   - Horizontal
   - Diagonal left to right
   - Diagonal right to left

Basic Kinaesthetic Eye Movement Patterns

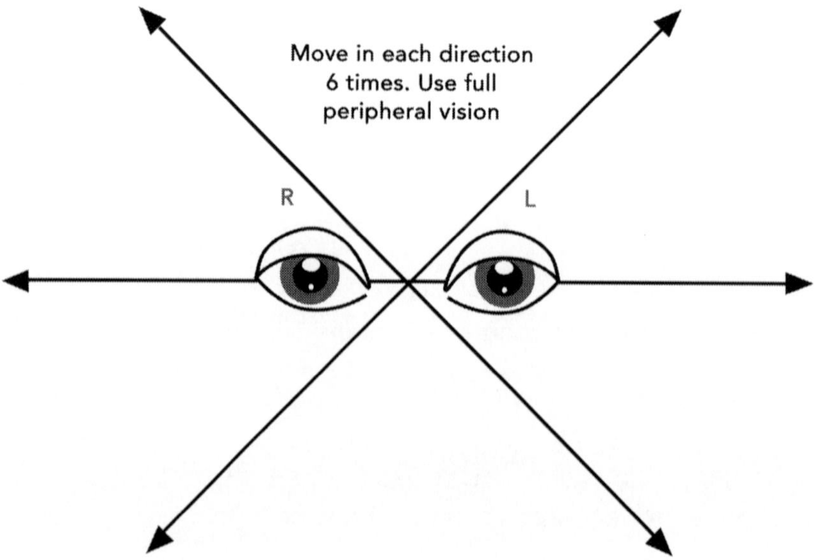

10. After completing the eye movements, you can ask the participant:

> ***"And when you think about this memory now, what do you notice…?"*** (wait for an answer).
>
> ***"And what do you notice or experience with that feeling now?"***

A variety of answers will be given; however, many people will struggle to bring the memory to mind. If this is the case I may ask:

> *"That memory was vivid before the eye movements. Is it still as vivid?"*
>
> *"And the feeling, that was 6/10 is it the same or different? If different, in what way?"*

It is very unusual for there to be no change at all in either the representation of the memory or the associated kinaesthetic. For those who insist there is absolutely no change, we can accept this or ask one or two more pointed questions. Bear in mind this could be an indication of one or several of the Five Primary Patterns of Chronicity that we discussed earlier in the book.

Typical observations

Several changes are described by the majority of people who experience this exercise:

1. The memory becomes less defined, less vivid, or in some cases no longer accessible.

2. The memory or image appears to be more distant.

3. If the memory was an associated one, it often becomes dissociated and there may also be some age progression; i.e., if the memory was, for example, from childhood, they will view it from the age they are now, which is why the memory can become dissociated.

4. The feelings or emotions have reduced in intensity and in some cases disappear completely.

It is important to understand that there is a difference in how people feel in a memory and how the kinaesthetic component is organised. For some people, there is an emotional reaction to the actual memory, while others will be remembering how they felt at the time of the memory. This is something we cover more in the Level 2 Advanced Training.

If one or more of these observations are noted, I am satisfied that IEMT is a useful modality for this person.

Less typical observations

1. Images go from colour to black and white.

2. A 'movie' type of memory becomes a 'still' photograph.

3. There are changes in the audio component of the memory, e.g., reduced volume.

4. Feelings shift position within the body.

Resistance to Change?

Of course, no process is going to work for every person all of the time. In a minority of cases, a person will say they experience no change in either memory or feelings, and some will say the feeling has worsened or the memory either become more vivid or jumped to another memory entirely. This jumping memory can actually be an important part of the process of change, and when we look at what can be called the Integral Process, close tracking and calibration of eye movements is key to being able to reduce the number of eye movements required to create change.

If they go on too long, eye movements can be quite tiring for the client (and for the arm of the practitioner…). The basic rule of thumb is around 45 seconds per round of eye movements. We then stop, check in, and recalibrate if needs be.

After this first exercise, and even the model proper, the following observations or complaints may be heard:

> *"I feel dizzy."*
>
> *"It made me feel nauseous/sick."*
>
> *"I now have a headache."*
>
> *"It made my eyes hurt."*

Other responses including hysterical laughter and tears have also been known. Such physiological responses may be due to the fact that the person is slightly dehydrated, hasn't had any breakfast (eye movement and rapid brain process is likely to require a lot of glucose), may have a headache starting anyway, or any number of physiological variables. An interesting study by Chong-Hwa Hong et al (1995) found the following:

> *"Eye movements during REM sleep were associated with increased glucose metabolic rates in areas corresponding to the neural system that controls saccadic eye movements and in areas corresponding to both the parietal visual spatial attentional system (superior and inferior parietal lobules) and the midline attentional system (cingulate, medial frontal cortex and praecuneus)"* (1).

Also, Sandusky et al (2013) demonstrated that:

> *"Initial memory processing in the hippocampus causes a drainage of hippocampal glucose because of increased local metabolic demand."*

Their research also showed consistency with previous hippocampal data. They commented that:

> *"Avoidance training and testing caused an acute elevation of local metabolism within the basolateral amygdala, causing a decrease in ECF glucose and increased ECF lactate and glutamate. To our knowledge, these are the first microdialysis measurements of local metabolism in the amygdala during affective processing, and also the first attempt to compare neurochemical processes in the amygdala during consolidation and retrieval"* (2).

Hence, low glucose levels due to a rapid burst of use could be responsible for such undesirable effects after intense eye movements (3).

This research is important when looking at why some people may experience the above reactions after eye movements such as those during IEMT. Even during the brief 'test' process, memories are being retrieved and consolidated by certain parts of the brain, in particular the hippocampus and the amygdala. In fact, the more interesting question might be why so many people don't have such responses. I suspect that a person who may be experiencing a memory as a trauma and currently strongly affected by the memory may be more likely to experience an extreme physiological response. Of course, this is only my theory and it would require a vast amount of research to prove.

In some instances, the following responses to the above reactions can be useful:

1. Explain about the rapid use of brain glucose during a sudden burst of action such as eye movements, and how this can result in feelings such as dizziness.

2. Explain that when the mind is resisting change, the resulting inner conflict can cause a depletion of brain glucose.

3. You may add that such physiological responses can often pre-empt a huge emotional shift. I have seen this on occasion, and one in particular springs to mind from a training course. The person, though instructed not to choose a huge issue as this was just an introductory exercise, chose something very deep from childhood. They had a massive physiological reaction and possible abreaction. After a lie-down, they were elated that the issue had now gone. I know others have similar stories of such responses.

4. I usually wait for the second or third incidence of such a response to introduce the Three Stage Abreaction concept to the client. Those who may be consciously resisting the process could well have demonstrated an earlier signal of this pattern, as this POC would be useful as an explanation. Be mindful of a stage 2 or 3, however, as a result. Introducing this concept is at the discretion of the practitioner on a case by case basis.

5. Double check there are no contraindications. Sometimes people forget to put things down on the questionnaire; e.g., an eye or head injury or disease, or a recent case of labyrinthitis. Also bear in mind that some neurological tumours and disorders, including Parkinson's disease, affect eye movements. If a person finds it difficult to follow your fingers, it may be part of the resolution process or it may be a sign of disease.

6. For some people, IEMT is not the right modality right now. If after using the full protocol such a response or no change occurs, stop.

To give a little more information about point 5 above, there may of course be some psychological as well as physiological variables or issues that the practitioner or trainee/client is unaware of. I share the list of contraindications in the pre-course resources for online trainings or early on the in-person training, prior to any eye movement work, so that if a person thinks they have an issue that could be affected by eye movements they can indicate this to the trainer. This list is also found in the Case Study Guidance which delegates are asked to read pre-training. At one training, a lady had an intense physical response. She had not mentioned that she'd had laser eye surgery a few months previously. Eye surgery and head injuries must always be disclosed prior to working with eye movements.

Ruling out any physiological or medical condition, resistance to change may be the issue. Not everybody, even those who come to train in IEMT or attend a session as a client, are always fully prepared for real change to occur, or even on some level, truly desire it. Change can be scary for some people, especially when they have built comfort into their discomfort as a coping or protection mechanism. Acknowledgment of physical or emotional pain can also be a stretch for some, and finding a negative memory, even a low-grade one, with someone who may have other issues can cause a precipitation effect [(4)].

As practitioners, it is important that we learn to become comfortable with others' discomfort so as not to invalidate their experience. This can be difficult, especially for those who have been indoctrinated in the rules of building rapport and being non-judgmental, empathetic and understanding.

The truth is, I may be able to empathise with a client's situation and issues, but I am unlikely to be able to fully understand them, as everyone's brain is a unique set of neurology. Saying, *"I understand your pain",* for example, can just come across as condescending or untruthful. Telling a client that I don't understand what they are feeling may on the surface seem like dis-rapport, however it has never been an issue for me thus far. On the contrary, clients often appear relieved, especially when I go on to tell them that in order to be able to assist them with the IEMT process, I do not need to understand their pain or suffering, just to accept that that is their experience in the here and now. Also, that I also don't need to hear their life story, or require any disclosure for that matter if they choose not to offer any [(5)]. This approach often comes as a great relief to many.

Testing for Change

This exercise is hugely beneficial for the client and the practitioner. Some people coming for IEMT may have been holding onto an experience for many years, and they could well believe nothing can really create change for them. By choosing some old memory that they still have a negative kinaesthetic response to in the 'test' exercise, and noticing change in that memory and/or feeling(s), is a powerful convincer that IEMT works. Even though I ask clients not to choose a memory associated with the issue they have come to see me with, occasionally this does happen. It is very reassuring, even pleasantly surprising, for the client to know that change really can occur this quickly.

I ensure that I test this shift as a way of showing clients that the old memory is no longer successful; i.e., that the change is the success and the brain has the capacity to create these changes quickly and easily.

So, ask the client:

> ***"Please close your eyes if you wish and try to bring that memory back as vividly as you can; bring it back exactly as it was before... And now... try harder!***
>
> ***What do you notice and what do you experience?"***

Again, for the majority of people it will be difficult, if not impossible, to bring back the memory to the exact visual experience and feeling as before. Hence, we have now associated failure to the negative memory and success to the change.

At this point, if I haven't provided a drink for the client beforehand, I will go and get some water and a hot drink if they want one. This can be a good opportunity to give the client some space to process what has just occurred. Remember, they may have been holding onto this 'thing' (one of my favourite words when working with IEMT) for many years, yet in a few minutes the memory has changed, in some cases vastly, to the stage where they can no longer recreate or hold on to it.

As far as convincers go, this exercise is by far the most powerful and long-lasting of all the therapeutic modalities I have worked with. After all, I experienced this change myself on my first encounter with IEMT and I am pleased to say that the thought of that event from childhood now just brings a smile to my face. Indeed, my memory is now not of the event, but of the meeting in the top room of that pub in Brighton.

Chapter 6

The Basic IEMT Kinaesthetic Model

> **"How did this person learn to feel this way about this thing?"**

The above question is fundamental to the kinaesthetic process of IEMT, yet is sometimes forgotten after a trainee completes the course. So, if you are a practitioner, please memorise the question (see later) and ensure that it is always part of your reasoning for assessing when to use IEMT.

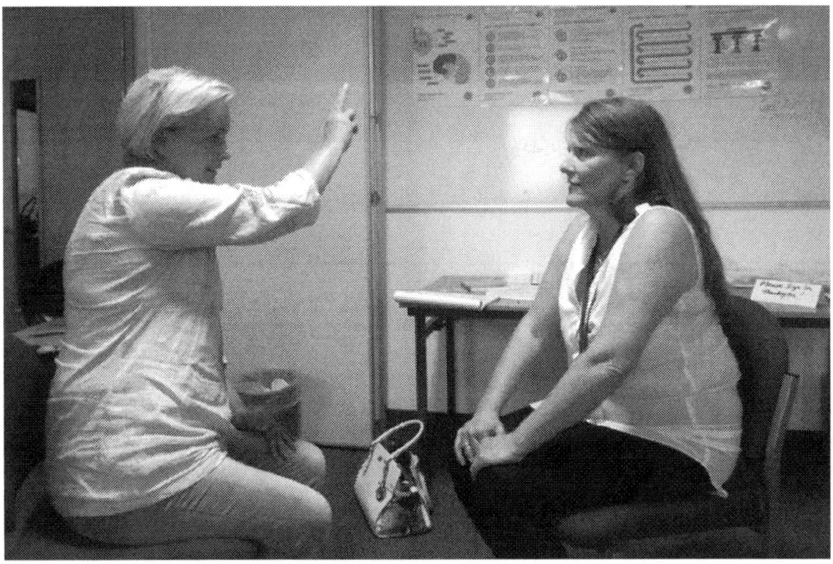

The Basic Kinaesthetic Model in Practice

In the previous chapter, I described how at the start of the IEMT Practitioner course there is a set of rules. Rule one is: Follow the instructions. When it comes to the wording of this model, that instruction is paramount. As mentioned earlier, this process and these words didn't just come about on a whim. Many hours of research, trial and error and experimentation through workshops helped the development of a robust process with specific wording that is able to elicit memory-based searches in order to access the answer to the question: "How did this person learn to feel this way about this thing?"

In IEMT, the closer we can get to this trigger or event, the more likely we are to be able to facilitate deep and long-lasting change. Also, the eye movements will indicate very accurately the processing of the memories and the bilateral movements are important in the processing, downgrading, completion and eventual storage (consolidation) of the memories that are now devoid of a strong negative emotional response.

The previous chapter looks at how to set up the session and the issues to look out for, including possible contraindications.

When moving onto the full IEMT Kinaesthetic Model, it is important not to allow the person's story to get in the way of the process. As we know, the brain has cognitive bias and can also introduce distortions, deletions and generalisations when a person is recalling and recounting their story.

I often find that for some people there is huge relief at not having to go over the same story again, as it may have been recounted many times to friends and family, a counsellor, midwife, human resources, work manager, GP and so forth. For those working with older children or teenagers, this can also be a huge advantage and again a sense of relief. With children I often use imagery to scale their level of discomfort, as they can find it difficult to articulate this. There are many images available on the internet for Specific Units of Distress scales. Something like the following chart, that has been created for me, can be adapted for feelings or physical pain, and you can ask the young person to point to a number to indicate where they are:

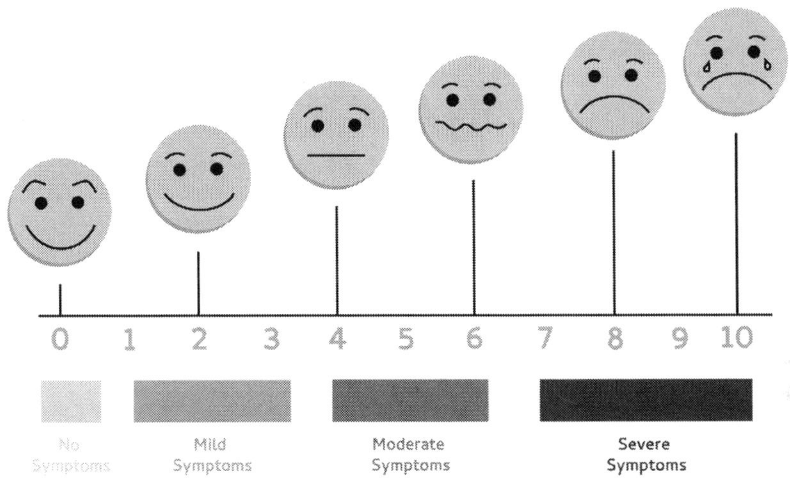

Current or Anticipatory or State Change

Now we come to the process itself. It appears extremely simple on the surface, as it only really comprises four questions, yet I never cease to be amazed at how, despite my course instructions, these few sentences can be generalised, distorted and even deleted by trainees. This not only happens on the course itself, but sometimes we see it in the case study videos sent in for Practitioner Certification. Suffice to say that if people ignore the process and decide to do their own thing, they will be asked to repeat their case studies. So, when working with this model, for the sake of repeating myself: PLEASE USE THE FOLLOWING WORDING!

Basic Kinaesthetic Pattern

From the client or participant, elicit the undesired state (whole body experience) or kinaesthetic expression (part of the body feeling). They may or may not tell you the name of the feeling; it is their choice. There is however some research that says naming emotions or feelings can improve resolution therapeutically [1]. I do encourage the naming of the feeling but never make the assumption that it is always best or make this a must-have, as those struggling to find a name may end up with a secondary feeling, e.g., of frustration. Also, when working with children, as mentioned above, the names of emotions may be difficult to elicit, hence the diagrams.

The Process Explained

- Ask the client to assign the feeling an amplitude on the SUD scale from 1-10, as follows:

(remember, the wording is key, so start with the word "*and*"):

"...and out of 10, how strong is this feeling, with 10 being as strong as it can be?"

It is preferable to use the word *'this'* as opposed to *'that'* feeling as *'this'* is a current state process, so the present tense is more applicable. After the process, when change occurs, we can then use the term *'that feeling'* (we explore other tenses and positions in the Level 2 course).

Wait for your answer - listen out for the **Maybe Man** pattern and challenge a non-specific answer in a constructive way. For example, if a person gives an answer such as *"7 or 8"*, I will always say:

"Now I like people to be specific with their answers, so is it 7 or is it 8?"

They usually correct this very quickly, often, not surprisingly, to the higher number.

Now ask:

"... and *how familiar is this feeling*?"

This question can sometimes cause some confusion or consternation. The client may ask:

"What do you mean by familiar?"

The temptation is to go into an in-depth explanation for the client here, however, by doing this we can be in danger of interrupting the process that will elicit the transderivational search (TDS) required with the next question we ask. For those unfamiliar with this term it has meanings in cybernetics and psychology. A psychological meaning can be seen in Ericksonian Hypnotherapy, where vague suggestions are made to clients to enable an intense internal search for their own experiences and information across time and space, without the practitioner interfering. They will elicit the facts such as episodic memory dates and times and sensory memory. This is why we give them time and a practitioner must never give them direct examples or suggestions 'just to help' move the process along.

I am of course also looking for a Three Stage Abreaction Stage 1 signal, which on occasion can occur here.

My response is to smile and repeat the question. I occasionally put a little more emphasis on the word '*familiar*' and incline my voice. This usually works well and gets a response such as, *"Oh... you mean how familiar?"* and an answer is often forthcoming.

On rare occasions, if still faced with a blank look or lack of comprehension, I will add:

"So, is it mildly familiar, familiar or very familiar?"

This strategy usually yields an answer.

If the person is still struggling with the concept (which is extremely rare), rather than let this lead to an impasse, I will say:

> *"You seem to be struggling with this, so compare it with something that you're really familiar with and then you will know if this is more familiar, less familiar or about the same."*

On occasion, the client will give you a score out of 10 for familiarity, so I will just check and get them to put it into the language of the process. For example, if they say 9/10, I'll just double check and ask, *"so are you saying this is very familiar?"* and await a reply. The person will now be comparing this feeling across time and space.

I just take whatever answer they give and don't change it into my own frame of reference.

- **When you have the answer, then ask the TDS questions:**

  "...and when was the first time you can remember feeling this feeling..? Now... it may not be the first time that it ever happened, but it is the first time that you can remember now...?"

Allow the client 20-40 seconds to access the imprinting event. Do not offer guidance or advice and allow the client to perform his or her own kinaesthetic transderivational search.

As talking therapists, it can feel odd to wait in silence for responses; it certainly did for me the first few times I worked with this process. But this will soon become familiar to you and something that you will become comfortable with.

Coaches are more comfortable with this concept of giving clients space to access their thoughts, memories and resources. Some therapy trainings may encourage a practitioner to step in to soothe things if we see the client is uncomfortable, to offer tissues or words of encouragement.

With IEMT, sit on your hands if needs be and refrain from speaking for a while. We need to learn to become comfortable with others' discomfort and our own. Give the client the time they need to search for and retrieve their memories. There may be the rare occasion when the client may be too distressed to continue, and I would halt the process, but this is few and far between. The distress may be genuine or a Stage 1, 2 or 3 abreaction, so also bear this in mind.

Remember, stop the person going into the story here, as this can send the whole process off on a tangent and away from the actual issue. At no point ask them to offer you an explanation or content.

- **When the client has accessed their earliest recollection, then ask,**

  "...and how vivid is this memory now?"

Again a question such as, "What do you mean by vivid?" could be asked by the client and I will follow a similar to the procedure as with the word 'familiar'.

Once the memory is located, instruct the client to ***hold this memory vividly, as vividly as you can***, in their mind for as long as possible... and to follow your finger(s)/pen with their eyes only - not their head.

There is really not much to add to this question, apart from if you repeat the process it may become more difficult to hold on vividly to a memory.

- **Eye Movements:**

  Guide the client to perform eye movements through the different access points as seen in the previous chapter. Periodically remind the client, "*...and if this memory fades, try very hard to bring it back... try as hard as you can to retain that experience...*"

  30 - 45 seconds per complete round is sufficient.

As per the Introductory Exercise image, ask them to focus on your finger or pen and follow this while keeping their head still. I will add that I am always watching for axial deviations from the first set of eye movements. However, doing this first round I am unlikely to indicate this to the client unless I need to repeat the eye moments. I will discuss this Integral Process later in the next chapter.

- **Repeat once or a few times until the client says they cannot retain or recall visual memory, or it is difficult to recall it.**

REMEMBER to re-ask **all** of the questions if you need to do more eye movements, because if there is a reduction in the SUD it is unlikely that the same feeling is being experienced, hence a different memory may need to be located. If an SUD score of 2/10 is reached it can be sufficient to stop here as the brain appears to continue to process for a 20 minutes or so, and a further reduction can occur as a result. I am not searching for what I call the 'Holy Grail of change' i.e., an SUD of 0/10, although of course it can and does happen.

- If after three rounds there is little or no reduction, stop the process and recalibrate the memory in relation to this particular feeling. In practice, I will have moved onto the Integral Pattern if there are any axial deviations, but if you are new to this process, please follow the Basic Pattern.

- If there has been sufficient reduction in the markers as seen earlier - i.e., memory intensity, distance, dissociation, kinaesthetic - the next stage is to test this change, as below:

Current state change

Test 1.
Ask, *"And what happens when you think about <u>that</u> memory now?"*

Test 2.
Ask, *"And what happens when you think about <u>that</u> feeling now?"*

(You may also add *"that was 9/10" or whatever number they started with)*

If the imprint event still triggers negative kinaesthetics, repeat the process, including the questions.

RE-SCALE, AS THIS MAY BE A DIFFERENT FEELING, HENCE A DIFFERENT MEMORY MAY BE ACCESSED SUBSEQUENTLY.

When asking test question 2, the person may say it's still exactly the same, so I will always rescale here. The original feeling may have been 9/10 and now they say it's 5/10 but exactly the same. This is important as it is a likely indicator to one of the Patterns of Chronicity this person is running, i.e., they are unable to notice or focus on the change because they are so focused on the problem. So, if the number changes I will explain that if this were the same feeling the number would be the same. I've not yet had any challenges to this piece of logic.

Test 3.
"So, either with your eyes open or closed I'd like you to 'try' to bring that memory/experience back exactly as it was before you moved your eyes around. That's it, 'try' again, 'TRY HARDER'."

It is unlikely that the person will be able to replicate the exact conditions of the memory/experience. However, some clients may say there is no change at all or that they can get it back exactly as it as before. It is possible that the three directions used were insufficient to create change and we need to look at using the Integral Pattern and some differently angled movements here.

Of course, IEMT may not be the right modality for this person at this current time. Alternatively, there may well be some change. However, a person's Patterns of Chronicity, where they do not want to admit to any change for whatever reason, could also be in action.

Unless there is a huge abreaction or some indication of trauma, I would attempt the Kinaesthetic Patterns again. It is important to go to the start of the model and check that we have the correct feeling in the first place before eliciting the memory. Eye movement-wise, I may go straight into the Integral Process, should it be relevant.

***Note: I am always looking to where the client is moving their eyes when asking the Kinaesthetic Model questions. I may well choose to start the eye movements at the place the eyes go to when the memory is first located, even when using the Basic Process and definitely during the Integral Process.**

Anticipatory state change:

If the issue is anticipatory i.e. a visit to the dentist or driving test nerves we can test for the change as follows:

> **Test**
> (this is optional, depending on the original issue the client had)
>
> **Ask: "...*And when you think about < XYZ, (ANTICIPATORY EVENT)> now, what feeling comes up for you now?*"**

If a negative kinaesthetic emerges, repeat the basic process and locate the next imprint.

Basic kinaesthetic Process Summary:

Elicit the undesired state (whole being) or kinaesthetic expression (part body feeling)

Ask client to assign amplitude scale (1-10). "*...and out of ten, how strong is* ***this feeling****, with ten being as strong as it can be*?"

Ask: **"*...And how familiar is this feeling*?"**

Ask: "*...And when was the first time that you can remember feeling this feeling... now... it may not be the first time it ever happened, but rather, it is the first time that you can remember now...*"

Allow the client 20-40 seconds to access imprinting event. Do not offer guidance or advice and allow the client to perform his or her own kinaesthetic transderivational search.

When the client has accessed their earliest recollection, ask: **"*...And how vivid is this memory now*?"**

Instruct the client to **hold that memory vividly** in their mind for as long as possible...

Guide client to perform eye movements through the different access points. Periodically reminding the client that, **"...And if this memory fades, try very hard to bring it back...try as hard as you can to retain that experience..."** (30-45 secs per round).

Repeat once or twice until client says that they cannot retain or recall visual memory.

Test 1.

Ask: **"And what happens when you think about that memory now?"**

Test 2

Ask: **"And what happens when you think about that feeling now?"**

If imprint event still triggers negative kinaesthetic, repeat process.

RE-SCALE, THIS MAY BE A DIFFERENT FEELING HENCE A DIFFERENT MEMORY, SO DO THE PROCESS AGAIN IF NEEDED

Alternative questions:

1. And when you think about that memory now, what happens/what do you notice?

2. And when you think about that feeling now what happens/what do you notice/how does it feel?

Test 3. (optional)

Ask: **"*...And when you think about <ANTICIPATORY EVENT> now, what feeling comes up for you now?*"**

If negative kinaesthetic emerges, then repeat basic process and locate next imprint.

Test 4.

As a final check you can ask... **"And try hard to bring it back exactly as it was before...try as hard as you can". If a negative kinaesthetic emerges, repeat basic process and locate next imprint.**

There are only 4 questions to this Kinaesthetic Process

Learn them verbatim so that the process becomes part of your unconscious memory, like the alphabet or a song like *Happy Birthday to You.* This will help you to become completely comfortable using the process whenever it is required.

Ask for specific scaling

Maybe Man can be unwittingly overlooked, so keep vigilant. This is one of the main points I notice with trainees - lack of recognition of the 5 POC and lack of challenge by the practitioner.

Learn to be comfortable with all aspects of IEMT

If you are uncomfortable with a client's discomfort and find it difficult to stick to the process and do testing at the end, engage in some self-reflection work as to why this might be so that you can clear such restrictions to enable you to work more effectively with IEMT. If you find it hard to apply IEMT for yourself, speak with your trainer or find a practitioner to work with.

Learn from your client sessions

Record sessions (with your clients' permission). You will learn so much from the replays – both what you did well, and more importantly, what you may have missed.

Chapter 7

The Integral (aka Complex) IEMT Kinaesthetic Model

“Getting their ducks in a row.”

Mike Richards

In many instances, the Basic Model is sufficient to deal with many kinaesthetically based issues, whether current or anticipatory. However, there will be times when more calibrated eye movements are required.

When working as a nurse in the field of neurosurgery, Andrew Austin would attend the pre-operative clinics of surgeons who were assessing the positioning, types and grades of neurological tumours. He watched as the doctors would take a pen or pencil and ask the patient to follow it with their eyes.

Andrew would notice that every now and then a patient's eyes would deviate momentarily from the pen. This happened in many cases, and when he asked the surgeons the significance of this, they replied that it was merely an artefact of no diagnostic relevance. When

Andrew asked the patients what had happened at those moments, they would often apologise and say, *"oh, I just lost concentration for a split second,"* or *"my mind wandered for a second."*

Given his background in NLP, and his knowledge of eye accessing cues and of EMDR, these events excited our intrepid IEMT developer, who felt that they did indeed have some significance. Not to the diagnosis of a brain tumour, but in the thoughts and internal images that the patients' brains were processing. He was quite excited by his 'discovery', and even phoned his mum to tell her about it (to which she responded, *"that's nice dear..."*). This occurred around 1996, and it inspired AA to develop the first 2-hour workshop to discover more about eye movements and memory in dealing with unhelpful emotions and behaviours. He later learned that these eye movements had been noted and commented on by others including Steve Andreas, so it wasn't actually his discovery. This gave him confidence - if other prominent trainers and innovators in the therapeutic world had also noticed these movements and were looking at the significance for change work, he was in good company.

Unconscious axial eye deviations - 'blips' as they are sometimes called - can be very subtle and it can take time to become accustomed to noticing them. Sometimes on training courses, very observant trainees will notice them when we do the Introductory exercise.

There have been several levels of research into the various unconscious eye movements, including some functional magnetic resonance imaging (fMRI) studies. An interesting paper by de Voogd et al (2018) on the subject with persistent fear-related disorders found that:

> "*Goal-directed eye-movements, like working-memory tasks, deactivate the amygdala, the core neural substrate of fear learning*" [1].

Several studies, including that of Similo et al, have investigated eye movements, comparing emotional images versus neutral images, and all seem to conclude that overt spatial attention first needs to be directed to emotional content before the event-related potentials (ERP) responses to emotional content could be observed. Event-related potentials (ERPs), also known as time-locked Electroencephalography (EEG) activity are very small voltages generated in the brain structures in response to specific events or stimuli [2]. These findings suggest:

> *"An involvement of higher-level processes in the interaction between emotion and attention. Moreover, both eye movement and EEG results demonstrated enhanced attention to emotional as compared to neutral scenes, supporting 'the emotionality hypothesis'"* [3].

Hannula and Ranganath set out to investigate whether the eye movements associated with relational memory would be correlated with hippocampal activity. Using fMRI they scanned the brains of 18 participants during a simple memory task [4]. They found that while the hippocampus alone may be sufficient for retrieval of implicit relational memories, this information must be communicated to the prefrontal cortex in order for conscious recollection and overt decision-making to take place.

Thus, hippocampal activity is closely correlated with the eye movements associated with retrieval of relational memories, even in the absence of conscious awareness. There also appears to be correlation between implicit and explicit memory retrieval showing distinct brain activation patterns. The authors suggest there could be far-reaching implications with their findings. Eye-tracking could be used to investigate memory function in infants, or to obtain past event information from those unwilling or unable to recall them. For example, schizophrenics often exhibit memory deficits, and Hannula has already used memory-related eye movements to show that they have difficulty noticing small changes in a previously learned scene.

When using IEMT, the practitioner needs to become used to tracking rapid unconscious eye movements, as this is a good indicator of the direction in which the eyes are to be moved in order for the client to create neurological change. A report in *Psychology Today*,

2015, reported that eye movements unconsciously give away secret personal information, as follows [(5)]:

12 ways your eye movements reveal personal information:

1. Rapid eye movements indicate impulsive decision-making.
2. Plodding eyes reflect a wandering mind.
3. Slow eye movements indicate your level of fatigue.
4. Tracking eye movements can shift your moral compass,
5. Gaze cues can reveal your political temperament.
6. Rapid eye movement (REM) sleep minimises painful memories of PTSD.
7. Rapid eye movement (REM) sleep increases positive emotions.
8. Jerky eye movements can predict neurodegenerative diseases.
9. Alterations in eye movements are an early indicator of Alzheimer's disease.
10. Involuntary eye movements can diagnose ADHD.
11. Lack of eye contact is the earliest marker for autism in young infants.
12. Abnormal eye movements can diagnose mental Illness.

https://www.psychologytoday.com/gb/blog/the-athletes-way/201505/12-ways-eye-movements-give-away-your-secrets

The online article contains links to studies for each of the 12 points above and there appears to be anecdotal evidence of these correlations.

Creating the Integral Process

After devising and using the Basic Kinaesthetic Model of IEMT, Andrew Austin realised there must be a way of utilising the unconscious saccadic eye movements that he observed while working in the neurosurgery department. In the early days of IEMT he may sometimes have to use the Basic Pattern many times in a session.

There was one client who called and asked for a session ASAP because he had to give a very important presentation the next day and he had become extremely anxious about it. When questioned about the issue, he scored it as 100/10 and the first time he could remember this feeling was related to something from a previous job. The process completed, when he was asked what he now noticed and felt, the man said everything was exactly the same. However, when AA enquired about the level of the SUD, the client said 80/10.

Here was a discrepancy. The client was reporting no change and yet the SUD had decreased. So, the process was repeated and the memory changed to something from school. The eye movement Basic Pattern was used and again, on testing for change, apparently everything was exactly the same. The SUD, however, was now 70/10. So, the process was completed one more time and the memory was now back to a younger child being forced by his father to stand up and sing in front of strangers at a party. When asked about possible change, the answer was again everything was the same, but the SUD was now 50/10. So, according to the client, the memory and feelings had not changed, but the SUD had dropped by half.

AA realised that he could keep going like this and the client was likely to report no change. At this point, he decided to change his approach. He had been tracking some of the unconscious saccadic eye movements and decided to see if working directly with these would make a difference. On this attempt, instead of moving the eyes in each of the directions as before, he started at a place where he noticed a deviation and kept going with eye movements until this set of involuntary saccades smoothed out. This time, when subsequently checking and testing for change, a shift occurred in the memory intensity and feelings.

Further experimentation using these targeted smoothing out movements found that this often reduced the number of eye movement 'rounds' required to create significant change, thus streamlining the process (and saving AA's arm and shoulder joint too much wear and tear!).

Thus was created what Andrew Austin termed the Complex Pattern, and this more calibrated and targeted method was at the time unlike any of the other eye movement modalities. I have debated with Andrew the term Complex Pattern because it actually makes the process sound like it may be complicated, which it really isn't, and he agrees. Since my trainer training in 2013, I have used the term the Integral Pattern, as it is these specific eye movements that the brain is unconsciously deviating to during IEMT and they are integral to the process of rapid neurological change. I will continue to use the term Integral Pattern and hope other practitioners decide to adopt it.

This form of targeted, smoothing eye movements can take a bit of practice, as sometimes the axial deviations are very subtle. Sometimes, however, people's eyes jump markedly away from the direction in which the practitioner is leading them. These huge jumps can be very significant; as though the brain is wanting to avoid memories/images in that particular place. However, it is to this place the eyes need to be directed, as continual avoidance will not enable the brain to process and consolidate the memories in order to neutralise the emotional impact.

I like to term this smoothing out of the axial deviations as getting people's ducks in a row. Once the memory has been processed, the eyes glide more smoothly - just like ducks moving effortlessly and easily through water. The memories and feelings become easier to handle and can eventually slip deeply into parts of the brain where they are no longer easily accessible.

We will now look at the process of using the Integral Pattern in a client setting. One interesting point with these eye movements is that, due to their subtlety, the client is not always aware the deviations are occurring.

How to use the Integral Process

One thing that often surprises people is that there are no differences in the questioning process between the Basic and Integral styles. I encourage practitioners to go straight into this way of working once they have had some practice in the Basic Pattern and are confident they are able to calibrate axial deviations quickly and easily. This will reduce the time they are spending on eye movement work within the session, which is of huge benefit to both client and practitioner.

- On trainings and in client sessions, we start with the Basic Pattern questions using the full process.

- Being observant as to the unconscious eye movements clients are making during this process is key to calibration and to the place you will start the eye movements from.

- As soon as you start asking about familiarity and *when is the first time…* etc, be vigilant of the eye movements as the client will go to where they are locating the memory and away again, sometimes very quickly, to where they feel more comfortable.

- On locating a vivid memory and asking the client to hold this memory, again look at where the eyes deviate to and the direction, e.g., is it horizontal or diagonal tracking, and start there. You can also instruct the client to…

"…Just allow your mind to move through time to different events, locations, memories and experiences, the logic of which is irrelevant."

Also you can instruct them as follows:

"***You can talk to me as we do the process if you wish to, tell me what images come to mind now.***"

- It is likely that there will be access deviations almost immediately, however not always. Look for the saccadic movements or axial deviations where there is a sudden shift. Note where it is and on returning the eye movements to this place verbally mark the 'blip' with rhetorical questions such as...

  ...And what was that...

  ...Oh, what happened then...

  ...And again, just there...

  *And so on, continuing in the same direction until the deviation smooths out and change direction (*or stop – see point 8 below).*

- Watch closely for state shifts and changes in representation and mark them verbally (as above). It can be important to get a person to discuss these representations so that they can now talk about the past experiences while being anchored into the present. So, now they are remembering in a more detached, updated way. In some cases of incidents from childhood, this means they are now remembering from a current adult position and perspective, rather than a childhood perspective that may be more fear-based. However many won't speak and the process still works really well in most cases.

- Repeat the process for other deviations. If, however, you track a direction and there are no blips, change direction.

- It is really important that we only run this type of eye movement work for a maximum of 45 seconds. Any more and the eyes can become overwhelmed. This is usually sufficient time to locate at least one memory access point and axial deviation and work on it to smooth it out.

- You may notice some huge jumps away, so bring the eyes back to the starting point and move away. Smooth this out.

- If you are at 40-45 seconds, STOP. Give the person a second or two and advise them to take few breaths if they need to, then recalibrate

- We use the questions from the Basic Pattern, asking the client **what they now notice about that memory and what the feeling is like now.**

- Re-scale if you need to and remind them that a change in the SUD valency means this is not the exact same feeling or emotion, so we use the questions to find an appropriate memory for this feeling. Occasionally, it may be the same memory, even if it has faded. Remember, we rarely experience situations with single emotions and feelings, hence the same memory may be brought up more than once.

- Repeat the process if required.

- Sometimes, people will break eye movements, smile, laugh or make a comment; these usually indicate that the change has occurred.

- Remember to **test** the change and ask them to, ***"Try and get the memory back exactly as before... Try harder"*** etc.

- The client can now see that the old memory is no longer successful in its ability to create the old, outdated feelings or emotions. **We have now created success inside the problem state** and as such the person has now indeed changed state at a neurological level with regards to the issue.

"But I can't visualise..."

Some people can struggle with visual memories. However, pieces of music that can trigger emotions, a kinaesthetic response, even smells and tastes can be used as key memories, especially for those with visual impairments and in the very rare cases of aphantasia (the inability to visualise).

I am yet to encounter a true case of aphantasia, yet I know some practitioners who have. Some people say, *"I can't visualise",* so I ask them to *"imagine"* or *"remember a time when...".* I will sometimes ask them to imagine themselves outside their front door turning the key in the lock, then ask what colour the door is. I've never yet had anyone unable to tell me the colour immediately. This can act as a good demonstration to the person of their own ability to remember, imagine, or indeed visualise.

Seeing lots of deviations on one axis?

Sometimes a person's eyes will do two or more blips along a horizontal or diagonal axis. There appears to be some correlation as to what this may indicate. There is no scientific evidence of the following, however, there appears to be anecdotal evidence and I have witnessed this myself on a few occasions.

With axial deviations, the aim is to smooth out as many 'blips' as possible, as an indicator that the episodic memory and emotional memory is now being processed, consolidated and encoded (stored) i.e., 'put to bed' if you will. Or, as my husband would say, it's about "getting your ducks in a row."

Examples of Axial Deviations

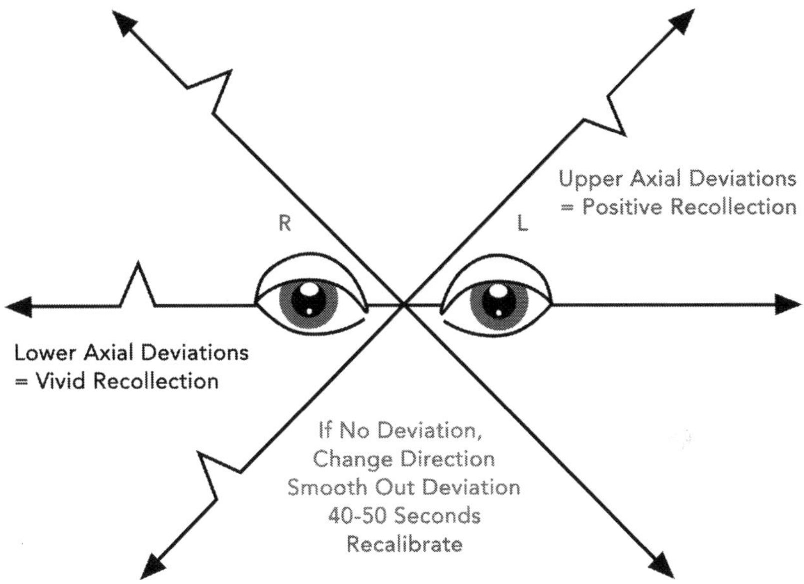

- Three or more blips in the upper area on an axis can indicate some sort of positive revelation. The client may say things such as, *"I never thought about it that way before"*, or *"How interesting, that makes sense now"*.

- Two or more blips in a lower area can indicate a vivid recollection, usually a positive one, and draw comments such as, *"I'd forgotten all about that memory"*, *"That's nice, I remember the colour of my birthday cake"*, etc.

Quick learning points of the kinaesthetic models

1. We are working on the premise that a person has ***"learned to feel this way about this thing".***
2. We are working with the **MEMORY** and not the feeling.
3. Whether using the Basic or Integral Model, keep the eye movements at a good pace, reach the peripheral boundaries if the eyes allow this movement, and keep it brief at 20-45 seconds per round.
4. Be vigilant and observant for unconscious eye movements when the client is locating memories.
5. Learn to become confident when instructing clients what to do.
6. Learn to work in a more "Integral Way".
7. Stop and recalibrate. If there is a fall in the SUD to 3/10 this can be enough to stop. Ask the client - they will tell you if it's okay to stop or if they wish to continue.
8. Re-ask the set of questions if working with a new feeling.
9. **TEST FOR THE CHANGE.** This can be an amazing, rapid experience for clients, so embed the learning.
10. Always be listening for Patterns of Chronicity, feelings that are demonstrating via the 3 Pillars Model (see in a separate chapter), signs of language that may indicate a trauma. Stop and deal with these if required.

Chapter 8

The Great Big Identity Conundrum

> “Be yourself; everyone else is already taken.”
>
> Oscar Wilde

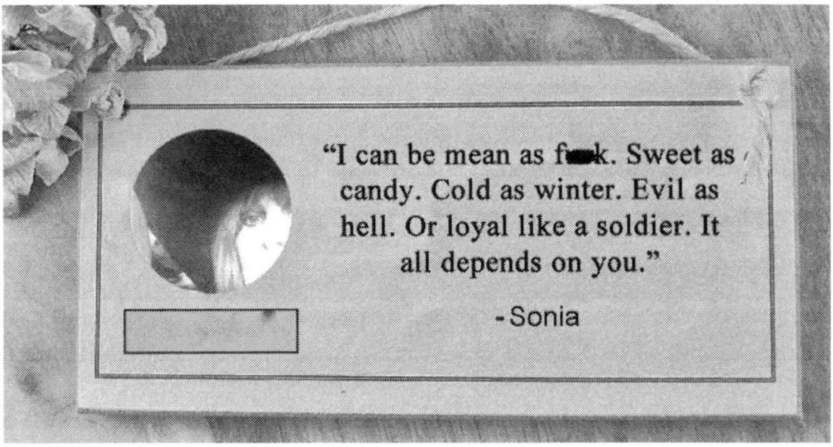

Identity can be a difficult concept to evaluate and quantify. Often an umbrella term related to all things related to “the self”, it is a nominalization, i.e., the word is commonly used as if identity were a physical thing, which of course it is not (it can’t be easily or comfortably placed in the proverbial wheelbarrow to be moved around). Even looking up a definition in dictionaries can lead to confusion. So, let’s just say that in its simplest definition when it comes to human beings, identity is, to quote the Oxford English Dictionary:

“The fact of being who or what a person or thing is.”

The French philosopher René Descartes is famously quoted as saying: "***Cogito, ergo sum***" - ***"I think, therefore I am"*** [1]. In other words, the reason I as a person, an ego if you like, exists is because I have cognition. Descartes didn't actually realise that he was referring to the ego, and it took another 300 years for Jean-Paul Sartre to put this into a more accurate context. He looked at the above statement by Descartes and very deeply and suddenly realised, in his words:

> *"The consciousness that says, 'I am', is not the consciousness that thinks"* [2].

I have a brain capable of thought, not just automatic response to my environment. Here's the thing though, so do other mammals, especially the great apes. So, do they have a sense of identity as humans have a sense of identity?

The philosopher/guru Eckhart Tolle says:

> *"The philosopher Descartes believed he had found the most fundamental truth when he made his famous statement, 'I think, therefore I am'. He had, in fact, given expression to the most basic error: to equate thinking with Being and identity with thinking. The compulsive thinker, which means almost everyone, lives in a state of apparent separateness, in an insanely complex world of continuous problems and conflict, a world that reflects the ever-increasing fragmentation of the mind"* [3].

Tolle goes on to explain the Sartre statement as more accurate than the Descartes one, and asks:

> *"What did he mean by that? When you are aware that you are thinking, that awareness is not part of thinking. It is a different dimension of consciousness. And it is that awareness that says, 'I am'. If there were nothing but thought in you, you wouldn't even know you are thinking. You would be like a dreamer who doesn't know he is dreaming. You would be as identified with every thought as the dreamer is with every image in the dream."*

I feel there are merits in both viewpoints; after all, that is what philosophy is about - opening up thinking into the human condition and posing questions that inspire us to discover more about who we are. These concepts of what makes us human have been debated for millennia and will continue to be questioned for many more to come.

Unfortunately, what we as practitioners and therapists see is that many people live life like sleepwalkers, trapped in mindsets that are outdated and defunct, running schemas that keep creating old and even nightmarish realities. Being aware of a dream, awake in it, brings in another dimension of consciousness. Somehow, the person needs to end the dream and come back to reality. For some, this can mean updating old identities that want to hold onto the past and even cause internal fights to remain, which can lead to mental health issues.

The Integral Eye Movement process has a highly innovative way of helping with the internal wrangling that keeps people rooted in the past and can prevent emotional growth in some or all aspects of a person's life. This is often seen when trauma occurs during childhood, and also in people with certain types of addictions. Of course, the two are not mutually exclusive. Interestingly, researching scientific papers relating to identity and neurology yields far less research than papers pertaining to emotions and neurology. I think this is analogous to the ways in which we approach health issues in the West, more so than in Eastern medicine and philosophies.

In the West, we are largely focused on the 'effect' and the symptoms. When looking at symptoms, we often take them individually. Several fields of medicine may be involved, a person is often treated by several doctors and given a huge cocktail of pharmaceuticals, many of which have never been tested in tandem, so the interactive effects cannot be truly known. It is rare that a physician in the West will look at the bigger picture of that person's life, their feelings or issues about themselves as well as others. Traditional Eastern medicines often start here, before looking at the symptoms [4] [5] [6]. In IEMT work, we know that just ameliorating feelings is unlikely to result in a fundamental shift neurologically and maintenance of that shift.

One of the most prolific researchers and writers on personality and identity work was the psychologist Erik Erikson (1902-1994), famous for coining the phrase 'Identity Crisis' and credited as one of the originators of Ego Psychology [7]. His theory of psychosocial development is based on eight stages of how various psychosocial crises are resolved, unlike Freud who believed in a set of psychosexual stages [8]. Erikson's stages start at around 18-months-old with Trust vs Mistrust, and progress to stage eight at 65 years and Integrity vs. Despair [9]:

Erikson's Stages of Psychological Development

Approximate Age	Psychological Crisis/Task	Virtue Developed
Infant to 18 months	Trust vs Mistrust	Hope
18 months to 3 years	Autonomy vs Shame/Doubt	Will
3 to 5 years	Initiative vs Guilt	Purpose
5 to 13 years	Industry vs Inferiority	Competency
13 to 21 years	Identity vs Confusion	Fidelity
21 to 30 years	Intimacy vs Isolation	Love
40 to 65 years	Generativity vs Stagnation	Care
65 years and over	Integrity vs Despair	Wisdom

Each stage is defined by two opposing emotional forces known as contrary dispositions or 'syntonic' and 'dystonic' positions. Each initiate a crisis or task that a person needs to resolve or master. Once resolved, the person acquires some basic virtues and a sense of competence. Failure to achieve this can lead to feelings of inadequacy, lack of self-belief, self-worth and so on. The third column in the table denotes the virtue that is developed, according to Erikson, once the crisis or task is completed.

There are some limitations to Erikson's theory, and some details it doesn't address. For example, the type of experiences needed to complete each stage and how a person moves onto the next stage. However, as a framework for movement and psychosocial development through a lifespan, it demonstrates the social nature of humans and the importance of social relationships in development, maturity and identity.

I will briefly say that in Metaphors of Movement (MOM) [(10)], another modality developed by Andrew Austin, we see how this lack of development of healthy social relationships can, metaphorically and in reality, stunt emotional growth and keep people trapped, usually via some metaphorical container, at one of the less mature states of psychosocial development. In other words, their identity becomes limited, in some cases entrenched, in a certain position. Hence, the possibility of change or refinement at the identity level can feel frightening or even threatening.

The great thing about the human condition, however, is that even those who are struggling with their own identity or those who appear entrenched in a position that is causing some emotional turbulence, can with the right stimulus, social interactions and motivation, start to find movement. And, as we see in IEMT and MOM, a maturing or 'growing up' is possible via integration and updating.

Who Am I?

> *"Knowing thyself is the beginning of all wisdom."*
> Aristotle (384-322 BC)

It is safe to say that the question, "Who Am I?" is one of the great identity conundrums of all time. Human beings have developed from a group of animals doing whatever was needed to survive and procreate more than 1 million or more years ago, to a species that in many cases feels the need to find some reason for existing or some higher purpose for being. This has led to many different philosophical beliefs and identities, a lot of confusion in some and, in some, hatred of those seen as "other".

We can view identity in terms of "core" identity and "peripheral" or "acquired" identity. Some may also add "didactic" identity and "digital" identity. Core identity has no one true definition and it will vary from person to person. Sometimes it is described as a deep understanding of the 'self'. It is a set of beliefs based on a visceral interaction within our own bodies and minds and between our relationship to others.

I have a fundamental understanding and belief about who I am, deep down, today. It is unlikely to change, so I would describe this as a 'core identity'. The Earth's inner-most core is formed of iron at a temperature as hot as the sun, but it remains solid due to the intense pressure of the rest of the planet. This is an analogy to core identity; the more I adopt other external layers of identity, the more stable the core identity becomes. It has been noted that each time we shape our surface beliefs and values around our deeper ones, the deeper ones become more deeply entrenched [(11)]. The outer layer of the Earth's core is of course molten and as such is able to move and flow. This is somewhat analogous to our peripheral identity, which is more open to change.

Identity seems to be rapidly becoming one of the most vehemently debated topics of our current age, and the explosion of gender identities is leading to numerous conflicting views and a whole lot of Maybe Man thinking for some who would possibly never have questioned their own sense of self on the basis of gender. I am not offering an opinion on this, just stating some observations based on clients I have seen, usually teenagers or young adults. I think it is fair to say that, possibly for the first time in our history, this sudden explosion of opinions and beliefs has, instead of freeing more people to express themselves, led to more confusion, instead of less, for some.

All humans, be they XX, XY, or some other combination, begin their developmental journey at the same point, and gonads remain undifferentiated for several weeks.

However, the Y gene in those who have it will begin to express itself from around 6 to 7 weeks' gestation. Testes will begin to form and testosterone starts production from around 9 weeks. This has a direct effect on the developing brain as well as primary sexual characteristics. Interestingly, female phenotype is not reliant on the secretion of ovarian hormones for female sex differentiation [12].

So how much of our identity can really be considered as core? From the moment of conception our sex is determined, so in terms of our first core identity it begins here. Now, for a small number of developing embryos (about 1 in 1,000) this is not quite so straightforward; a duality can exist and both sets of genitalia can be produced [13]. So, for such individuals, what we understand as a core identity is not one particular gender. Historically, it has very often been the choice of the parent, with medical advice, to assign a gender to these children. Sometimes this appears to have no lasting physiological or psychological effect, but unfortunately sometimes it does. In terms of identity rather than biology deciding a person's core identity, a parent decides, so for some even that core fundamental identity is given to them. They may grow and develop feeling entirely different to the gender that has been assigned to them.

As a Trainer of IEMT, MOM and hypnobirthing (peripheral identities), I find it extremely interesting that many therapists, coaches, practitioners, and other professionals who attend trainings have a goal of helping others to know themselves better and change things that are unhelpful and sometimes dangerous to mental and physical health; yet they often don't know who they are, or indeed where they stand. So, on day two of the IEMT training, which is primarily identity-based, I conduct the following exercise. There are no right or wrong answers in this exercise, but it can be very revealing to the person examining their inner self as to who they feel they are, and sometimes who they think they are. I also conduct this exercise with all clients prior to IEMT identity work. This can be a deeply profound experience for some.

The Who Am I exercise

According to Kath Woodward in her book *Understanding Identity,* "Who am I?", will have a reference to "you", "us" "them" and "others" with whom I have contact [(14)]. Who I am is interwoven into my own beliefs and those of society and it can be one of the most difficult of all questions to answer, because who I am right now may alter from who I am in the next moment on some level according to belief, value and experience. In other words, identity is essentially a contract or a story we tell others and ourselves; i.e., a construct.

One of the starting points for having an understanding about ourselves is a sense of roots and belonging. This can cause profound issues for some who have been conceived by anonymous sperm or egg donor, and for some adopted as babies. The drive for these people to search for their birth parents can be a fundamental need to know their roots, their story and who they are. In terms of MOM, there may well be a fulfilment issue; e.g., *"If I don't know who am, then how can I be happy, whole, complete?"*

The following exercise can be conducted in pairs or solo.

1. Take a clean piece of paper and write the question:

   "Who Am I" at the top with the date.

2. If working in pairs, one person can ask the other,

   "So, Who Are You?"

3. Give the person time to do an inner search and write the answers down for them. If you're working alone, you may choose to mind map this exercise on a whiteboard or flip chart:

4. Keep the paper or photograph the board so that you can review it after the IEMT identity work.

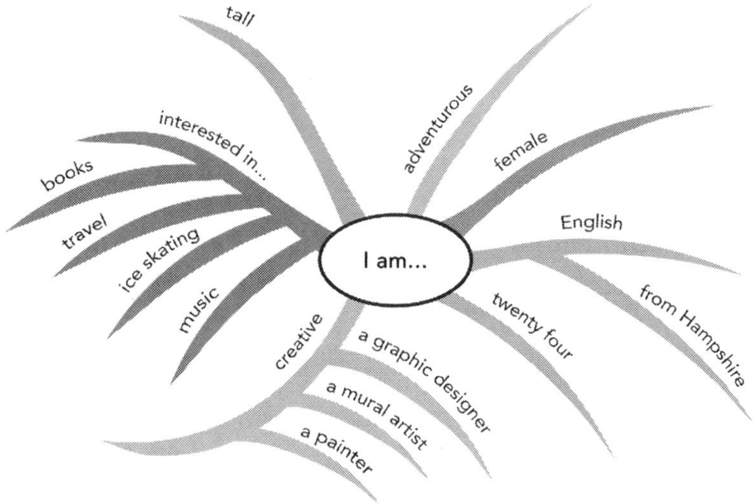

This exercise can create a host of different scenarios. For some, the "Who Am I" becomes more like "What Am I". There will be a list of labels and titles, often work, pastime and hobby-related, and often status-related: An army major, a doctor, a surgeon, a freemason, a business consultant, a cyclist, a cricketer, a dog lover, a fine wine connoisseur, a secretary, a therapist…

For others, it will be a collection of esoteric, philosophic thoughts: A free spirit, a healing soul, an innovator, a loving person, a feminist, a caring person, a change facilitator…

Some will create a more fundamental list of identities: I am a mother, a daughter, sister, a wife, a father, son, a parent, a guardian, a mentor…

And for many it is a mixture of things: I am a man, a father, a provider, a life coach, a toast master, a first aider, a Liverpool fan, a golfer, a generous person…

I tend to give 15 minutes for this exercise and some people rattle through it rapidly, barely stopping for breath. Others, however, really struggle. I am watching and listening out for this because often statements such as, *"I don't really know who I am"*, or *"I don't usually think about myself"*, or *"I'm really struggling with this"* (watch out for the Three Stage Abreaction signals, look at body language) will come out. Chances are, when we come to the IEMT work, there will be a full-blown Stage 3 or lots of Maybe Man language and disparity within the locations and ages in the pronoun work.

Every part of an IEMT session should be crafted to ensure the practitioner can see and hear as much as possible. That is, of the person sitting in front of them, not the 'story' or facade they normally present to the world. It is not always comfortable for the practitioner at first, but it becomes easier over time.

The ability to help a person learn to understand themselves more and address at a neurological level the issues and behaviours they are ensnaring themselves in is a fabulous release for the client or trainee practitioner during a training event. At the start of each IEMT course, I always state that this is training, not therapy. The fact of the matter is that when people are working on true issues, as such, change for the better is very often going to occur. This not only acts as a huge convincer as to the efficacy of the techniques for the trainee; it also gives them a true sense of just how easily at times they can alter their own beliefs and mindset about their own issues. I have seen amazing releases of stuck emotional states and negative identity beliefs on the training courses I have delivered, no matter where in the world, in person or online.

Secondary Identities

One thing I want to briefly touch upon is purposely choosing a secondary identity. Of course, having a different public and private persona is not a new thing. People in all walks of life have been doing this for millennia, e.g., actors, barristers, musicians, comedians, trainers, those with different sexual identities such as a cross-dresser, territorial SAS personnel, government spies and so on. If fact, most people have a different face, front or identity at various times, depending on where they are and who they're with.

Not only is this normal, but I conjecture that it is likely a vestige of an evolutionary form of survival. The Fight, Flight, Freeze phenomenon also has a response called 'Fawn'. This is often seen in species with beta males; e.g., wolves and apes. Less dominant females in ape species, for instance, will 'fawn' to dominant members of the group in order to curry favour or even prevent themselves being killed (a survival response).

I do not want to engage in the debate on Dissociative Identity Disorder (DID, formerly known as Multiple Personality Disorder) here. However, as a psychological condition it appears to be gaining more traction in recent years. For those with this disorder, the creation of new identities as a means for what they often term 'survival' may have some relationship to what many people do as role-play in everyday life. However, in the case of DID, this mental role-play can become exaggerated; there have been reports of people who have created more than 100 personas in response to trauma, most often childhood abuse. In one extreme case, a woman reported having created more than 2,500 different personas [15].

The definition of DID is usually a person having two or more relatively distinct identity or personality states. However, this was updated in 1994 to what psychologists say better reflects their understanding; that this disorder is a fragmentation or splintering of existing identity, rather than a creation of new ones [16]. The fragmented identities can function without the awareness of the person's main identity/personality. It is thought that approximately 2% of people have DID and that women are more likely to experience this phenomenon than men. The key factor in DID is trauma and about 90% of cases involve some history of sexual abuse.

One of the more disturbing definitions of DID is that the personalities 'take control' of an individual. This has been described by some as 'possession'. Other side effects are amnesia; a sense of being detached from oneself and one's emotions; a blurred sense of identity; a perception of the people and things around the person as distorted and unreal; significant stress or problems in relationships, work or other important areas of life; inability to cope well with emotional or professional stress; and mental health problems such as depression, anxiety, and suicidal thoughts and behaviours [(17)].

When it comes to the IEMT work discussed in the following chapter, secondary identities can be an issue on occasion and this may interfere with the process. Hence, there is a need to be mindful of the language being used as this can often offer a significant indication of possible secondary identity disorder issues.

I had a case recently where the person had seemed to fragment off part of their identity as a response to a very traumatic event so as to continue to function in their work and personal life. The person also felt they had lost part of their identity as a result of this and was in turmoil over wanting to find that part of their identity again. In order to get some understanding about this, we did some work with the PTSD model discussed later in the book.

If you suspect something that goes beyond secondary identity, such as schizophrenia, where a person's sense of reality is distorted and is often not trauma-related, it is important to have a discussion with the client with regard to engaging with a local medical mental health professional so that the person can access specialist help. Schizophrenia is a serious mental illness that causes hallucinations and delusions, with other symptoms such as jumbled thoughts, jumbled speech, and difficulties expressing emotions. People with schizophrenia may hear or feel things that are unreal or believe things that can't be real, but these aren't separate identities [(18)].

An interesting paper on the subject of identity and schizophrenia by Mary V. Seeman reports that individuals with the condition find it difficult to define to themselves and others who they truly are [19]. Also, according to the author, schizophrenia is also called the "I am" illness, meaning that it:

> *"Affects an individual's core identity, the qualities, characteristics and continuities that distinguish one person from another."*

As we know, identity is never static, and for schizophrenics in particular it can be associated with fluidity. Autobiographical recall and changes in self-representation are inconsistent over time. Seeman goes on to say:

> *"Perhaps for this reason they make attempts to change core aspects of themselves. These attempts may be delusional, but are too often unjustly dismissed as delusional before the potential value of the change is considered. Instead of facilitation, obstacles are placed in the way of hoped-for body modifications or changes of name or of religious faith."*

It would be an interesting study to see how many of those with body dysmorphia and go to great lengths to physically alter their appearance – whether that be with tattoos, piercings, and/or surgery - may actually have undiagnosed schizoid tendencies. Additionally, to discover whether the increase of such traits in recent years also mirrors an increase in schizophrenia or other identity-based disorders.

For those interested in mental disorders such as schizophrenia, the work of R D. Laing, such as *The Divided Self* [20], is a great place to start. I was only introduced to this work in 2018 and it has given me a deeper understanding of the construction and methodologies for IEMT and MOM. Although first published in 1960, the theories are still relevant today, perhaps even more so with the recent explosion in the identity and gender debate.

Laing's work on ontological insecurity and the loss of the sense of self is now manifesting in those who previously had a very secure ontology. The subject of removing gender separation for female toilets, changing rooms, sporting events and so on makes some women feel that their sense of themselves as a being female is being erased by society in order to make a minority feel more ontologically secure, hence perpetuating their ontological insecurity; e.g., society no longer recognises me as a woman who is separate from you, hence I as a woman no longer exist. Laing said:

> *"It is difficult for a person with such sense of his integral selfhood and personal identity... to transpose himself into the world of an individual whose experiences may be utterly lacking any unquestionable self-validating certainties."*

And yet politics and society seem determined to force this transposition onto the majority of those who have no concept of ontological insecurity.

So, we now have the Three Stage Abreaction pattern manifesting itself in the social and public psyche. 'You' the majority have to change in order to make 'me/us' the minority, feel better. 'I' can't say that 'I' have any answers to this on a global scale and I think this ontological existential crisis will get worse before it gets better, if indeed it actually ever does.

The tangled web of identity is becoming bigger and more complex. The Maybe Man phenomenon is therefore also likely to increase globally, especially in children and young people who are now, in some cases at very young ages, being confronted by the beliefs of parents that they are gender-fluid and therefore have no specific gender identity, even if they feel strongly male or female and favour certain colours, toys and ways of behaving. I can only see this leading to even greater numbers of mental illness in young people, which is already increasing at an alarming rate.

Chapter 9

IEMT Identity Elicitation, Integration and Updating

“How did this person learn to be this way?”

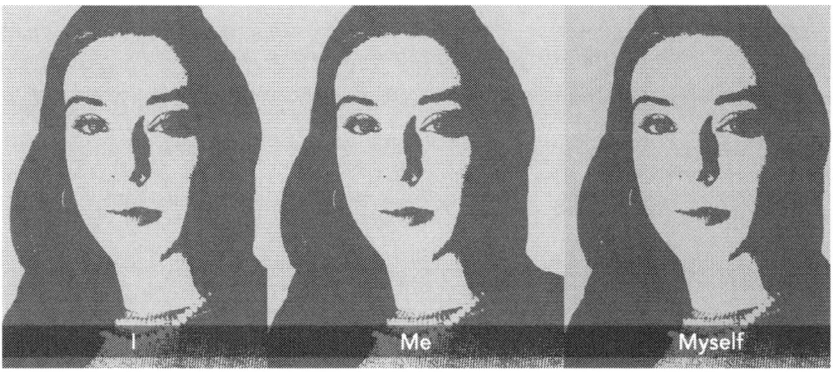

The above question is part of the conundrum of identity. What are the genetics, events, experiences, beliefs, values, social constraints, family interactions and so forth that shape a person's identity, their ego, their ontological security or insecurity, or sense of self with respect to themselves or to others?

The following body of work and techniques devised for use in IEMT sessions was in part influenced by the work of David Grove (1950-2008), a New Zealand-based psychotherapist. Grove was the founder of a communications methodology process that has become known as 'Clean Language'. He also developed 'Clean Space', moving the understanding into a spatial format with clients moving about a room or even outside it as a means of enabling them to discover a new self-knowledge [1].

Grove started working with 'Clean Pronouns', the purpose being for a person to understand that at any one time and in any situation there is the possibility of more than oneself that may respond. This is not the same as a schizoid experience; rather, it is a phenomenon that all humans will experience. However, prolonged imbalance in one's sense of self and responses to life based on such imbalances could, in certain circumstances, lead to mental illness if not addressed.

This is one of the areas in which IEMT has a different approach to issues and their resultant behaviours compared to other modalities that work on purely kinaesthetic change. Ameliorating a person's feelings about an issue is not getting to the cause. Merely dealing with effect - as seen in parts of the medical profession, when drugs may be given to treat a symptom rather than finding out why the symptom is there in the first place, is not ideal. It must be added that some parts of the medical profession are very open to the use of complementary therapies as an adjunct to the wellbeing of patients or service users. Midwifery is one such field, where approaches such as hypnobirthing, mindfulness, aromatherapy, reflexology and acupuncture have been well integrated for the benefit of patients and staff. Mind-body based approaches to better health or to improve normal outcomes such as in birthing, have been seen to have great benefits in improving anxiety-based physiological issues. Irritable bowel syndrome (IBS), for example, is a condition for which hypnotherapy is included in the UK NICE guidelines' (National Institute for Health and Care Excellence) recommended interventions.

The ability to connect the work of Groves into eye movement work is inspired, and those taking IEMT training who may be highly qualified in the field of psychology, for example, often comment on how this identity-based work is unlike anything else they have encountered. I will add that at first it can cause some Three Stage Abreactions at level 1 and 2 in such attendees, as it is so far outside their own comfort zone. However, once they experience just how deeply and simply this process can work, it often creates the most profound changes, not only in issues they are working on for themselves and with others, but in their own presuppositions regarding this work.

We have looked at emotional imprinting, where a person lays down a new kinaesthetic response to some issue, situation or experience. The question posed was: *"How did this person learn to feel this way about this thing?"* This part of the work is more suitable for remedial change; i.e., current situations that are causing issues interfering with life such as anger, anxiety, depression, and PTSD. With identity imprinting, we know that the development of a person's identity is usually a lifelong process characterised by cycles of exploration and consolidation as well as experiences of competence and vulnerability. According to Fandrem in 2015:

> *"Although the process is lifelong, it takes new dimensions during years of youth because of the confluence of physical, cognitive, and relational changes during this period"* (2).

However, it is still very pertinent to ask the question: ***"How did this person learn to be this way?"*** even if identity is ever-evolving, because it has been shown by Erik Erikson and others that many of our earliest beliefs about our identity are the most ingrained and can, if they don't sit well in later years, especially the teenage period, cause internal turmoil. Indeed, Erikson believed that identity begins long before there is even self-awareness, and it is in the nascent bonds of intimate relations (primarily with parents) that identity assumes its earliest expression:

> *"Identity grows and is nurtured or frustrated in a complex bonding of self and society"* (3).

For Erikson, identity is both a personal and a social construction, due to the strong interplay between the psychic self and the social self. This being the case, the IEMT Identity Process is far more suited to creating generative change; i.e., to generate or create something new that builds upon itself and creates a deep contextual shift (4).

When hearing expressions of identity, the IEMT Practitioner listens and looks out for certain 'red flags' that alert us to possible identity-based issues; e.g., where a person takes on the identity of a problem or a disease. For example, instead of *"I have asthma"*, the person will say *"I am an asthmatic"*, or *"I am a depressive", "I am a diabetic", "I am a loser"*, and so forth. Such statements can come across with an air of hopelessness, learned helplessness or even victimhood. Once a person begins to own this identity, it can be difficult to shift. As we know, often such labels will afford the person a particular status that can be difficult to give up if there is some perceived advantage in ***being this way.***

Working with Pronouns

Until a few years ago, the concept of pronouns was relatively straight-forward. Most were divided into genders and pronouns of self and others. Personal pronouns were single for one person and plural for pairs or groups. Then came the gender explosion and it became, in some cases, almost a crime to use grammatical language with regards to certain people. In fact, using the word 'person' may be mis-speciesising someone who identifies themselves with another animal, plant or inanimate object. The propensity to be offended by what is normal grammatical language used in what is thought to be the usual way has become not only politically correct, but has resulted in some people being prosecuted for 'mis-gendering' some individuals.

For the purposes of this book and of IEMT Practitioner training, we use pronouns as they were originally intended. Those reading this book who wish to use other pronouns will have to adapt it accordingly. Also, those whose first language is not English will have their own grammatical rules with regards to pronouns.

So, let's look at the following four personal pronouns:

I, Me, Self (Myself) and You

In English, pronouns are usually used in place of the noun to avoid repeating it. According to several sources, there are 12 different types of personal pronouns, including the four above, that can be singular or plural depending on whether they refer to one or multiple nouns. Personal pronouns can be subdivided into three classes:

- 1st Person - the person speaking; e.g., I, me, we, us.
- 2nd Person - the person spoken to; e.g., you.
- 3rd Person - a person or object being spoken about; e.g., she, he, they, it, him, her, them [(5)].

The pronoun, 'myself' is known as a reflexive pronoun. Such pronouns end in the word 'self' and are used when the object is the same as the subject of the verb. This particular relationship in terms of the identity issues that we encounter is of particular importance when using IEMT. Examples will be littered throughout pre-session questionnaires or in conversations with clients; i.e., *"I love myself", "I hate myself", "I challenge myself"* and so forth. We can see this relationship emerging between "I" and the "self" and for most people this will be just a figure of speech, with no particular meaning.

Reflexive pronouns can act as objects or indirect objects. There are nine English reflexive pronouns: *myself, yourself, himself, herself, oneself, itself, ourselves, yourselves,* and *themselves*. If you are fascinated by all things grammar, I suggest visiting the Grammarly website [(6)] as we are not going to delve into grammatical concepts in any depth here.

Let's look at how in IEMT we incorporate Grove's work and the definitions and interpretations he put onto pronouns with respect to our identity.

Starting with "I"

When working with clients, there is little point in launching into the Identity Protocol without explaining what we are looking to achieve. This way of working is unlike anything most clients and even trainee practitioners are likely to have encountered previously. The skill here is to explain enough to a client without leading them into what they think it is that you want to hear when asking the relevant questions. This ID process works best when the client is working spontaneously and not trying to over-think or over-intellectualise the process.

I have had quite a few people abreact to the ID work during trainings because it is an unknown and often outside of their comfort zone, yet I've had very few clients abreact to the work. It is often those who come with a perceived status who want to mess with the model (the term meta-meddle has been used to describe this) and add what they think is required to enhance this work who fall foul of the process. This can completely interfere with the exercise both for themselves and the unfortunate partner they are trying to 'therapise' with their genius, rather than just follow the instructions and work by following the process. Some think they know better and will attempt to re-word the questions in ways that simply do not work and then wonder why the exercise does not achieve much.

So, to relate this back to "I", there may well be a notion of:

> *"I know better than this trainer"* or
>
> *"I don't need to follow these instructions"* or
>
> *"I will do what I want"*

There may even be,

> *"Don't you know who I am?"* lurking in there somewhere.

When listening to what people are saying with reference to themselves, "I" is often the more dominant referential index. In fact, "I" can be rather bossy or pushy. To generalise, it is often associated with the 'left brain', speech-driven, conscious mind and the neocortex. Those who work in terms of ego states may see "I" as the "parent" ego state. This is of course a generalisation, but as with all generalisations, there is an element of truth.

The "I" used in the above statements is of course grammatically correct and these statements on their own may not raise any insights or concerns as to the person's inner way of being; i.e., who they are being. One thing that may be seen is that a person using "I" excessively in correspondence or speech may have a tendency towards narcissism. Again, this is not a scientific definition or even a particularly strong indicator; in fact, it could just indicate a more limited vocabulary. There are of course much better indicators of such ways of being, and it is always useful for anyone working in the change work arena to apprise themselves of such conditions and ways of spotting particular personality traits so that IEMT is only used where and when appropriate, especially with the Identity Process work [7].

There are several theories and deep philosophical discussions regarding the meaning of "I", and we discussed the "Who am I?", exercise earlier. One of the more interesting, and for some controversial, viewpoints is from neuropsychologist Professor Bruce Hood in his book, *The Self Illusion.* He says:

"You are your story - a matrix in your mind that produces the illusion of a coherent individual. But we would be wise to recognise that stories can be wrong."

This resonates with Grove's work of the fragmentation theory [1] of identity, as discussed later.

Hood says that after waking in the morning, the "I" part of our identity is the initial conscious awareness part, the here and now. He says that as we gather consciousness the "I" becomes the "Me"; as he calls it, "*the person with a past*" - i.e., the autobiographical experience via autobiographical memory [8]. He believes we are born with a brain that has conscious awareness, but we don't have a fully formed autobiographical memory, so this needs to develop. We know that the hippocampus does not appear fully functional in very young babies and that early life stress can delay its development.

He also states that the "Me" is crucial to the development of the "Self". This is only the tip of the iceberg as regards his theories.

Looking at "Myself/Self"

Self-concept is a generalised term for how we think about, perceive and evaluate ourselves. To have self-awareness is to have a concept of oneself physically, emotionally, socially, spiritually, and in terms of any other aspects that make up who we are [8].

It is part of the human brain's normal function to have internal dialogue, although some say they do not perceive this as words. That inner voice, which we know as 'self-talk', is not always supportive, and that can lead to issues pertaining to self, such as self-doubt, low self-esteem, and even eventually self-harm.

Again using a generalisation, the "Self" concept of identity can be said to be more 'right-brained'. It exists more at the unconscious level, which is more emotionally driven. When looking for possible ID statements that may flag an issue, "I" statements on their own may not be a red flag. However, when combined with "Myself" we have a more likely prospect of some internal conflict being demonstrated.

When reading pre-session and pre-training questionnaires and speaking with clients, my antennae is always scanning for reflexive pronoun statements such as:

"I keep telling myself to lose weight, but I never do"

"I really need to give myself a good talking to"

"I seem to have lost myself"

"I don't trust myself"

"I hate myself"

"I just see myself that way"

And so forth...

So "I" and "Myself" have this linguistic relationship that is not only grammatically correct, but can demonstrate to the trained ear the different internal representations or aspects of a person that are in conflict with each other somewhere in space - internal, external or a mixture of both - as per the work of Groves. When working with pronouns in identity-based work it is important to know that "Self" is expressed by "I".

Those who have trained in and use IEMT will become so aware of these language patterns that they seem to jump out everywhere, and it can be hard to resist making people aware of these linguistic discrepancies or conflicts. However, for the sake of your own sanity and theirs, it is best to lower your tuning when outside the therapy room!

When clients are made aware of these linguistic patterns, they will often be astounded that they have never heard them before, thought of 'it' (the issue) this way, or had any concept of the consequences to themselves mentally, emotionally, even physically. It's hardly surprising, because as a rule this way of listening out for unconscious language patterns demonstrating possible identity issues is not taught in school or college, and is rarely taught even among the various therapeutic modalities. It was not until I happened upon IEMT that it became fully apparent to me.

Of the many things I have learned from this modality, the identity-based work was the most revelatory in terms of my own and clients' issues. It's not always comfortable to work in this way; which is as it should be, after all real neurological therapeutic change rarely comes as a result of being comfortable.

So many of the issues that may seem kinaesthetic are actually a result of who the person is being, rather than how they are feeling. The feeling can be viewed as the being 'at effect', the identity is more core and thus more 'at cause'.

There are so many words in the English language that are prefixed with the word 'self' that it is impossible to list them all here; below are a few that we may encounter:

Self-Abuse	Self-Acceptance	Self-Centred
Self-Confidence	Self-Control	Self-Depreciation
Self-Development	Self-Denial	Self-Disgust
Self Esteem	Self-Fullfilment	Self-Harm
Self-Hatred	Self-Indulgence	Self-Injury
Self-Knowing	Self-Motivation	Self-Obsession
Self-Pride	Self-Punishment	Self-Sabotage
Self-Sacrifice	Self-Torment	Self-Worth

Let's break down some of the 'I' and 'self' statements to begin to gain more clarity for working with clients or ourselves.

"I hate myself"

This is one of the statements we use on trainings to explain the nuances of what we are looking to explore with the client.

We have two issues here: The "I" that hates and the "self" that is hated.

The obvious questions would be:

What is it about the self that is so abhorrent to "I" that it is worthy of hate? Hate is an extremely strong emotion.

However, on further investigation "I" is an aspect of that person capable of "hate". So, what is it about "I" that it is able to be provoked so to be capable of hating?

I would investigate the above using the IEMT Identity protocol that we will discuss later.

"I keep telling myself to lose weight, but I never do."

The "I" is assuming an air of authority over "myself"; that parental role as discussed earlier. "I" wants to lose weight, but it is deflecting that responsibility and action onto "myself".

"I keep telling myself to lose weight, but I never do, and I hate myself for it."

So, here we have a culmination of statements heard by many practitioners. "I" is in the authoritarian role and also the role of hater. So, we can start to see the sort of internal turmoil that people are battling with. This statement could easily be about smoking, alcohol, gambling, drugs, etc. So not only is there a possible chemical substance creating inner turmoil, there is internal discourse, which can also be external be dialogue, compounding that turmoil. With IEMT, we are looking to generate a better internal dialogue and relationship between these aspects so that the person can be more balanced and equipped to deal with their challenges.

It's All About 'Me'

As David Grove showed, the pronoun 'Me' acts in a different way linguistically to 'I' and 'Myself'. However, this distinction between 'Me and 'I' was first talked about in psychology by W. James in 1890 in the debate about the 'self'. The debate continues today and we are not going to get embroiled into arguments of cognitive science versus conceptual distinctions here. I recommend the paper by Mateusz Wożniak for those interested in exploring this in more depth [(9)].

Grove treats epistemological metaphors connected to clients' symptoms as containers holding bits of information that have become fragmented from one another and from the adult ego state. The approach identifies these experiential fragments by location, giving them structure and animating them so that they may continue their migration in experiential time and space.

Like pieces of an exploding bomb, the foreign parts move out of the self, while the pieces of the experience that belong to the client are allowed to sort themselves out, finding their useful forms and locations within a more coherent self-structure. In this manner, congruence takes on structural meaning - integrity in a literal sense.

Grove said the difference between 'Me', 'I' and 'Myself', is in almost metaphorical terms. Linguistically as well as somatically, 'Me' tends to act like a receptacle or container – it is often where things of an emotional nature go. It is also important to understand that 'Me' is often a recipient of 'You', hence the container element; e.g., "*'You' fill 'me' with hope"* (...or *dread, anxiety, rage, happiness* and so on). It is unlikely that anyone would say, "*'I' fill 'me' with love*" (...*hate, dread*, etc.). However, they may say, *"'I' fill myself with anxiety"* (...*joy, hope*, and so forth).

The type of statements people may make are as follows:

> *"It always happens to me"*
>
> *"This makes me feel empty"*
>
> *"It fills me with dread going into work"*
>
> *"I won't let them get to me"*
>
> *"That book really upset me"*
>
> *Why do you always make me feel this way?"*

And Finally, Let's Look at 'You'

How many people, I wonder, use the term 'You' in place of 'I'? Now that I am tuned into this phenomenon, I notice that almost everybody does this, some more than others. Even those who have undertaken our trainings and are made fully aware of this phenomenon may forget and slip back into old, inaccurate language patterns. Even I have on occasion...

When talking with clients I often have to point out when the word 'you' is transposed in places where it can make a conversation confusing. 'You' actually means, 'YOU' - the person being addressed not the person talking. It doesn't mean 'I', 'me' or 'myself', yet some people use it interchangeably with all of these.

If 'you' listen carefully you'll start to notice these patterns. See what I mean about it getting tad confusing...

Here is an example of what a person may be saying in a conversation:

> *"Well, **you** know, **you** just don't feel safe out there anymore. **You** read the papers and see things on the news and if **you** go out on **your** own, **you** just don't feel safe in town. **You're** always thinking someone will mug **you."***

This is not the same as:

> *"Well, **I** know **I** just don't feel safe out there anymore. **I** read the papers and see things on the news and if **I** go out on* **my** *own **I** just don't feel safe in town. **I'm** always thinking someone will mug* ***me."***

When the person is using the word '**you'** instead of **'I'**, 'me or 'myself'**,** they not only mean **'You',** the person they are talking to, on some linguistic level, but they are operating from a position of belief and value**.**

If a person says **'I'** in the above conversation, this is from a position of their own experience. If they say "'**you'** *don't feel safe",* and if 'I', as the recipient of this wisdom, start disagreeing, chances are they'll disagree back; they don't want to change their beliefs so readily and they will defend them. I prefer to stay out of beliefs if I can (i.e., the 'what if' scenario). A person stuck in their own beliefs and values often uses the term **'You'** as a way of forcing their belief onto others to gain a consensus. This can be in order to assuage their own anxiety regarding the issue they are discussing.

Indeed, there are some schools of thought that infer a person constantly using 'You' instead of 'I' is more likely to be an anxious person. Also, that those using 'I' disproportionately may have narcissistic tendencies [(10)]. Those using 'One' as a first-person pronoun may have delusions of grandeur.

Interestingly, there are gender differences in the use of first and third-person pronouns. An article by James Pennebaker in 2011, who used computer algorithm studies, concluded that:

> *"Most people think men use 'I' more, because men are more narcissistic and self-congratulatory. But across studies and cultures, we found that women use 'I,' 'me,' and 'mine' more. Women are more self-attentive and aware of their internal state. Men use more articles: 'a', 'an', and 'the'. That means men talk*

about objects and things more. You use articles when you're referring to concrete objects, because articles precede concrete nouns. Women also use more third-person pronouns - 'he', 'she', and 'they' - because women talk more about people and relationships, and they're better at managing them. And in many ways, relationships are more complex." (11).

We will look at some use of third person pronouns with the Identity Model later.

YOU and the Feedback Model

The way we work this in IEMT is that every time your client transposes 'I' to 'You' or is speaking from a position of their belief and values, don't feel the need to correct it, as it is so unconscious and can happen so often it will drive you both nuts. In the IEMT model we have a very simple pattern, as follows:

- '**I**' in a session instead of '**You**': Every time the person uses the word '**You**' in a session instead of '**I**', my response is to act as though they're talking about 'me', because at some abstract level they are. I tend to act a bit confused.

- If they say something like, *"Well **you** know, **you** just feel anxious all the time."* My reply would go along the lines of (with a confused expression): ***"**What do you mean **'I'** know **'I'** just feel anxious all the time? Are you talking about me here?"* They may reply with something like: *"What? I'm not sure what you mean?"*

Feed the pattern back every time the person uses the word you, and they will respond accordingly. I find people often catch on very quickly and say: "Oh no, sorry, not you, I mean me!" They will often start to self-correct once I've fed this back a few times. However, they are unlikely to hear this language pattern outside the session or self-correct ongoing unless it is explained that their language tends to exhibit they can be operating outside of their own experience. Once this is explained to a client or course attendee, "Aha…" moments can occur and some will start to change this ongoing.

One of the best ways of tuning into this phenomenon is listening to the radio, e.g., news-based shows such as the Jeremy Vine show on BBC Radio 2, and TV chat shows. Many guests and presenters will be heard speaking from a position of their beliefs and values, using 'You' as a way of trying to bring us, the listener or viewer, into their experience and create a consensus with their view. For those who are anxious, feeling that others are agreeing with them can help to temporarily assuage their anxiety. However, it won't last long; perhaps only until they come into contact with the next person with whom they feel the need to bring into their position of belief and values.

Using Eye Movements to Deal with Linguistic Identity-Based Issues

I often spend part of the Practitioner Training or follow-up practice sessions looking at examples from client questionnaires. Using highlighter pens, the trainees work in groups to elicit core identity statements, conflicts or mismatches, and Patterns of Chronicity, and this is exactly what I do with every client questionnaire I receive. If this is not carried out in the class setting, it is part of the required assessment coursework for those wishing to become certified practitioners. This preparation, especially to elicit POCs and potential ID issues, saves a lot of time in a client session. I am also vigilant for any identity-based sentences in the session.

Written permission is obtained to record each session, because some of this identity and Patterns of Chronicity-based language flies past so quickly that it can be missed, and when working online, Zoom makes recording sessions so easy. Listening back to the session can be very helpful for any follow-up work. Also, if clients wish to review the session themselves they can. It has to be said I get very few requests for the recordings, possibly because I send a post-course email with the learning points from the session and provide lots of resources so that they can do some self-development and self-use work in their own time.

In a session, before initiating the Identity work, I will start to talk about identity and give examples, usually from the person's own questionnaire, as these are of the most relevance. Elaboration is given if the client is not quite understanding the concept of the linguistic markers that can be causing issues for them. Having already performed the "Who am I?" exercise and discussed the concept of "I" with examples from their questionnaire, talking about the 'Self' and 'Myself 'is the best place to start, as most people understand the concept easily. I will give examples of words such as *'self-confidence', 'self-esteem', 'self-obsession', 'self-determination', 'self-worth', 'self-loathing'* and so on. I will then talk about the relationship between "I" and the 'self' and hopefully have one of their examples to use. If not, I'll use examples such as *"I wonder how often you would say 'I like myself'?", 'I hate myself', 'I can't stand myself', 'I love myself'* and so on, and discuss such concepts with the client.

When discussing the pronoun "Me", I talk about how this seems to operate differently linguistically and again give examples; usually there will be a "Me" example from the client's questionnaire. If they are operating outside of their own experience a lot, using "You", or talking from a position of their own beliefs and values, I may have already fed this pattern back as seen above. If not, I will mention this too.

Taking an example of one of their ID statements to see how they respond and feel in relation to this is important. If a big emotion/feeling comes up for the client when eliciting the information or working on the ID eye movements, we go back to the Kinaesthetic Process and work on the feeling so that this does not sabotage the rest of the work. It is important to be mindful to observe a sudden change of state; e.g., into anger, which may be a type of abreaction either of the 3-stage variety or the more somatic release variety, so vigilance is important

Set-up: Dynamic ways of resolving identity-based issues - give examples

- Discuss identity with client; explore themes and issues that are both culturally common and specific to the individual.

- Introduce the concept of different aspects of identity, "**I**", "**self**", "**me**" and "**you**." (I use my flip-chart and write this out so that the client can see it clearly).

- Give examples from what they have said or written: e.g., **I** am sure that it won't hurt **me, I** often say to **myself**, **you** know **you're** just being silly.

- Do not shape their answers, take the answer **THEY** give you. It is important that we don't overlay our interpretations, metaphors, etc., onto the client's thoughts and experience.

The questions for elicitation of information

1. **Locate the identity components of the client (as per David Grove's work)**

2. **Now ask:**

   ... And - when you think about "I" whereabouts is "I"?

   ... And - how old is "I"?

   ... And - what's happening around ... "I"?

- The client may ask for clarification on the third question – maintain your own state and offer no guidance. If the client gets stuck, repeat the question.

Repeat sequence for "**me**", "**self/myself**" and "**you**."

- Now discuss any of the answers that show some sort of mis-match; e.g., the aspect could not be located or it is outside the body. I remember one lady telling me "Self" was over on the Waitrose car park that I used to live opposite.

- There may be an age mismatch such as "Me" is aged six, or is pre-born, or older than their age now. Sometimes the answers will be ageless, timeless, or older and wiser. I even had one chap say this his "self" was 1,000. This was a smoking client, to whom my reply was, *"interesting, in the 1,000 years that self has been around it still hasn't figured out how to stop smoking".* The chap was in his 60s and this was a huge 'Aha' moment. After just one round of the eye movements, all his age discrepancies resolved ('me' was in its cot around 1 year old, 'I' was 14 - the age he started smoking). He stopped smoking after that session and subsequently referred several members of his family to me.

- Also, look for any events that are negative, traumatic, stuck states, etc., as this may be an area to work on.

Eliciting the Pronoun Identity-Based Information, Sequence and Updating Identity Imprints with IEMT - Simple Form Technique

What to look for in the eye movements

The eye movements are circular, like a lazy '8' or infinity type of symbol. Axis deviations are usually observed on the edges of the circles, corners or up top.

Set up: Revive the states/ experience/ the answers

1. Instruct the client to hold the representation vividly in their mind for as long as possible. Guide them in eye movements through the different axis points (lazy 8).

2. As you start to do this, instruct the client ***"...and you can talk to me as we do this..."*** Suggest to the client that they can allow their memory to, ***"...move around through time to different events and memories, the logic of which need not make any sense..."***

3. While continuing the eye movement sequences, instruct the client: ***"...and you can talk to me as this happens, tell me what images and past experiences come to mind as we do this..."***

4. Observe closely for state shifting, physiological changes and changes in representation. These are often represented by saccadic jerks and blips of the eyeball. At each shift, prompt the client, ***"...and what was that one...?"*** etc.

5. Stop after 40 seconds and recalibrate. Go again if there are still things going on, let them process what has happened, or carry on.

6. Do it again when you come round to that axis deviation, **change direction**, look for a new axis deviation, **change direction** again and so on.

7. Keep going until there are no more axis deviations.

8. If there is more than one, **change direction** on the first one.

9. If no deviations are seen at all check the head is not moving.

10. Continue until the state change is complete and representation is now current.

11. Recalibrate the answers to the elicitation questions.

What can we see when moving the eyes?

The eyes almost cut the corners of the big lazy 8s and can't follow for some reason: Something specific happens at that axis deviation

Deviations at the central points where the eyes cross from one side to the other, although this is not as common as the above

People break off completely, often when the process is complete, however it can also be because the image is uncomfortable. Some kinaesthetic work may be required here.

After working in the initial basic way, we can begin to work in a more Integral way. This is similar to the integral kinaesthetic pattern in that we are observing the axis deviations and work with them, as follows:

Integral Method for Identity Elicitation Work

Desired Changes:

- **Updating and reintegration:** i.e., the ages for different aspects become the age the person is now, not when the event happened. Externally sourced aspects, i.e., Self - *'I can't find myself', 'Myself is out in front of me', 'Me is in the chair at school aged 7'.*

- Change in spatio-temporal locations (somatic change).

- The above phenomenon of updating, integration and somatic shift can be quite dramatic. Some trainees are suddenly overcome emotionally and have to go out of the room. This work can be life-changing for some, and many seasoned 'therapists' and 'coaches' have never experienced anything like this work before.

- Some people will ab-react when asked to do this work and will want to change the questions to fit their own model or language patterns. I am always looking for the first signal of their discomfort, i.e., Stage 1 of the 3SAR, and will remind them firmly about following the rules and the wording. Interestingly, abreactions occur more often with therapists and professionals who exhibit status issues than they do with clients. However, in trainings some of the most ardent ab-reactors, after they actually engage and persevere with the process, have very pronounced positive responses, making them huge converts and advocates for this process.

Chapters 8 and 9 have taken us through some background and philosophy regarding identity as well as explaining the first-party pronoun work that can on examination indicate a spatio-temporal separation and fragmentation that can lead to issues with cohesion of identity and can compound issues pertaining to the self.

The following chapter is a more in-depth explanation of how we can work with the identity-based statements that people use, whether first- or third-party, as well as how certain names, titles or labels such as disease states can become problematic and feed outwards into behaviours and actions.

Chapter 10

Interpretations and Applications of the Identity Process for Specific Issues

"The tool is not the skill..."

Sonia Richards 2011

When training IEMT, emphasis is always placed on the importance of the information gleaned from the pre-session questionnaire that all practitioners and Association members are asked to ensure clients complete. The purpose of the medical history part of the questionnaire is two-fold. Firstly, we need to rule out any contraindications to IEMT, and we ask for basic health information in case there is a need to ask the client for permission to contact their medical practitioner.

All information is kept in line with GDPR regulations and therapists holding such information should have an ICO registration certificate. Additionally, the questionnaire seeks information about the issue the client is seeking assistance with, and this can yield some rich information regarding any Patterns of Chronicity they have, metaphors they use, the identity statements that could be significant as to why and how the client is keeping an issue in place, and identity-wise, the 'who' they are being or not being.

Here is an example of the sort of information in the questionnaire that other types of therapists may dismiss as figures of speech or not having any real significance. To the person trained in IEMT, this can be an indicator of the 'cause' of the issue that other therapists have not been able to help the client with.

Male client, aged 28

Q1. What do you want?

A1: *"Well, I sort of think this maybe sounds a bit naff, but I want* *to be able to get on better with my work colleagues. I am anxious around them and just don't feel like anyone takes me seriously. In fact, I just can't seem to be myself and this really makes me anxious. You just can't relax and so you make mistakes which makes things worse. I beat myself up about this a lot."*

Q2. *On a scale of 1-10 how much to you want to change the problem?*

A2: *"I think I'd like to change this about 7 or 8 out of 10."*

One of the first things to look out for is when the person doesn't actually answer the question. The question is *"What do you want?"*; it is phrased in the present tense. It is interesting how many people answer the question from a past or future perspective, or don't answer the question at all, e.g.:

"I have anxiety/depression."

"I don't want to have this phobia anymore."

"I can't drive on motorways."

"The thought of going to the dentist makes me panic."

"I am really petrified of dogs."

"I keep thinking that I'll die in a plane crash so can't go on a plane."

These statements are not actually answering the question as stated, so when we see the client we need to clarify the issue. We may say to them:

"So to the first question, 'what do you want?' You have given me an example/a diagnosis of your problem, but you haven't actually told me what you want, so what do ***You*** *want?"*

or

"You have told me here what you don't want, but actually the question is - what do ***You*** *want?"*

or

"You have told me what you currently can't do,
but what do ***You*** *want?"*

So, we are not just going to accept whatever they have put on the questionnaire unless it is an answer to the question. This can quickly indicate the Maybe Man people who are unable to tell you what they want. In the examples above, the person who keeps thinking they're going to die in a plane crash is an example of a Great Big 'What If' pattern. Often, the Patterns of Chronicity a person is running will be demonstrated by how the person does, or more likely doesn't, answer this question. Many of the above answers are also demonstrating the client being "At Effect".

On the surface, the issue for the client who wants to get on better with his workmates seems straightforward. He's said the word 'anxiety', so it would be easy to just focus on that, look at the 3 Pillars, work in the kinaesthetic of the feelings, and perhaps do some self-confidence boosting techniques. Those who do 'tapping' might tap on the anxiety, others may do some hypnotherapy, or NLP 'swishing' of the anxiety might be used. And the person may well leave feeling less anxious or even feeling good. This will help him with the issue of what he is feeling or experiencing, but not always with "How" he is being or "Who" he is being.

If we look more forensically with our IEMT lenses in place, these few sentences yield much more information about 'how' this person is being and 'who' this person is being, so we can do some further work at an identity level.

Let's take the first part of the sentence:

"Well, I sort of think this maybe sounds a bit naff."

Immediately, we can see that this person is highly likely to be running the POC of the Maybe Man, a person unsure of their own experience and one who is even willing to denigrate their own issue and discomfort as being *"a bit naff"*. This is a person who is lacking in self-confidence who could also have low self-esteem, as is reinforced by the scoring:

> ***"I think** I'd like to change this to **about 7 or 8** out of 10."*

Also, in terms of the Five POC, this person is likely to be "At Effect", rather than "At Cause".

> ***"I** want to be able to get on better with **my** work colleagues."*

This is a future-based statement of intent answered per the question - so that is a good start - coming from the **'I'** - often the more dominant ego state. The 'I' in a sentence is often more active. He obviously doesn't feel able to do this now, but wants to be able to do this in the near future. Also there is a possessive pronoun here - ***"my"*** *colleagues*.

He could have said: "*I want to get on better with the people at work"*, but instead he says, *"my colleagues"*. So there is a feeling of some emotional investment and ownership for the client here, and such feelings, if not reciprocated, when termed in the possessive, can be perceived or felt as rejection. So, we may have an element of 'hurts' going on here with this person.

> ***"I** am anxious around them and **I** just don't feel like anyone takes **me** seriously."*

Again, the dominant **'I'** is anxious around **'them'**.

So, we have several ways to approach this. Working on the feeling of 'anxious' is a good place to start, as a big feeling or emotion can overwhelm if not worked on initially. This is also an opportunity to bring in the 3 Pillars Model, and the anxious person is likely to be cycling around a set of connected emotions/feelings. Coming back to the Identity markers, we have two here - a first-party and a third-party:

> *"And when you think of **'I'** whereabouts is **'I'**... and how old is **'I'**... and what's happening around **'I'**?"*

*"And when you think of **"Them"** whereabouts are **"Them"** ... and how old are **"Them"** ... and what's happening around **"Them"**?"*

I have just altered the words slightly so that it is more grammatically cogent; i.e., 'is' to 'are' with respect to **'Them'**.

The word 'Them' with respect to 'I' denotes separation, lack of connection. A connected person would be more likely to speak in terms of 'us' or 'we'. Sometimes, a person will say words like 'they' or 'them' with force or even venom, so this will indicate emotions such as anger or jealousy. Watch the associated body language and micro-expressions.

***"I** just don't feel like anyone takes **me** seriously."*

Now this is getting interesting; we have a dynamic between the **'I'** and the **'Me'.** The **'Me'** is almost phrased in the child or victim state here. The word 'just' is significant in this type of mindset. He could have said:

"I don't feel like anyone takes me seriously."

This has the same type of meaning, however the *'just'* gives an added emphasis to a possible unfairness. I can almost hear this person saying, "**it's not fair**", with that sort of language.

*"So, in relation to this issue... And when you think of **'Me'**, whereabouts is **'Me'**... and how old is **'Me'**... and what's happening around **'Me'**?"*

Let's also look at the last word "**seriously**".

There are a few possibilities here.

We can ask: *"And this 'Me' that is not taken **seriously**, whereabouts is this **'Me'** and how old is this **'Me'**...and what's happening around this **'Me'** that is not taken **seriously**?"*

I would add: *"And when is the first time that this 'Me' wasn't taken seriously by other people?"*

Now that may seem a bit harsh, but it is unlikely this is the first time in this person's life that this sort of issue has happened. This person may actually be running a schema with this sort of way of being. Remember the questions, "***How did this person learn to feel this way about this thing?"*** and ***"How did this person learn to be this way?"***

So, this person who is "At Effect" needs to get to being "At Cause". As practitioners, we need to be able to help guide the person to "Cause". This way, they can start to learn to take more responsibility for their own way of being and get out of the victim mindset. Without guidance, this person could go from job to job where the same issue occurs again and again; of course, the common denominator is less likely to be others, and more likely themselves.

I am reminded of the story of the chap who said he had social anxiety, he couldn't make friends and nobody liked him at work. It was then pointed out to him that he had extremely poor personal hygiene and this may well be the reason why. A bit of a red face perhaps, but he needed training in cleanliness more than he needed therapy for social anxiety. Not surprising he had no friends, nobody wanted to be anywhere near him! You may not be surprised to know I have no issue taking action with clients or former work colleagues if they have poor personal hygiene, and advising them to get it sorted (ask some of my former band mates…I've even been known to spray them with deodorant and air fresher before taking to the stage with them!).

Now onto the next sentence, in which we have the trinity of personal pronouns:

> *"In fact, **I just** can't **seem** to be **myself** and this really **makes me anxious."***

This is a very identity level-rich sentence involving '**I**', '**myself**' and '**me**'. We have that classic interplay relationship between 'I' and 'myself'. When we break this down into the identity aspects of the person, he is saying there is an inability for the 'I' and the 'self' to be a combined force; there is a fragmentation here as per Groves' observations on identity. These phrases, on first inspection, appear to be everyday linguistic phrases, however on some deeper level, at an identity level, there is a disconnect.

The client is also adding "*just*" and "*seem*", so there is an element of the indecisive Maybe Man POC here and a bit of the victim mindset again.

Eliciting information about this "I" and "Myself" is interesting and, to throw in a curve ball, can 'I' ever actually be 'Myself' in any event?

"And when you think of 'I' whereabouts is 'I'.... etc., and when you think of 'Myself', whereabouts is..." and so forth.

Hence this disconnect then **makes** (in the present) **"Me"** anxious. So, this is real-time anxiety response - this is an experience that this person is currently having/living.

Again, test for the kinaesthetic of 'anxious' in the here and now, and if there is something that can be worked on first, we can do this before returning to the Identity work.

*"And so, this "Me" that is anxious, whereabouts is this "**Me**"?"* etc...

All the above questions can be asked exactly as before when we are generally gathering the information for I, Me, Myself and You, as we do in the trainings, but they can be applied in relation to this specific issue and within the frame of what the person wants.

An example of this would be:

> *"And so, this **'Me'** that isn't taken seriously and is anxious... whereabouts is this "Me" ... and how old is this "Me" ... and what's happening around this "Me" that isn't taken seriously and is anxious?"*

By phrasing the questions in this way, we are getting into the actual issue of the client and who they are being in relation to this issue that they have come to change.

If somebody says a statement such as ***'I hate myself'***, we can break this down into:

> *"And so this "I" that hates, where about is this "I" that hates and how old…?* etc.
>
> *"And also this "myself" or "self" that is hated, I wonder what it is about this "myself" that "I" hates, that makes them hateful?"*
>
> *"And so, when you think about this 'myself' that is hated, where about is this 'myself' that is hated? And how old"… etc.*
>
> *"And on a scale of 1-10, with 10 being as strong as it can be, how strong is this feeling of hatred for 'myself"?*

Here we are building a up a picture of the issues that the person wants to change, and a picture of the person with reference to internal identity struggles that are creating the unwanted feeling i.e. hatred. So we should also work kinaesthetically here on the feeling of 'hate'. In other words the 'who' they are being affects the 'how' they are being.

In life, the following may be hard for people to think of or to be:

If 'I' am a kind and benevolent person, 'I' am unlikely to be feeling discomfort and anxiety about 'myself' and the situations that could befall 'me' or that 'I' find 'myself' in. Even if 'I' have a blip now and then, 'I' have within 'me' the ability to regain my 'self' worth.

So even the odd 'if' or 'what-if' statement should not always be enough to create chronic anxieties when a person has a solid identity.

Next, we have one of my favourites:

> *"You just can't relax and so you make mistakes which makes things worse."*

This is a very interesting sentence, because now he has switched from this issue being termed personally to coming from his belief and value set. This is a way of drawing the reader into his own experience, while on some level meaning the reader. This is an unconscious attempt to create a shared experience or rapport as a way of justifying the issue or problem state the person has. Because of course, "You" just can't relax (can 'you')...and "you" make mistakes, (don't 'you').

So, we can continue with:

> *"And when you think of this 'You' that can't relax and makes mistakes, whereabouts is this 'You'...and what age is 'You'...and what's happening around 'You'?"*

Interestingly, for those of us in the UK, (and I suspect other countries, as I have heard this use of "You' in people where English is not their first language), there can be another reason for this use of the second person singular **'You'** instead of the first person singular **'I', 'me' or 'myself',** depending on which part of the country a person is from. I lived in Brighton, England, down on the South East coast, for 30 years and I noticed that the colloquial use of 'You' appeared to be less frequent than on Merseyside, North West England, which was my place of origin. After moving back to the North West a few years back, this use of 'You' in place of 'I' became a real annoyance because it is used so frequently.

Being an IEMT Practitioner means making a concerted effort not to correct this with people who are not clients, so I had to learn to dial down my ID receiver on this. Unfortunately, I'm sure you can guess what began to happen; yes, I began to substitute 'You' for 'I', especially when chatting with family members. So now my concerted effort is not to fall into this trap.

There is some conjecture that this substitution can occur in close-knit communities. In these communities, there is a great level of common knowledge and common identity, where individuality appears to be of less value than in more disparate communities; e.g., in the north of England versus the south of England. An example would be behaviour on the London Tube, where nobody tends to talk to each other. Up north, we are more likely to engage in a comment or conversation with a person unknown to us on a train, in a bus queue, the supermarket, etc. However, this common knowledge and the use of 'You' instead of 'I' can jar when assumptions are made by one person and the other person does not agree or hold that opinion. I have certainly challenged this on more than one occasion, when I have been dragged unwittingly into someone's opinions, points of view, or experience when I do not share them.

In 2017, Orvel et al performed experiments on the use of "You" instead of "I" and concluded that:

> *"Across six experiments, we found that generic-you is used to express norms in both ordinary and emotional contexts and that producing generic-you when reflecting on negative experiences allows people to "normalise" their experience by extending it beyond the self. In this way, a simple linguistic device serves a powerful meaning-making function."* [(1)].

Internal versus External You

Eliciting the location and age information for 'You' can cause some consternation in trainings and afterwards. On the course, we talk about how using the pronoun 'You' should mean somebody external to the client. But of course the phrasing of the question is rather confusing. Because if I, as the practitioner using the term 'You' direct it towards the client then I do actually mean them. So we may get answers that refer to an internalised 'You' or an externalised 'You'.

Example of externalised 'You' pertaining to themselves:

> *"'You' is here in this room, my age now, and what's happening is that I'm in a therapy/coaching session."*

Example of an internalised 'You':

> *"'You' is in the chest, it's younger than I am now, about 7, and there's confusion."*

Example of external 'You' pertaining to non-self:

> *"'You' is, well, you, out there, whatever age you are and you are talking."*

There are other examples, but these are the most common types of responses.

Other Pronouns and Identity Markers

What's in a name?

In IEMT, we can extend Identity work beyond the restrictions of first-party pronouns and into the peripheries of our wider experience. We have looked thus far mainly at core elements of personal identity and the inner conflicts and imbalances that can occur on a linguistic level that have a much deeper impact than first meets the ears. One of the more personal core elements of identity is our name.

After the sex of a child is determined, which can now occur pre-birth, choosing a name is often a huge undertaking. Some parents will just go with what they like the sound of, some will want to make an artistic statement, naming a child after a musician or actor, for example. Some will make a political or religious statement, some will choose a name to please other family members such as parents or grandparents. Hence, there can be a lot of emotion invested in the choosing of a child's name.

There can be family disagreements when one parent or grandparent expects a child to be called one thing and they are registered with another. An acquaintance of mine was registered with the names Philip Paul by his father and grandfather while his mother was still in hospital after the birth. She had wanted him to be called Paul and a huge family row erupted. The mother insisted on calling the child Paul, and the grandparents, with whom the family lived for several years, would call him Philip.

After moving to another part of the country, the child was called Paul by his parents, brother, neighbours, etc., but he hated the name. He felt he had no connection to it, so when he went to senior school aged 11 he requested that the school use the first name as seen on his birth certificate and not what his parents had chosen to register him with for the school. A very understanding headmaster agreed to his request and the name on the register and his school records was changed to Philip Paul. His mother so was irate about this that she went to the school to try to have this changed back to Paul Phillip (i.e., *you need to change to make me feel better/this needs to go back to how it was before).* However, the school was adamant, this child would be called the name as seen on his birth certificate as per his request. His friends soon got used to the name change, however, to this day his parents refuse to call him by the name that he identifies with, Phil. His mother even told him: *"I gave birth to you, so I have the right to call you what I wish."*

His parents' lack of respect for his identity led to much conflict over the years, though after IEMT Phil now shrugs it off, no longer angered but amused at their behaviour. Such intolerance on the part of parents to respect the identity of their own offspring can lead to some children becoming withdrawn, socially anxious, angry and rebellious, with many knock-on issues possible along the line. It may even be enough to trigger behaviours such as addiction, the use of substances being a way to anaesthetise feelings pertaining to the self and others. Not all traumatic childhood triggers are huge events, if a child perceives a hurt or rejection etc. deeply enough it can manifest as a trauma this can affect their behaviour years down the line.

As children, we are given a formal name, but this may be shortened or altered to a nickname by family or friends. For example, Michael could be called Mickey, Mick or Mikey as an affectionate name by family. He may prefer to be called Mike by friends as he gets older, and work colleagues might decide to call him Mick, which he may or may not identify with or even like. As children, we often know if we are in trouble with our parents because they will use our full name rather than the family term of endearment or nickname they normally use (e.g., *"Michael! Come downstairs!").* A feeling of foreboding, fear, irritation or anger may result from hearing this formal name said in this particular way, and may set a whole lot of programming in place.

Children can be cruel and may level insults at those who aren't in their clique or posse or are seen as a 'geek' or uncool. Names such as *four eyes, fatso, ginger, shorty* are levelled. One nickname-come-insult given to a friend of mine who was very thin as a child was *Skel,* short for skeleton, which he grew to detest as his association with the name was of being bullied, sometimes in a very extreme way. IEMT helped him to deal with his emotional responses when they name came up later in adulthood, when he met up with old school mates. When this name was used inappropriately to his adult self by his old friends, I could see this person visibly wince, his body physiology tighten, his hands form fists and he would start experiencing feelings of extreme irritation and anger.

Imagine how the poor child landed with an unusual moniker would feel, that some parents like to give their children, such as for example *Pythagoras*, when they become self-aware and gets to school to find their name highly unusual? On a scale of 1 to 10, how does the name *Pythagoras* feel? The choice of silly or 'artistic' names by parents can have a huge effect on the self-confidence, self-esteem and self-worth of a child when they are judged by others, especially their peers. To be fair, the name doesn't even have to be that outrageous. David Bowie's son was originally named Zowie, and he changed this name firstly to Joe and finally to Duncan.

As a young child, I detested my first name as I felt it was too old for me and too different to those around me, the Janes, Susans, Debras and Karens, etc. For years when playing make-believe games with kids (this is well before the days of mobile phones, play stations and TVs in kids' rooms, when the imagination created the most wonderful play), I would say, *"I'm called Tina"*. I have no idea why I chose that name, I can only think that I saw Tina Turner on a T.V. clip one time and was highly affected by her fabulousness. Incidentally my favourite doll was also named Tina.

It wasn't until I was 12 when my own name suddenly seemed to fit. At senior school, my unique first name (there were no other Sonias), suddenly felt good. My family also had a unique surname in our small town because my Dad was Indian, so there was only ever going to be one Sonia Mazumder in the school. I liked being the only Sonia Mazumder and, as my teachers would attest, once met, never forgotten...

My unique name served me well over the years. After coming to the attention of various music luminaries in Liverpool in the early 1980s, once again that name was remembered and even mentioned on a few records by the bands I sang with. So I was very happy with my identity; I finally knew who Sonia Mazumder was, what she was all about.

This aspect of my identity was an unconscious acceptance and never in doubt until I met my first husband. All of a sudden there was a societal expectation that in getting married I should adopt the last name of my husband's family - Griffiths. But I didn't feel like a Sonia Griffiths, and on a sensory level could not accept it. So I didn't for the first eight years, until my passport came up for renewal. It was only then that I finally accepted this new addition to my identity and it felt extremely uncomfortable for a while.

After 11 years as Sonia Griffiths and gaining a lot of new qualifications in that name - BSc, MSc, diplomas in Hypnotherapy, Hypnobirthing, Complementary Therapies, NLP, IEMT and so on - my marriage ended, very amicably, and we remain great friends. Andrew Austin says it's interesting how, after a separation or divorce, people tend to stay married or attached to the bad stuff and divorce the good stuff. Luckily, I am one of the exceptions to that rule, however, I now had another identity dilemma. My passport, driving licence and a myriad of qualifications were in the name Griffiths and I now identified as Sonia Griffiths. I wasn't sure that I wanted to go back to Mazumder. Much as I love my original surname, it felt past, not current.

To throw one more conundrum into the mix, I met the person who was to become my new husband and here we go again, the name Richards was thrown into the mix! The names Steve and Sonia Griffiths were very well known in the world of hypnobirthing as Steve is the person who introduced the first-ever method, the Mongan Method, into the UK and we ran a very successful practice and trainings. Blimey, I now had a status issue to consider, something that I had never been bothered about before. Should I ditch the name Griffiths and go back to my maiden name? Should I keep the name Griffiths professionally, even after my new marriage? Should I accept the name Richards and force it into my identity; or would this need be a new identity in order for it to feel okay? Yes this was me exhibiting Maybe Man behaviour about this issue!

Here is the one thing that nearly scuppered my taking on my new husband's surname. If you have read the introduction to this book, you will know that I had an unpleasant encounter with my primary school headmistress. She was a scarily strict woman, who thankfully was generally nice with me because I was usually very well behaved and had a good voice, so I was picked out to sing and do readings in assembly quite frequently. However, instead of calling me 'Son-ia' like everyone else, she insisted on calling me 'Soan-ia' which made me cringe and feel alienated among my peers who would often snigger on hearing her booming voice calling my name.

The only time I was hauled in front of a teacher in primary school was by this headmistress, because I'd had the temerity to call another teacher by her first name in the playground. She chastised me with a very harsh voice, and I felt hugely guilty and ashamed for committing this heinous crime. I didn't like her one bit after that. Her name? Mrs Richards! Irony of ironies…

> *And when you think of the name Mrs Richards where about is Mrs Richards?*
>
> *And how old is Mrs Richards?*
>
> *And what's happening around Mrs Richards?*

I had the opportunity to work on this very thing during my IEMT Trainers' Training. We were practising working on other identities. I had only been re-married for two years and had resisted changing my name to Richards (again, the irony of a change practitioner resisting change!). However, my ex was also now about to re-marry and his fiancée, who is lovely, was very uncomfortable with me still being called Griffiths on Facebook. She wanted me to change my name, of course to make her feel better, but in fairness I decided that it was actually time to deal with this aversion to the name Richards once and for all.

And whereabouts is Mrs Richards? – *"In her office sitting in front of me."*

And how old is Mrs Richards? – *"8 years old."*

And what's happening around Mrs Richards? – *"Being talked to sternly, being told to give my monitor badge back, feeling ashamed."*

We did lazy 8s on the representation and straight lines on the feeling, and I remember suddenly grinning when the image and feeling began to fade. We did the tests - close my eyes and try to get the memory and feeling back, close my eyes and try to make the image bigger - both of which just made the memory get further away. The feeling had actually turned into one of amusement. So afterwards when I thought about the name Mrs Richards, I had no bothersome feelings and instead one of actual amusement. From that day on I was very happy to be called Sonia Richards or Mrs Richards, and when my husband pointed out that Mrs Richards was the name of the cantankerous old partially deaf woman in an episode of *Fawlty Towers*, it made me laugh out loud. I'm glad to say that many years on, it still amuses me and I remain very happy to be called Mrs Richards.

The one thing we didn't work on that day was the "*Soan-ia*", so I did that for myself later, because many Americans with whom I've worked, trained or taught over the years also pronounce my name this way. Again, I now find it rather quaint and amusing.

Now this is a rather long-winded way of demonstrating that given names or names that we acquire through relationships can at times cause a disquieting, or to quote *Star Wars*, "disturbance in the force", that if left unchecked can have ripple effects to all levels of identity and behaviours, so that both the 'who' and the 'how' we are is affected. Oh, and just one last thing on this subject, today I looked up my old school, Cathcart Street School in Birkenhead, to see if there were any old photographs, perhaps even from the time I was there. I almost fell off my chair; the current headmistress is called, yes, you guessed it, Mrs Richards!

Over the years I have worked on many first and last name issues with people, in addition to nickname issues, titles depicting status, the growth or loss of status, some through marriage and divorce and some via occupation. Being able to accept our names and titles in the here and now is very important in updating identity and getting us out of child-related or former years thinking, and in integrating and owning our current identity. Of course, many still struggle, as is seen in some of the gender-related issues that have dominated social media of late.

One interesting case was of a consultant anaesthetist who came to my first Brighton IEMT Practitioner training. She hadn't used the title Dr on her booking form or in her email address, and it was only when we did this exercise that she told me she had issues with being addressed as such. This lady came from a working-class background and was obviously extremely gifted as she became a consultant at the age of 30. One of her issues was that she would be walking along a corridor of the hospital where she worked, and somebody would call to her - e.g., *"Excuse me Dr... Dr ..."* - and she would not recognise this person be called as being herself. The title felt alien and 'other', even though she was now in her early 40s. So she worked on this aspect of her identity in the training which was a very profound experience of change for her. She commented that the integration felt like this aspect actually physically entered her body (this experience has been observed in trainings and client sessions). From that day on, she had no issues with being addressed as Dr, just accepting it as a job title without any status implications.

Have a think, is there a name or title that causes discomfort or that you find difficult to identify with? If so, you can attempt some self IEMT on the subject. If you find this tricky, call on a practitioner who will be pleased to help you to deal with this.

Third-Party Identity Markers

There are many other pronouns and names that denote identity which can be troubling or bothersome. Some will be confined to self and some will be about others. These little words can often become associated with emotional connections and somatic experiences. Third-party pronouns are often used because they refer to people, places, or things that are not the client.

Whereas the previous category featured actual nouns or titles more heavily, these words can sometimes be used in place of naming a person. For example, when somebody is so angry or disgusted with another person or their actions a third-party pronoun may be used with invective and at times as an insult.

The words we are concerned with here are as follows:

Him, His, He, Her, Hers, She, It, Its, They, Them, Their, Theirs

People often differentiate the above from themselves and those they are connected to in some way, as in the following terms:

We, Us, versus Them, They, The others, That lot (often colloquial).

So when working in this area we can also use these terms. This also comes into play with some of the Advanced IEMT protocols. Examples:

i. *He never cleans up after himself.*

ii. *She's an absolute a disgrace, that one.*

iii. *They think they're better than the rest of us.*

iv. *It's not fair, it doesn't belong to him.*

v. *We don't like to associate with them*

Of course, there are many examples, and when reading through a client questionnaire do watch out for such statements as well as in any pre-session chats. These sorts of terms can be contributing to a negative mindset and way of being, i.e., *getting themselves in a twist, getting wound-up, getting their back-up*, to name a few idioms.

Of course, these third-party pronouns are not always used in the above context, but people rarely come to see a practitioner or coach because they are totally sorted about everything and everyone in their lives, e.g., *she's such a treasure, I appreciate him, they are always there to lend a hand*. Those examples are not really going to create troublesome kinesthetics or insults to a person's sense of identity.

I remember as a child being chided when using the word '*she*' to describe a person instead of using their name, as this was deemed to impersonal and impolite. The phrase: *"Who's 'she', the cat's mother?"* would be trotted out if I did. This idiomatic phrase goes back centuries in the English language and other languages have similar sayings.

When working on potentially troublesome pronouns, we need to ensure that the person notices a change in the internal kinesthetics when using the word in a partial way. For example, the pronoun '*him*' will feel different if a person is saying, *'I like him'*, compared to *'I hate him'*.

During a Practitioner Training in Las Vegas I noticed one lady kept saying that she had nothing to work on, that she had sorted out lots of stuff in her life, which of course may well have been the absolute truth. She participated in the exercises, but I could see that the normal engagement and "aha..." moments weren't really happening for her; until this exercise. After describing the use of third-party pronouns - the implications and the emotional and kinaesthetic effects these small words can have that can cause huge sticking points for people, and describing with some invective the words, *"he, him, his"* - there was an audible intake of breath and the words: *"Oh my God, this is my issue, I'd never even thought about this before, but it's all about* ***him!****"*

The lady was divorced and her ex-husband was a nightmare whenever he was in contact, messing her and the children around, making every issue about 'him' even now, after being divorced several years. She realised that she was holding a lot of animosity and tension about "*him*" and when using this word out loud to others including her children, or internally, it caused inner conflict which then led to external arguments with 'him' when 'he' was around. This made 'them', i.e., the children, uncomfortable, sad or even angry at times.

In a client session, we go through any examples from the client's pre-session questionnaire and establish any associated bothersome feelings. We can also look at these third-party pronouns in relation to the I, Me, Myself and You. We can explain, with examples, that the person understands the concept of "representations" in three-dimensional space, e.g:

> **Ask: "What representation do you have when you hear, 'Him'?" Elicit visual representation and what the representation *means* to the client.**
>
> Approximately 75% will have a negative representation for one of these words.
>
> **Ask: *"And when you think of 'Him' whereabouts is 'Him'?" "And how old is 'Him'?" "And what's happening around 'Him'?"***
>
> You could even ask:
>
> "***And whereabouts is him in relation to I, Me, Myself or You?"***

This depends upon how the client has phrased the third-party pronoun, e.g., "*I am so angry with him", "Him and me always argue",* etc.

Work also on any potent feelings or emotions that come up as a result of exploring 'Him' or any of the other third party pronouns that have been chosen, e.g. *"He really bothers me", "They just don't understand who I am"*, *"I keep comparing myself to them"* , and so forth.

The word "**It**" can be very information dense and be used in place of a noun or other pronouns at times. I have sometimes heard people describing a person they don't like as "it", e.g., *"Just look at it; the state of it - mutton dressed as lamb."*

The word "it" can almost become anthropomorphised. Here is an extract from part of a statement using "**It**" (there was much more in this questionnaire):

> *"I want to be able to say to myself 'I know it feels like you can't survive without 'using' food today, but really, you don't need it, so don't think about it/don't eat it, move on, you are strong enough'. Ideally, I want to be able to not even think about it or have to go through this process – I just want it to be natural, just a fleeting thought, 'Am I hungry? No, ok, fine' and that's that."*

Further explorations can take place with words from the following list (which is not exhaustive):

Boyfriend, Girlfriend, Husband, Wife, Daughter, Son, Mother, Mummy, Mum, Dad, Father, Daddy, The Ex, The Mrs, The Wife, The Kids, My Girl, My Fella **and so forth. Pet names can be included, e.g.,** ***Bunny, Baby, Honey*****, etc.**

Pet names are interesting, because not everyone likes the name that a partner affectionately calls them, or sometimes it is not so affectionate and can have connotations of insult or a putdown, even gas-lighting and abuse. It could be a work colleague or boss using terms which have bullying undercurrent and the person may feel too insecure to ask them to stop. Feelings of fear and/or resentment can build quite easily and friction in relationships follows.

Perhaps upon reading the above, various names or third-party pronouns have come into your conscious awareness as bothersome or even emotionally painful. IEMT is a wonderful modality for creating remedial and generative change in order to deal with the emotional and identity-based issues that can arise. If you are trained in IEMT, use the techniques yourself to work on this, or find a practitioner to do a swap with. If you are not trained in IEMT, seek out a practitioner to work with you. The more emotional baggage we ditch, the lighter the load and the easier it is to traverse the landscapes we inhabit, both internal and external.

Putting Our Identity Into Perspective

I recently saw the film *Marvellous*, which is based on the life of Neil Baldwin. He was born with learning difficulties in the UK in 1946. He was picked on and bullied as a child, but the one thing that made Neil different from so many supposedly 'normal' people in a fantastic way was a decision he made as a youngster. *"**I** always wanted to be happy, so **I** decided to be,"* he said many years later when being interviewed.

Neil's belief in himself and in the goodness of others led him on a life of amazing adventures. He had decided as young boy that he wanted to be a clown in the circus, so he left home and did just that. He also worked, unasked and unpaid, as a meet-and-greet person at Keele University, where his mother worked as cleaner. His friendly, infectious nature won him lots of friends among students, lecturers and visitors. He loved football and ended up running a university football team whose president was at one time the former Liverpool and England star, Kevin Keegan.

A lifelong Stoke City Football Club fan, Neil's love of the club led him to befriend its manager, Lou Macari. He was offered the role of kit-man by Macari after their first meeting outside the stadium in 1991. They remain friends to this day, Macari making a cameo role in the film of Neil's life. He is friends with bishops, archbishops, footballers, university professors, medical consultants, politicians and royalty. Keele University awarded him an honorary master's degree in 2013, he was awarded the freedom of the city of Stoke-on-Trent in

2015 for his services to the city, and in the New Year Honours 2019 he was awarded the British Empire Medal. [2]

Neil's belief in himself - i.e., who he is, his own identity - and in the good of others has enabled him to create a "marvellous" life for someone who could so easily have been another social services statistic. In IEMT, gaining a comprehensive understanding of the many nuances of identity that can affect a person is more important than merely reducing the intensity of a feeling. If we are unhappy with who we are, it affects all aspects of our lives on all levels, core and peripheral. Ongoing, that will be seen in emotions, feelings and behaviours; the 'who' we are and the 'how' we are being. Ultimately for many, this is actually our own choice.

Chapter 11

Using IEMT When Working With Trauma Issues and PTSD

"My Memory is My Worst Enemy"

Anon

One of the main differentiators between IEMT and other eye movement models is the work we do with post-traumatic stress disorder (PTSD) and the models that have been created for this. In IEMT Practitioner Level 1 training, I teach the model as per the work of Andrew Austin, with its original intent for those with PTSD. However, the model is extremely useful for trauma in general and the occasions when people need to see things more clearly about a current situation. These uses and adaptions are taught on the Level 2 (Advanced) training.

It must be mentioned that although these models and the subsequent eye movement work are extremely successful and often very precise in their ability to help those experiencing PTSD to obtain relief, this will not work for all people all of the time. Remember that PTSD is a psychiatric classified disorder and a person with PTSD may have other psychological or psychiatric conditions. For this and the reasons discussed previously, such as Patterns of Chronicity or resistance to change, no apparent change may be reported. However, IEMT has enabled many people with lasting and seemingly unchangeable PTSD symptoms to find freedom from what can feel like a lifelong prison sentence.

The models within IEMT were initially developed for those suffering from what is still termed PTSD, as opposed to the more latterly defined Complex or CPTSD which was first described in 1992 by the American psychiatrist Judith Herman in her book *Trauma & Recovery* (1). The definition for PTSD came about as a result of observations following various armed conflicts, the most notable being the Vietnam War. Psychiatrists in the USA eventually came up with the term and it was officially recognised in 1980 by the American Psychiatric Association in the third edition of the Diagnostic and Statistical Manual of Mental Disorders (DSM-III) [(2)]. Prior to this, it had been called various things, including shell shock in World War One and combat fatigue in World War Two.

Of course, PTSD is not a condition exclusive to military personnel, and there are many examples of circumstances that can lead to diagnosable symptoms. It has also been recognised that an event does not have to be what would be termed as 'extremely traumatic' for a person's brain to respond by creating such symptoms. Events such as natural disasters, road and rail accidents, violent attacks (even if the person was not injured or was an onlooker or a first responder), childbirth (even if the birth was classed as 'normal') can be imprinted on the brain as trauma.

Some people who have been formally diagnosed with PTSD may seek help via eye movement work, and of course some who have not had a formal diagnosis will also seek help, so it is important that practitioners are aware of the symptoms that may indicate the condition. Apart from practitioners who are medical doctors and psychiatrists, we are of course not qualified to diagnose disorders. However, we do need to be aware of how they can manifest, as we may need to suggest to some potential clients that it is best for them to speak with a doctor before having IEMT. Guidelines are available on the Association's website and practitioners should read these and keep a copy.

Signs and Symptoms of PTSD

Re-experiencing

Signs and symptoms vary from person to person and may manifest differently in children and adolescents. The most common effect of PTSD is known as **re-experiencing,** where a person involuntarily and vividly re-lives parts of a traumatic event. These unwanted traumatic memories can intrude into the here and now, causing overwhelm.

These can take the form of:

- Flashbacks
- Nightmares
- Repetitive and distressing situations, images and sounds.
- Physical sensations, e.g., pain, sweating, nausea, trembling. [(3)]

Avoidance and Numbing

Emotional avoidance is often a reaction to trauma and hence is seen in cases of PTSD. A definition of avoidance is: *"Actions designed to prevent the occurrence of uncomfortable emotions such as fear, sadness, guilt and shame"* [(4)].

It may also include avoiding certain places, people or activities, listening to music that reminds the person of the trauma, or talking to people about the incident. Avoidance may be useful in the short-term to prefer temporary relief, however, long-term it may exacerbate the symptoms of PTSD.

Hyperarousal

A person with PTSD often experiences heightened anxiety due to a heightened sensitivity to external stimuli and events. They are in a state of increased sympathetic activation of the nervous system. This can lead to:

- Irritability
- Anger outbursts
- Sleep issues
- Concentration issues
- Hypervigilance
- Muscle tension

- Increased pain sensitivity
- Increased cardiac output
- Heightened startle response
- Shallow, rapid breathing
- Flashbacks

Other Issues as Effects Related to the Trauma

As a result of the unresolved trauma, the knock-on effects to the mental and physical functions of the body can include:

- Depression
- Anxiety disorders
- Phobias
- Substance misuse
- Eating issues
- Self-harming
- Chest pains
- Stomach and bowel issues
- Migraines
- Dizziness and vertigo

Andrew Austin's Experience

The PTSD model as used in IEMT was developed by Andrew Austin from many observations of trauma within his nursing career as well as working with clients both in the UK and overseas. He wanted to ascertain why two or more people could be exposed to the same traumatic event and some would go on to experience the effects of PTSD, often long-term, and others wouldn't; or if they did, it would resolve itself with little or no intervention. He began to notice certain patterns arising in some PTSD sufferers, hence I decided that it would be best to have him explain the circumstances himself. An interview with Andrew on this subject is available for course attendees on my website: www.integraleyemovement.com

The section below is taken from the interview and a few communications we have had on the subject:

"It started in 1998 when I went to South Africa. I stayed three months and left, never to return, owing to the horrific crime levels and the fact that I had witnessed some things I wish I hadn't. During my stay there I met with many victims of crime, including women whose husbands had been murdered in front of them. They had grief compounded with trauma, and this is where I first began to notice the two things PTSD patients want and which actually serves them badly:

1. Time travel - they want to go back in time to how things were before, or they want to go back to be the person they used to be; i.e., to change history.

2. They need others to understand; i.e., to change everyone else.

But I didn't really get the second point until later, when an acquaintance was on regular combat rotation with the military. I recognised that he and his friends were really cool about their experience; despite what they had been through and the losses they had sustained, they suffered no flashbacks or signs of PTSD. What really stood out was their acceptance, when they were in the company of people such as me and others (in the pub mostly), that they didn't need to explain anything. They had a shared knowing and didn't need to get anyone else to understand. Later, one of their group who I'd not met before appeared on the scene. He was a deeply troubled man and clearly was rapidly descending into alcoholism. He had a desperate need to get me to understand his experiences. The others had all learned to ignore this and just keep buying him more beer.

Something else that began to make sense was that certain jobs make marriage to someone outside of that career almost impossible. For example, at the hospitals where I have worked there are some departments, such as A&E, where what the staff do on a standard day cannot be comprehended by anyone who hasn't worked in such a role. Successful long-term relationships among these people were mostly to other emergency service personnel (fire, police, etc.) or other hospital staff. Many staff were single, and it wasn't uncommon for people to say things like, *"this is not a place for married people"*. Other staff members were engaged in serial short-term relationships or were simply having affairs.

The ones who were in long-term relationships or married to people outside of the services were typically people like my acquaintance and his friends; they had a different attitude and accepted that everyone had different realities.

I'm sure this is probably connected to Theory of Mind [(5)] and an attitude that says a person can empathise with people having a different reality from themselves, but don't need people to empathise with their own reality."

Sonia writes… To interrupt Andrew's monologue, this is a good place to talk about the Theory of Mind. This refers to the ability to understand the desires, intentions and beliefs of others, and is a skill that typically develops between the ages of 3-5 years. This will usually not apply to those who are not developing typically in childhood, i.e., children with autism [(6)]. Interestingly, a study on eye tracking in 2009 showed that adults with Asperger's syndrome seem to compute Theory of Mind differently to those without autism or Asperger's [(7)]:

> *"We showed that, like infants, neurotypical adults' (n = 17 participants) eye movements anticipated an actor's behaviour on the basis of her false belief. This was not the case for individuals with Asperger's syndrome (n = 19). Thus, these individuals do not attribute mental states spontaneously, but they may be able*

to do so in explicit tasks through compensatory learning."

One of the earliest tests for the Theory of Mind is the 'False Belief Test' which demonstrated that this is impaired in people with autism. The test was developed in 1985 by Baron-Cohen, Leslie and Frith [8]. The classic example is as follows:

> *"A little girl named Sally puts a ball into a basket and goes out for a walk. While she is away, another little girl named Anne takes the ball out of the basket and puts it into a box. When Sally comes back, she wants to play with the ball. Where, the children are asked, will Sally look for the ball? 'In the box,' children with autism answer, unable to imagine that Sally might be operating under a false belief."*

Now, to continue with Andrew's monologue: "Another phenomenon I became aware of in the early 1990s working in A&E was the issue of trauma and compensation. There is a saying that '*whiplash doesn't heal until the compensation is paid'*, and we saw lots of examples of this, though at least some of those whiplash patients were undoubtedly genuine.

But I also saw traumatised clients with flashback-type symptoms who would not permit themselves to heal for the same reasons. When attempting a therapeutic intervention, what I used to call "the excuse machine" would kick in, or less commonly they'd abreact.

Initially, I'd think of this as simple secondary gain, but as time went on, I began to reject this as an over-simplification and projection onto the complex system the client was presenting. I was not convinced that in the non-malingering clients' secondary gains were actually what was going on.

It seemed to be more of an issue about a sense of injustice and having wrongs righted than one of monetary gain, and people who are living under an injustice suffer terribly. The trick would be to frame the intervention as a way of improving their mental wellbeing so they could be in a better position to deal with this injustice.

Later on (around 1999-2000) I was listening to a Richard Bandler audio set where he was recounting a story about a couple arguing in the supermarket. The story goes that Bandler went over and apologised to both of them for what had happened to them to give rise to the argument. I forget what the rest of the recording said, but it gave me the concept that for many people it doesn't matter who apologises to them. We see this often, for example when the mayor or some other public official apologises to a family for whatever police injustice has happened. It seems that the important aspect is that the person who apologises needs to be seen as an 'authority'. It's very unfortunate that so many therapists appear weak or compensate for this by being cocky or arrogant.

The apology gives rise to, *"I acknowledge your reality, I don't need to you acknowledge mine"*, and can leverage subsequent therapeutic intervention.

It goes wrong, of course, when therapists use reframing, reassurance or explanations, because this violates the above and says, *"I reject your reality, so here, please accept mine."*

All of this is what allowed me to begin to recognise the Lynchpin Model, where a knowing/understanding of the lynchpin (LP) is communicated to the client without them having to explain it."

The Lynchpin (LP) Model

Sonia now takes up the narrative again... In the years since my original training to be a Complementary Therapist and Hypnotherapist in 1999, I have attended many courses to improve my knowledge and skills. This CPD has included several trainings in working with trauma. I have gained some amazing insights and knowledge along the way and have been introduced to several important areas of work that is both mind- and body-orientated. The most profound and innovative piece of work encountered thus far has been the introduction to working with the PTSD Model in order to locate a lynchpin for a particular trauma and how this can be released, in many cases within one session.

This knowledge - that the mind can hold a complex structure such as trauma in place, usually by a tiny, seemingly inconsequential part of the overall experience such as a piece of memory, often accompanied by an internal narrative, not only a visual representation – is, I believe, ground-breaking in the field of trauma resolution work. The fact that it is still relatively unknown among mental health professionals is anathema to me. I'm sure the IEMT Practitioners reading this book who have used the model and witnessed the relief from mental torture which it can achieve will agree it is nothing short of astonishing.

My field of work focuses quite significantly on childbirth-related traumas. I have worked with many women, and a few partners, in whom the events of or around birthing have led to issues such as post-natal depression and post-natal PTSD. Time after time, women especially don't often cite the birth itself as the thing that caused the trauma, even if it was traumatic or not the experience they had hoped for. By listening to their story – and this is one area where the story is important because for many, the fact that they felt they were not listened to or had their preferences/wishes ignored or dismissed during the event is the issue - and the resulting lynchpin can become obvious to a trained IEMT Practitioner.

Some women who have had what to many would seem an ideal birth will come for hypnobirthing classes during a second pregnancy with fear and trauma-like symptoms. Often, women will say, *"I know I should be grateful as I'm okay and the baby is fine, and the birth wasn't traumatic, but..."*

Here lies the rub; women's trauma is often dismissed by health 'care' professionals because of the assumption that if there is no visible trauma, all must be well. *"You have a healthy baby, be grateful for that"*, and other words to that effect are often quite dismissively bandied about. It is not surprising then, that the rates of PND and PNPTSD appear to be increasing year-on-year. In fact, the NHS glibly states on its website:

"Post-natal depression is a type of depression that many parents experience after having a baby. It's a common problem, affecting more than 1 in every 10 women within a year of giving birth. It can also affect fathers and partners" [(9)].

Data from the Office for National Statistics (ONS) found there were 464,437 live births in England and Wales between January and September 2020, so a potential 46,443 cases or more within that time period.

Not all women suffering PTSD experience PND and a study by Czarnocka and Slade (2000) suggested it is possible that 25% of women who have PTSD could remain undetected due to a lack of PND symptoms [(10)]. Finding up-to-date statistics is proving difficult at the time of writing, however according to the Depression in New Dads website in 2020, research suggests that up to 15.7% of UK women will develop trauma-related symptoms following childbirth (around 9% in the United States) [(11)].

The Lynchpin = What They Did or Didn't Do

It may seem that I have gone off on a tangent here, so let's bring things back to the PTSD LP Model. It is imperative when working with those with trauma, whether PTSD or not, to listen for tell-tale phrases and watch for body language clues for the lynchpin.

A good definition of a lynchpin is an essential component of a system or structure (often something small or singular) that keeps the other parts in place and functioning. Hence, when we look at working with PTSD we are looking at the structure of the trauma, and what small piece of the structure is keeping it in place and functioning in the brain. Find and remove this, then the complex structure of the trauma can disintegrate, often quite rapidly. To give it a plumbing metaphor, it's like taking the plug out of a bath full of water, release the plug and the water can quickly flow away.

For traumas that are health-related, it is often what a doctor, nurse, midwife, etc., said, or the look (often perceived as disdain) that they gave; e.g., in relation to a question or request, that a person finds difficult to get past. Also, and I have heard this many times in birthing scenarios, it is often what the client felt they were unable to say that is the lynchpin. This can keep going around and around in their brain; *"If only I had said X, Y, Z, things would have been different"*. Trauma can be a feeling of 'powerlessness' which Carolyn Spring defines as "life-threatening powerlessness" [12]. When those with medical "authority" appear to dismiss a person, it can feel devastating.

Here are some examples of statements I've heard often over the years. The fact that I am still hearing statements like this after more than 21 years in the birthing world demonstrates that the medical profession still has much to learn and change regarding the verbal language (words as well as tonality) and the body language used around vulnerable and emotionally compromised individuals:

"I wished I'd said X", "I felt I couldn't ask for Y", "The doctor glared at me, folded her arms and stood in front of the door and said I wasn't going anywhere as he was going to induce me". "I'll never forget that look she gave me", "I was made to feel stupid so said nothing more", "I was threatened that if I didn't push harder they would call for the doctor and I would end up with forceps or a ventouse". "I was shouted at", "They kept saying 'good girl' as if I was a child, I felt totally patronised", "I was laughed at and told I wasn't in labour, so I said nothing, even though I could feel the head"...

This last one also had the following statement going around her head:

"This young girl thinks she's in labour!"

This came from midwives who were deriding her because of her calm demeanour, which they took as a sign that she was not in labour. She birthed in the hospital corridor half an hour later. The physicality of the birth, although quick, was not traumatic, however the events that her brain fixated on, including the above words, felt traumatising.

In many cases, however, there will not be such an obvious lynchpin or lynchpins (sometimes there are more than one). So, using the model and drawing it up on a board and then describing a story - not the client's actual story, but it can be similar if desired - can then lead to the uncovering of the LP so that it can be removed and the complex structure of the trauma collapse. This needs to be approached carefully; to do so carelessly can result in this elicitation looking like an apportioning of blame.

The principle behind this comes from the simple observation made by Andrew Austin which runs contrary to what most clinicians appear to practise:

PTSD sufferers are haunted by the part that they played in it all, not by what happened to them, **but by** ***what they <u>did or didn't do back then.</u>***

The above statement may sound like a 'blame', hence it is easy to get it wrong. It is also observed that when clients raise their own 'shame' in therapy, this tends to be quickly dismissed by clinicians/ therapists with phrases such as, *"well that's understandable, don't worry about it..."*

Many therapists appear to be especially adept at dismissing their client's experience without realising they are doing it - just as the client's trauma may have been initiated due to the attitude of a medical practitioner in the first place. It's a like a weird form of Catch 22.

This is how Andrew Austin describes what a client may experience in a therapy session:

i. **Their experience is reframed** In the need to appear therapeutic, the clinician changes negatives into positives. In reframing in this way, the clinician is essentially dismissing what the client has reported, i.e., their actual experience as they remember it.

ii. **Their experience is blamed** When the clinician hears the potential for the inference of blame, "*that is not your fault*" is a common form of reassurance, but this can backfire, because even if the client doesn't say it out loud, they might well think, "*but I didn't think it was my fault anyway*!"

iii. **Their experience is ignored or lost** For example, in the recollection, "*My teacher shouted at me again, called me stupid, and then hit me*," we have several emergent themes; the teacher, the fact that shouting has occurred previously, the name calling and the violence. Which one of those does the therapist address with first?

iv. **Their experience is filtered out** Clinicians have their own built-in biases (they are merely human after all). The result of this may be that their filtering process is engaged when they listen to their clients and they might only pursue things that fit their most recent learnings and study, and so on.

v. **The therapist avoids that which is uncomfortable to talk about** Instead, they stick with the stuff that they find safe.

Eliciting the LP and Drawing Out the Model

IEMT PTSD Lynch Pin Model

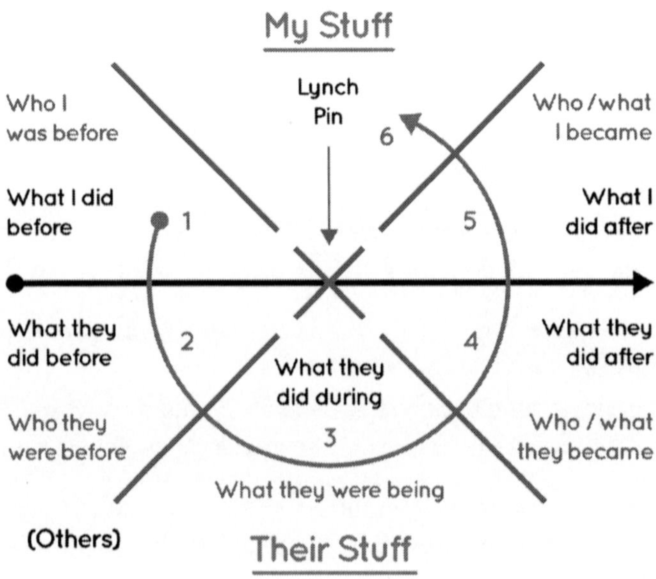

- It is important to cite other examples when working with a client so as not to engage the person directly into their trauma and re-trigger it - hence do not go straight into their issue when they are presenting with PTSD. Of course this can sometimes not be avoided even with this process.

- When a person who has come specifically with a trauma/PTSD issue, talk through the process briefly to give them information about what you will be doing. You will have to use your judgement as to when using the model will be appropriate for that person.

- Listening and watching for signs of possible trauma and lynchpins is important, as they can be missed when someone has presented not with trauma/PTSD, but with an anxiety issue or depression, for example.

- When you reach the lynchpin, say to the client, ***"do you have something like this?"*** There is no blame here at all. They may call it *"shame"* or some other emotion - we go with whatever they call it and never presume we know what they are feeling or experiencing.

- Draw out the client's scenario if required (note - it may not always be required). Elicit the information as shown below – this may take some time.

- Draw this on a flip chart; if the session ends before identifying the LP, keep it safe for next time. If using a whiteboard take a photograph so that you can recreate it for the next session if required.

- Don't rush this work; some additional episodic memory work may also be required. This will be described later.

How to Use the PTSD Model

This model works best when the trauma is attached to an event that involved another person or people. In this case, we construct a timeline, as follows:

Prior - During – After

1. What **'I'** did before... Additionally, you may work on *'Who I was before'*, as the loss of identity after trauma can be a significant factor for people.

2. What **they/others** did before... Additionally, you may wish to do some work on *'Who they were'*, e.g., is this/are they strangers or significant person(s) known to the person?

3. What **others** did during... Additionally, 'What/who they were being'.

4. What **others** did after... Additionally, 'Who/what they became'.

5. What 'I'/**Self** did after... Additionally, 'Who/what I became'.

6. **The Lynchpin –** The client doesn't have to disclose the Lynchpin. IEMT kinaesthetic eye movements are often used here. If the client has engaged with the memory of the Lynchpin we do have to go through the full question protocol here, so ask them to move their eyes as directed while thinking of the memory. Watch for the axial deviations.

    - Stop and recalibrate if needed.
    - If working on 'Who they are/Who they became', some identity questions may be appropriate along with the appropriate eye movements.
    - Episodic memory (See the image and description below) Move the person forward in time with the statement, *"And then what happened?", "What happened next?"* etc.

Updating the Episodic Memory Model

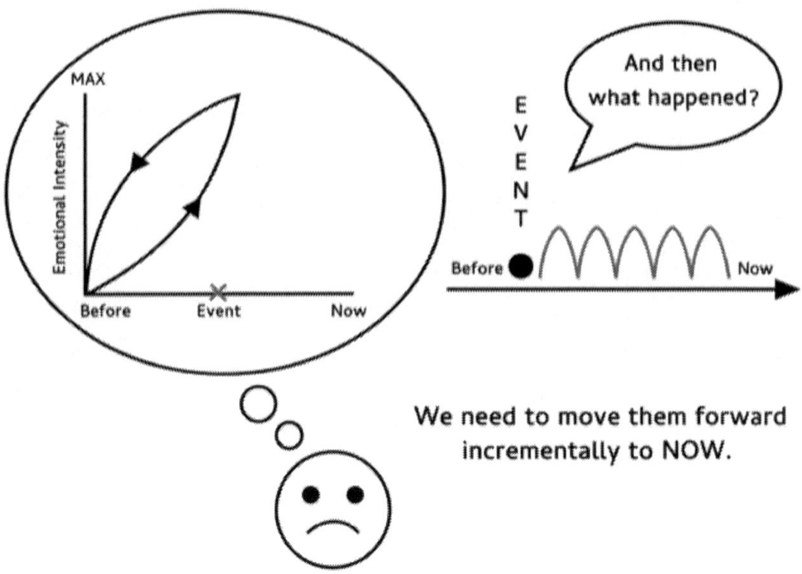

When researching PTSD, one of the phenomena AA encountered was the living death scenario. Those who have studied Metaphors of Movement will be familiar with this representation. This is where we hear statements such as, *"I died that day", "My life ended there", "I have no life any more", "I am dead to the world"* and so forth.

Such statements are of course untrue and depending on the scenario I may well make the observation: *"Oh, well if you died that day then how come you're sitting in front of me/talking to me now?"* or *"Well you seem pretty alive to me right now..."* etc.

At the time of writing I have never been contradicted on my observations. There may be a bit of laughter, or the even stage 1 of the 3SAR, but never an argument to counter this.

One of the stories AA cites is that of a lady he encountered in India. She was on the run, having skipped bail after being charged with driving while drunk and ploughing into a crowd of revellers one evening. He found her sitting in a huddle, hugging herself and rocking in a cafe somewhere in Kolkata. He was asked to help by the cafe owner who, when asked what the problem was, said she had been there all day and had only bought one coffee.

Andrew joined the lady at the table and mirrored her body-hugging, rocking motion, and eventually asked her what the issue was. She recounted her story and explained how she kept going over the events preceding and up to the crash and couldn't get it out of her mind. AA, in typical provocative style, said that while to do what she did once was appalling, to keep maiming those people over and over again in her mind was totally unacceptable. Having met her with some mirroring and pacing, he was then able to lead her and move her beyond that particular point in time by getting her to acknowledge subsequent events were in the past and to fill in the missing details of her life up to the present day. He moved her along her timeline, asking:

> *"And then what happened?".... "And what happened then?"... "And what next?"*

By getting her to extend her internal movie beyond the events of the trauma, he was able to get her unstuck and stop the incessant cycling around from just before, up to and including the trauma and back again. This is extremely important for those frozen in time, both emotionally and sometimes physically, as in the case of those who experience extremes of trauma and enter the Freeze part of the Fight, Flight, Freeze (F/F/F) response. This lady had done the sympathetic nervous system flight part, having fled to India, and was now in the pre-trauma discharge stage of the un-myelinated parasympathetic nerve fibre component of the response which is Freeze.

Again, those wishing to understand more about this phenomenon can access the work of Carolyn Spring, or read Stephen Porges' book on the Polyvagal Theory (13).

Porges changed the understanding of the autonomic nervous system as being only divided into the sympathetic and parasympathetic branches first named by British Physiologist J.N. Langley in 1903 (14). Pre-ganglionic fibres of both branches are cholinergic; i.e., myelinated using acetyl choline as a neurotransmitter. Post-ganglionic autonomic nerve fibres in the sympathetic and parasympathetic nervous system are unmyelinated as they are C-sensory nerve fibres that support temperature sensation. Myelinated nerve fibres are usually more rapidly responsive than unmyelinated fibres, activating the body's responses with energising ways; i.e., movement, alertness, exuberance. They support the stress response (F/F/F).

The parasympathetic nervous system facilitates the slowing down of systems (rest and digest) and is composed of the unmyelinated vagus nerve. This connects to organs below the diaphragm such as the intestines. In addition, a small number of unmyelinated nerve fibres connect the heart and these can cause a very slow heart rate.

In his polyvagal theory, Porges explains that there is an important third component to the autonomic nervous system - the myelinated vagus nerve, which is located above the diaphragm and branches to the face, head, lungs and heart (15).

For those who have already trained in Level 1 IEMT, I hope this chapter has been a good revision for how we work with trauma and PTSD cases, especially where this has been created at the hands of another person or people. For those new to this modality who have struggled with the concept of finding a Lynchpin and what this is, the important point to remember is that it is rarely the whole of the traumatic event that leads to PTSD. Rather, it is that point of contact in the mind where the trauma hinges - i.e., that small piece of internal response - that is causing the feelings of shame or guilt that are often Lynchpin-related. The *'if only', 'why did I?', "why didn't I?', 'I should have'* internal dialogue is so often key to keeping trauma in place. As we have seen, those who are able to come to acceptance of an event will either not suffer PTSD-type symptoms, or tend to find resolution more quickly.

I also feel, based on the clients that I have worked with, that there is a possible link between those who favour the Metaphors of Movement taxonomy called 'the hurts' and PTSD. However, there will also be differences between those who have experienced a one-off event of trauma and those who have experienced long-term exposure to trauma, e.g., childhood abuse. As we always say, IEMT can help many people who have been through one or more therapeutic approaches where change and resolution has eluded them. However, it is not a cure-all for everyone.

Chapter 12

Physiological State Accessing Cues (PSAC)

Tiny Tweaks for Big Changes

In trauma and PTSD situations, there is a down-regulation social engagement system (SES) as described by Stephen Porges. The SES picks up signals from others, such as body language, vocal tonality/quality, and facial expressions, and if the SES finds these signals unthreatening and acceptable it calms people down at the unconscious level, hence we are unaware of this. We have no idea that the SES is overriding stress hormones that others and certain situations activate in us (1).

This down-regulation can keep a person in a state of hyperarousal via the sympathetic part of the autonomic nervous system (myelinated fibres) and/or disconnection via the unmyelinated vagus nerve, or in a coping mode, i.e., avoidance. Each of these responses is a means of survival in optimal safety, and a person's nervous system can become primed to react to cues based on past traumatic experiences that may not fit a current situation.

In IEMT, we encourage practitioners to be constantly observant of body language. When somebody is talking about an issue and accessing their associated state, shifts in physiology can be detected. This may be very obvious or very subtle.

Here, the practitioner can use the Subjective Unit of Distress (SUD) scale to ascertain the level of discomfort the person experiences as they lock into a physiological response. By making the person consciously aware of the way they are holding their body, we can elicit small shifts in that physiology and ask simply, *"Is this feeling* *the **same** or **different**?"* Then we can ask, *"Is it **better** or **worse?**"* If better or worse, we ask, *"What score would you give it now?"* The next step is vital to the process; this is when we ask the person to: ***"Put your body back to the position it needs to be in order to get back to the original feeling or state."***

This demonstrates the relationship between a person's physiology and how they feel. With a subtle change in that original stance, there is a real and tangible shift for most people most of the time. This can often be another big "aha..." moment; when people understand that if they want to stop or downgrade the strength of a particular feeling or state all they have to do in the moment is a subtle shift. This may be as simple as moving a finger to a different position, sitting back slightly on a chair, or turning one foot out or in from its current position. It may even be enough to take a controlled breath in and out.

Such physiological changes using the PSAC model do not necessarily create long-term neurological change, however, over time, if a person becomes more aware of how their body can affect their mind, they can start to exercise such changes more regularly. Thus, with repetition, neuroplasticity can start to create new neurological pathways and delete those that are no longer used.

When experienced by people who say they find it very hard to change, this quick and easy exercise may be the first breakthrough they have consciously achieved for a long time. Now they are suddenly enabling themselves to make changes that can help them to feel better. It is not necessarily going to deal with 'cause', however if the 'effect' is so powerful that therapy can seem impossible, this tiny movement/tweak exercise can be the first step towards creating change for the better. The person can learn the process and implement it themselves in situations when a familiar unwanted state can be triggered or created.

How many people, for example with low mood or depression, wear one particular colour and sit in one particular chair in one particular position and as a result start to run and embed the vicious cycle of their particular physiological state loop? With this resource skill, they can make the choice whether to remain locked into a particular state or not. IEMT is about teaching skills to people inside the problem state, not just 'doing therapy' with them.

When teaching this to IEMT students, other exercises we use include the practitioner asking the client to exaggerate a stance, or the practitioner mirroring the stance to exaggerate it. Depending on the rapport between practitioner and client, even elements such as using taboo words or concepts can be introduced. However, this must never be seen to be personal to the client; it is merely a way of illustrating that the behaviour can be changed quickly, even with humour.

Here are few ways in which we can work with clients' PSAC:

Exercise #1 – Eliciting the State Access Strategy

- Use rapport and state elicitation to enable the client to access the recurrent negative/problem state:

  Ask: "*Do you have something currently that is a problem for you, something troublesome for bothersome*?"

  Ask: "*How do you know*?"

- As the client answers, you can add "*Show me...*" indicating that the client is accessing the problem state physiologically.

- Score 1/10. If required, increase the score in increments, up to 10 if possible.

- Observe what the client is doing and calibrate the physiological shifts they use to access the state. Mentally make a note of these.

- Now make some micro-adjustments of the client's physiology. With each movement ask, ***"What happens when I do that? Same or different? Better or worse?"*** They can score it again if they wish.

- Clients can make their own adjustments, especially if they are children or you are working with them online.

- If you are working online, ensure the client is far enough away from the screen so that you can see a good amount of their physiology. You can also ask, *"what is your right foot doing?"* etc. If it can't be seen, then instruct them to move it slightly.

- Then instruct the client, ***"Put it back to how it is supposed to be/how it was before."*** Repeat this exercise a few times and ask the client for feedback.

- Clients are often astounded that such small movements can create such huge physiological shifts and bring a sense of relief.

- This is the PSAC exercise I use the most with clients. I always teach them how to do this for themselves so that they can manage their own change when required.

Exercise #2 – Exaggerate the State Uncomfortable Enough to Create Change

- Ask the client to access the bothersome state as before and score it.

- This time, mirror the client; as you do so, you can comically exaggerate their movements while encouraging them to increase muscular tensions, posture, etc.

- Ask them how it feels (it should feel a little worse).

- Encourage the client to hold this posture until it becomes too uncomfortable to maintain.

- Break the state and ask for feedback.

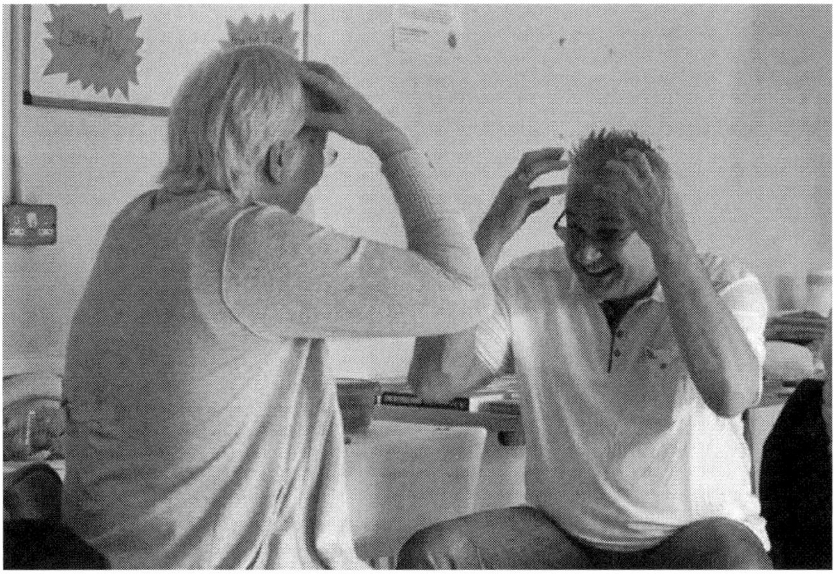

Exercise #3 – **Incapacitating the Unconscious Physiological Access to the Negative State**

- Use rapport and state elicitation to enable the client to access the recurrent problem state.
- Feedback to the client the physiological shifts that are necessary to access that state.
- Exaggerate the client's movements with your own and offer absurd verbal descriptions of the movements (*not of the client themselves).
- **Use humorous, rude, taboo statements and ridiculous concepts.**

***Only reference the movement/behaviour, not their body, appearance, or anything that isn't a behaviour-related to the accessing of the negative state.**

Tiny Tweaks

The idea of tiny physiological changes that can create real physiological changes to improve state, mood and even mental performance is finding traction among psychologists. Dr Amy Cuddy has an excellent TED Talk based on her research of body language. She discusses the use of 'power posing' and the temporary shifts in various hormones that can help people overcome nervousness in situations such as public speaking. [(2)]

In IEMT, we have been using very similar approaches with PSAC for many years and it's good to see this work being ratified scientifically now. I do encourage those of you who are interested to watch Dr Cuddy's TED Talk, the link for which is in the references.

Chapter 13

The Three Pillars Model: The Power of 3!

> **"Our anxiety does not come from thinking about the future, but from wanting to control it."**
>
> **Kahlil Gibran, 1923**

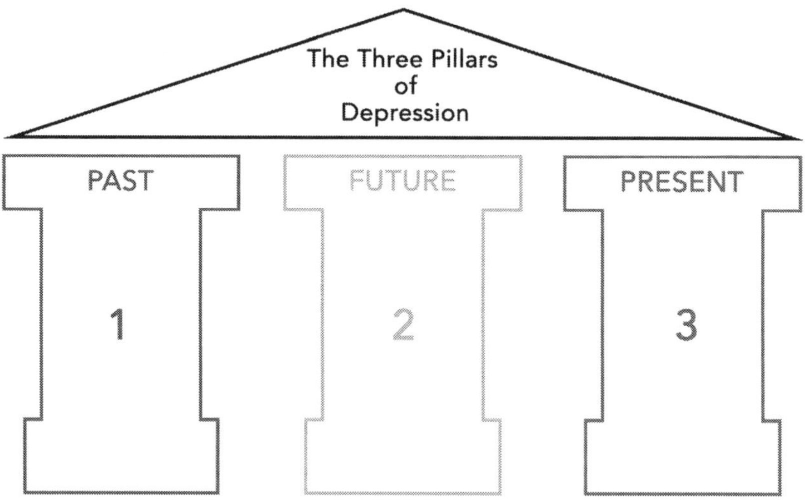

I've given this model the additional title *The Power of 3*, because there are other models, such as Sydney Banks' Three Principles, that highlight three elements to initiate change [(1)], and I don't wish to confuse the Three Pillars with anything else. When we are working with clients and the words '*anxiety*', '*anger*' or '*guilt*' appear on assessment forms or in sessions, this model of the Three Pillars should immediately spring to the IEMT Practitioner's mind. A bit like PSAC, this model is sometimes forgotten, which is a great shame because the beauty of it is in its predictability and recursive nature. It is also something many clients can relate to.

This model is primarily a focus for people who report feeling anxious or anxiety. However, looking at the supporting emotions to anxiety is also key. Anxiety can present a very broad set of feelings and physiological responses that can range from butterflies in the stomach to full-on panic attacks, so establishing what type of experience a person is having can be useful. Again, we don't need them to go into the content of their story; just factual information will suffice.

Like the Five Primary Patterns of Chronicity, the Three Pillars model was inspired as a way of working with anxiety and depression-related issues. The model is one of the 'chaining of emotions' and is predicated on two elements: (i) Time (ii) Rules.

I will discuss the above elements later. First, let's think about emotional chaining, what that means and how it manifests. Andrew Austin's original model of the Three Pillars arose from his observations of the emotional states clients would present when they came to a session. For example, a person would turn up feeling guilt or shame about the reason for seeking therapeutic help. However, after around 20 minutes their emotions would have shifted to, e.g., anxiousness or worry. A person arriving in an anxious state may after a period of time be exhibiting temper or anger. The person who turned up angry, perhaps because the train was late or someone cut them up for a parking place, would after a period of time start feeling regret or remorse about their outburst, and so on.

Such observations led to the formulation of this simple and extremely effective model, which can be used with clients regardless of using eye movement work. This cycling is also seen in people with PTSD and other trauma-based issues. Like all the techniques and models in IEMT, the skill is in recognising the patterns, traits and cycles people are running that keep them stuck in situations, and then integrating the knowledge of this into the remedial work, be it eye movements or other models that will result in neurological shifts and changes for the better.

As previously stated, the feelings/emotions from the original model are divided into groups based on (i) Time and (ii) Rules. In practice, I have over time added more feelings/emotions based on my experience with the many clients who have presented with issues in which the Three Pillars model is appropriate. I work in a bespoke way with this model because, although the original model will absolutely work for the majority of people, I have had one or two surprises over the years regarding the emotional chaining of some people. Thus, I will engage the original model and tweak it if needs be.

When demonstrating the model to clients, which I do via images from my manual, drawing the model on a whiteboard or sharing a course training presentation with online clients, the number of "Aha..." moments is huge. After describing the model, I always ask them:

"So, how familiar is this cycle to you?"

So many reply, *"Oh my God this is so familiar, this is me"*, or *"You've just described me/my life exactly!"* Or *"**I** really recognise this in **myself**"*. Interestingly, such statements also impact on identity: *"This is **me**", "**You** have just described **me** exactly!"* Hence, the IEMT Practitioner is not only listening for confirmation that the client recognises this cycle, but also for identity-based statements that can also be worked on. Remember, the **Who** we are being is just as important, if not more so, than the **How** we are being/behaving. Dealing with both is crucial for improved mental/emotional health long-term. In reality, the **Who** we are often drives the **How** we are. If we think of the Pattern of Chronicity of ***'Being at effect rather than being at cause'*** we can take it to this identity level - the **Who** is often the ***'cause'*** and the **How** the ***'effect'.*** An example of the **Who** is the perfectionist, the **How** effect is never being satisfied with external things or themselves; always finding fault with others; rejecting anything that is not perfect in their eyes (whatever that means!).

The original set of feelings/emotions are: **Guilt, Shame, Regret, Remorse, Anxiety, Worry, Panic, Temper, Anger.**

I tend to use the word 'anxious' or 'anxiousness' in place of 'anxiety' for the feelings a person experiences. I use 'anxiety' to describe the over-arousal of the autonomic nervous system, primarily the sympathetic nervous system fibres, and I educate clients and course attendees about this concept. Not everyone attending a course is a therapist or had any medical/scientific knowledge, so may not know about this, or about Fight Flight Freeze. Subsequently, adding the word 'anxiety' to the model seems inconsistent. On discussing the inclusion of other emotions/feelings into the model with Andrew Austin, he says:

"I don't think it matters - there may well be a cluster of related emotions that fit in there, but that might begin to complicate things, as it ends up becoming a model for how narcissists rapidly cycle through their inner turmoil."

This conclusion comes, as Andrew informs me, from material published by Sam Vankin, who is one of the world's experts in narcissism and is himself a self-professed narcissist. There are many videos of his work available on YouTube.

Why Anxiety Gets Mis-Treated

Before continuing with the model explanation, there is a very important point concerning anxiety that all IEMT Practitioners should be aware of from their training. Anxiety or anxiousness is created as a result of something else. In the model we can see that past-based emotions such as guilt, regret, shame, and remorse can link into the next column of future-based emotions and the future-based emotions can then link into the present-based emotions. Hence, before we dive straight in and begin the eye movement techniques, we need to explore what caused the anxiety in the first place.

I have seen video case studies from trainee practitioners where there is an anxiety issue, but the practitioner forgets about the structure of anxiety and starts with the Basic Kinaesthetic Pattern to attempt to downgrade the feeling of anxiousness. I'm not saying this doesn't work, of course IEMT can have a fantastic effect here. However, it is an attempt to affect an "effect". Working on one specific issue may not deal with the issues and ways of being that led this person to be this way in the first place.

I am now going to divide the above list into three columns or pillars with reference to Time.

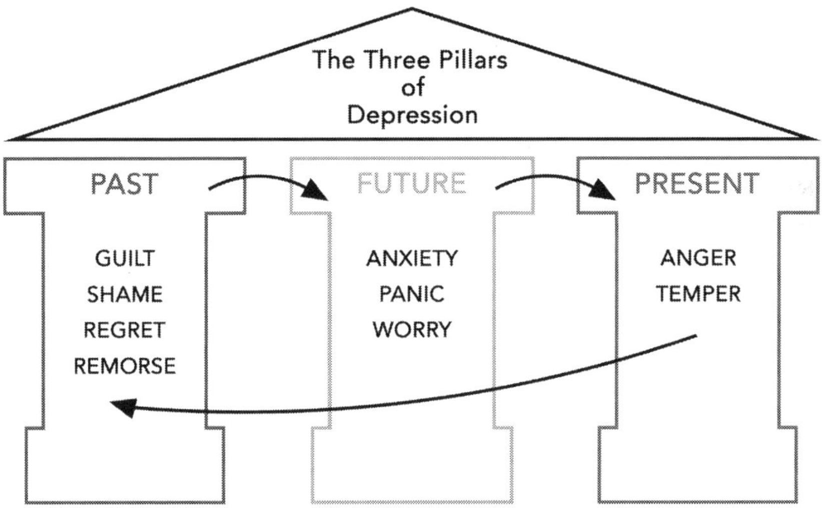

The Three Pillars Original Model

Looking at the table of the original Three Pillars Model, we can see that they are divided into Past, Future and Present. They are put in this order because this tended to be the order of the orientation in time of the state/emotional shifting that was being observed. Also, this cyclical model of emotional chaining will tend to link emotions that are more likely to follow from one to the next. Although movement between extreme emotions cannot be ruled out, people will usually shift between two extreme emotions such as 'love' and 'hate' by one or several link emotions. For example, a chain could be *joy – happiness – surprise – concern – worry – fear*. This sequence may move rapidly or not, depending on the situation.

The cyclical nature of this model occurs often in people who are anxious or have a tendency towards anxiety. Often, this trait can be traced back to childhood. It is very rare to see a client who wants help with anxiety and says this is a new phenomenon. Even if they do, once we start going back to memories, older memories of anxiety-provoking events normally surface. This way of being can feed forward into Identity and can make a person's day-to-day life exhausting. We can then get the person who identifies themselves this way, i.e., *"My name is Jane and I'm an anxious person."* Or, *"Hello, I'm Jane and anxiety is a part of me."* Or, *"Hello, my name is Jane and anxiety is part of my life."* And, *"Hello, my name's Jane and I'm always anxious."*

Of course, this lifelong type of anxiety can have many causes. I often discover a client's parent or parents also exhibit this behaviour, so when we think about *"how did this person learn to be this way?"* we have a very good idea of how. If you are working with Metaphors of Movement with a client, you may find this anxiety manifesting as a 'container metaphor' with an elevation element (although not exclusively). We know this is lifelong or brought through time and space from childhood, and is family-related. 'Family' can be broadened to those with whom the person grew up as a child, so this can be seen in looked-after children and those who have been in children's homes. The elevation element can manifest in many ways, such as on a cliff edge, on a pedestal or column, balancing on a chair or pole. Listen out for such statements as, *"I'm always on edge"*, or *"I'm up in the air about this"*, or *"I feel like I'm locked in a suspended bird cage"* and so forth.

Coming back to this model, we can look at the emotions that have been subdivided into the Time and Rule concepts relating to Past, Future and Present, as follows:

Time Concept

Past - Guilt, Shame, Regret, Remorse

These feelings/emotions tend to be expressed with respect to something that has happened, rather than things that are happening or might happen, although there can be exceptions to the rule. Working in the childbirth arena, some women will express feeling guilty about thinking of not breastfeeding in the future, or having thoughts about a caesarean section rather than a natural birth, even though they haven't had the baby yet. However, in general guilt tends to be felt in relation to something that has happened.

Guilt and shame can sometimes be mixed up or interchanged, however there is a difference, and for some the metaphorical representation and somatic experience will be different. People can feel guilt without anyone else ever knowing they have something to feel guilty about, while shame, which clients sometimes confuse with guilt, tends to need an observer in order for it to manifest.

Guilt is generally carried metaphorically and somatically, internally or externally. Many describe it as a heavy weight, e.g., like a big stone inside or a sack of coal on their shoulders. Guilt can be felt without any observer of an action and it can occur from a thought. Guilt can also be a learned emotion. For example, some religions will indoctrinate the need for people to feel sin simply for being human or alive. Hence, we can feel guilt for something we did or didn't do. As we discussed in the PTSD model chapter, it isn't always what a person did, i.e., their direct action, that leads to a feeling of guilt. Rather, it may actually be what they didn't do; their inaction in an event or situation. Some young children may observe others, especially key adults, doing guilt and learn that this is how people are supposed to feel and behave as part of everyday life. Remember "*how did this person learn to feel this feeling*", and "*how did this person learn to be this way?*"

Shame, as mentioned above, is sometimes confused with guilt until we get more specific, and it tends to need an observer in order for it to manifest somatically. Again in terms of metaphors, shame is often a viscous or sticky substance adhering to the person. Back in history, people were tarred and feathered in order to shame them in public. Some will describe it like treacle or wading through mud, so it tends to be an external manifestation as opposed to something carried internally, as guilt can be.

Shame is what we feel when we get caught doing something wrong. For example, if nobody sees a person stealing from the cookie jar, then most (not all) will have some feeling of guilt about their actions. However, only if the person is caught in the act will they be likely to feel shame; i.e., they have been caught and observed and now can be publicly shamed and be made to feel ashamed of their actions.

Regrets, I've had a few… (sorry, I couldn't resist that, but I have!). Regret operates differently to both guilt and shame. Its consequence is usually felt with regard to that person, rather than to others. I remember, aged nine and in a new school, being asked to look after a new classmate from Peru because - you guessed it - I was brown and so was she and the teachers thought we would have things in common (not that it was worded exactly in this way, but it was most certainly inferred). I resented this somewhat, and although I was friendly with her in school, I made no effort to be friends out of school.

Only later, when she went back to Peru and I found out she was pen pals with another girl in the class who had made the effort to go to her house and be friends after school, do I remember feeling deep regret that I had not bothered to be a proper friend.

Later that year, another girl from Venezuela came to stay and once again I was given the task of being her friend. This time, I did make the effort and this was a wonderful, fulfilling friendship. After her return home we corresponded for many years as pen pals. So, my feeling of regret in the above example was with direct consequence to myself. I felt bad that I had missed out on this friendship. I didn't, however, feel any remorse.

Remorse has a different focus to regret, even though they are often bandied about together. That focus is not usually with consequence to the perpetrator, but on those who have been affected by a person's actions to others, hence the difference between regret and remorse. An example would be a person who has been jailed for murder. In order that they can be considered for parole, a perpetrator must be seen to show genuine remorse for their act. They must be willing to show repentance and even some form of reparation towards others with no reference to themselves. Saying, *"I truly regret my actions",* is not the same as saying, *"I am truly remorseful for my actions."*

In researching this point, it is interesting how little information is available and how often people and scholars mix guilt, shame, regret and remorse together as if they are the same thing, when they most definitely are not. One thing that is known, however, is that remorse can fade over time because its focus is on others and not the self. Hence, this may not be the correct criterion to assess whether somebody should be freed from prison. One of the few more recent articles on remorse states: *"True remorse is never just regret over consequence; it is regret over motive."* (2)

The one thing all the above have in common is that they are usually based in the Past; i.e., as a result of actions and occurrences that have already happened. So when a person presents saying that they feel shame, we know this is likely to be a past-based emotion. We can then start to look to see whether they begin to feel anxious as they start to speak about issues, and whether this may in turn roll over into temper, anger or a similar. With enough time, they will cycle all the way back round to a past-based feeling such as guilt.

Sometimes the person is not running the cycle in the session (after all, clients are often on their best behaviour). If, for example, they have an anger issue, they may be ashamed to speak about it because it will make them feel anxious about the fact that the therapist may judge them. However, as IEMT Practitioners we are able to look for those little tells that indicate the annoyance, irritation and frustration that can be the prequel to anger in their body language, vocal tones, and responses. Some people deny that anger is an issue, or they say that they only ever direct anger toward themselves. This may be true and it may not be. Hence the reason I have added a few extra emotions to my 3 Pillars model.

Future - Anxiety, Panic, Worry

The above responses are in the Future column of the Three Pillars because people tend to express these emotions in relation to things that have not yet occurred, and indeed may never occur. Working in the childbirth world, almost every person on a hypnobirthing course, partners as well as mums, have some future-based anxiety or worry with regard to the upcoming event. There is a plethora of Great Big 'What If' scenarios, which is understandable, as there are a multitude of factors that can affect labour, birth and parenting that people may be worrying or even catastrophising about. However, many people behave this way for apparently innocuous reasons, making their lives and often the lives of those around them truly miserable.

Additionally, a person may be worried or anxious about an event that happened in the past, e.g., being unable to pay their mortgage last month, that can have knock-on effects now or in the future. The anxiousness comes from the consequences yet to be realised from that past event; e.g., "*Will this affect our credit rating?*" or "*Will we be able to pay this month?*" and "*Will we be evicted from our home?*" These are still future-based concerns and so belong in this category.

Those people who are worrying about the consequences of past events may also be doing guilt etc. about those past events, and anger etc. when being questioned about this. So, we can start to see that these issues are not always cut and dried or isolated to one column. Hence, the emotional chaining and cyclical nature some people get caught up in can seem like a whirlwind. Exhausting!

There has been much research into anxiety over many years - physiological, chemical, psychological even spiritual - and there is no shortage of theories as well as scientifically established hypotheses. The invention of fMRI has given scientists the unique ability to look at brain function without the need for dissection. Some researchers postulate that mood and anxiety disorders are characterised by a variety of neuroanatomical, neuroendocrine and neurotransmitter disruptions. Martin et al 2009, state:

> *"Identifying the most functionally relevant differences is complicated by the high degree of interconnectivity between neurotransmitter- and neuropeptide-containing circuits in limbic, brain stem, and higher cortical brain areas. Furthermore, a primary alteration in brain structure or function or in neurotransmitter signalling may result from environmental experiences and underlying genetic predisposition; such alterations can increase the risk for psychopathology."* [(3)]

This multitude of factors can be seen with clients. A person may say: *"Well this anxiety runs in the family you know, my mother is like this and hers before her",* and of course on some level this is true because, even if not genetic per se, the learned nature of this way of being can persist from generation to generation.

An interesting article in the online publication Business Insider looks at scientific research into how parents' behaviour shapes children. It includes a useful quote from Graham Davey, a professor of psychology at the University of Sussex, UK:

> *"Given that genetic inheritance is not an overwhelming contributor to the variance in our anxiety levels, this strongly suggests that anxiety may somehow be socially 'transmitted' within the family."* [(4) (5)]

This makes it sound like a disease and, to reference Metaphors of Movement once again, this behaviour that is family-related and lifelong will often manifest as a category of autogenic metaphors known as 'container metaphors'. Containers have two main functions: To restrict movement and keep us from leaving, i.e., like a prison; or to stop others entering, i.e., as a protective mechanism/ sanctuary. Either way, they can cause an element of anxiety: "*What will happen if I can't escape?*" Or "*What will happen if they get into my sanctuary?*"

Present - Anger, Temper

These emotions are very much about the 'here and now'. Given the above examples, we can start to get angry about the future consequences of something that happened in the past that affects us right now, i.e., a mortgage default that has happened - *"Am I going to be made homeless?"*

A person may start to get angry: "*How dare they do that just because I've missed a payment? Who do they think they are? I'll show that bank that they can't mess with me...*" and so forth.

But in most cases the anger is more likely to be a consequence of something happening now. Examples such as road rage, queue jumping, receiving an inflated bill for a house repair, being delayed at work and consequently missing an important event - the list is endless. Some people will manifest a slower response in three stages, as per the Three Stage Abreaction, and some will go straight to Defcon 5. Some of this will depend on their personality type and whether they have narcissistic or psychopathic tendencies. Those of us working in the change work/therapy arena should always be aware that at some point we are likely to work with such a person. Make sure you have some knowledge and resources in how to deal with this. This is why I prefer working online these days. We go into personality types in more detail on the Level 2 Advanced Training, where I do an introduction to DISC personality profiling.

What can we do when a person presents in a state of agitation or anger? Well, if we know they are very much in a current-time orientation, we can get them to back up time-wise. Rather than asking, "*Why are you angry?*", which will often lead to a diatribe of information and possibly expletives, we can work a question as follows:

> *"When did you first start to notice that you're angry?", or "When did you first start feeling this anger...?*

The reason this is such a great strategy is because the angry person now has to step away from the current time and do a memory search to locate a time point. Hence, we are taking them back and immediately out of the current anger state. This in itself can have an immediate calming effect on the person as they start to recount their story. Now, as you know in IEMT, we teach people to keep outside of a person's story, but on this type of occasion it can help to take the sting out of the tail, so to speak [6].

If the above questions don't work, you can ask, *"And when is the first time that you can remember feeling this anger?* Or, *"And when is the first time that you can remember someone else feeling anger like this?"*

This is one of my favourite approaches as it can make the person really focus on a memory search and thus start to calm them down from their heightened state of autonomic arousal.

Many consider anger a negative emotion, however this is not a term I favour; I just see it as an emotion. It is the behaviour resulting from that anger that is more important. If 'I' get angry about stuff and start hitting people or destroying property, that of course is a problem and we know that anger can spill over to extreme aggression and violence in some individuals. If, however, 'I' get angry and as a result change something that is causing myself or others harm, that is entirely different.

For example, if people weren't angered by the lack of affordable healthcare for the low-paid and unwaged in the UK, how much longer would it have taken for the National Health Service Act of 1946 to have been realised? How many of us would have been paying extortionate amounts for our covid vaccines now? So, let's not write off anger as always being unacceptable.

Other fundamental reasons for experiencing anger include the fact that it is part of our survival mechanism; the body's way of physiologically discharging stress. Remember Fight, Flight, Freeze? Well, Fight can mean a physical response or it can be extreme anger and shouting. Anger is embedded in our primitive requirement to survive; i.e., to live and protect ourselves against aggression from other humans or animals. It starts with the amygdala being activated via a testosterone production increase, heart rate and arterial tension increase, a decrease in cortisol (the stress hormone), and the left hemisphere of the brain becoming more stimulated (7) (8).

Part of our drives, (as seen when discussing the hypothalamus in Chapter 3), are then stimulated, which enables people to sharpen their focus and be vigilant about threats. When humans are provoked, threatened, or attacked physically or verbally, anger is automatically activated and pushes us to fight back and act quickly and forcefully to protect ourselves. In extreme cases, it may cause humans to self-harm. This can be seen, for example, in cases of PTSD and eating disorders (9). So, before we wade in to remove anger, we need to look first at its purpose as a possible resource and coping mechanism, then look at dealing with the underlying cause; e.g., a Lynchpin in cases of PTSD and other trauma-based issues.

The Rules

We have seen how sets of emotions can be grouped into various time-based categories and why this is so. Now we come to the division according to 'The Rules'. Once again, if we were dealing with a person's autogenic metaphor and rules were an issue, we would be seeing metaphors that feature obstacles, such as brick walls, fences, mounds of earth or rocks and so forth. Thus, each column has a different approach regarding rules. With the next Three Pillars image I have added the extra emotions that can be relevant. Others in a bespoke emotional cycle could also be added.

Past Column

These past-based emotions are based on rules that are usually personal to us. The rules for this column are based on the person's own rules being broken by themselves, hence the types of feelings and emotions that can ensue. For example, a person may not feel guilty about parking on a double yellow line to post a letter or quickly pop into a shop for a few essentials, and how many have exceeded the 70mph speed limit on a motorway? These are government rules, the laws of the land, but they can be shrugged off and disregarded when it is of some advantage to a person.

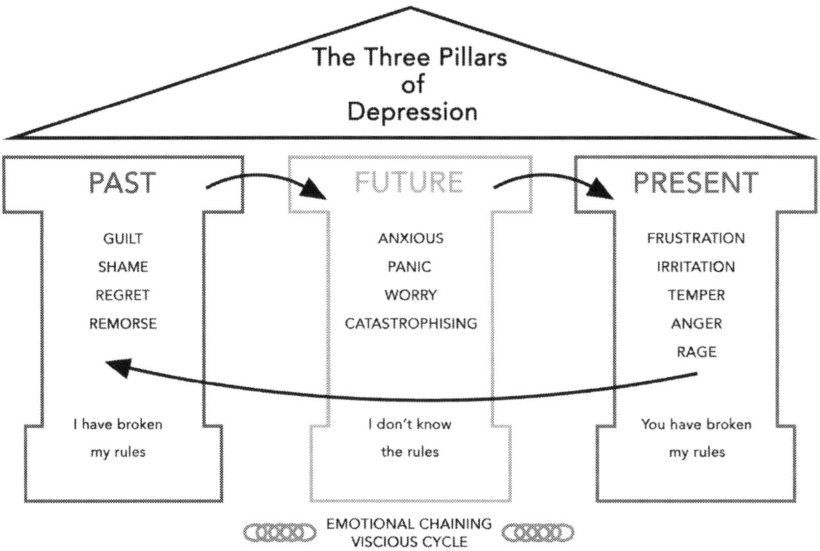

Consider how this differs from a set of personal rules that 'I' have. Some may call them ethics and values. Now, when we break one of these personal rules - e.g., I have decided to give up smoking and have even written out a contract with myself on the subject, then after a particularly stressfully day at work a colleague offers me a cigarette on my break and I smoke it, almost on automatic pilot - we then have the realisation of what we have done and, doh! We get that horrible familiar feeling of guilt, the head goes in the hands, the self-berating starts, because **we have broken our own rules.**

Now my display of guilt, or shame as there is an observer to the transgression, may be dismissed by others. *"What are you feeling guilty for, it's only one cigarette, cream cake, beer..."* and so on. But their dismissal or attempt to rationalise will often have little effect, at least initially, as these aren't their rules. A person may be carrying guilt as a punishment to themselves or as a perceived duty or responsibility and this can manifest in language as burden-based metaphors or attachment-based metaphors; i.e., shackles or ropes when holding on to something or someone out of guilt rather than love.

Remember, if I am feeling remorse this may fade and I'll have another cigarette, drink etc. Interestingly, unlike remorse, guilt is not time-dependent and many people will carry around guilt, even if they did something minor as a child, for the rest of their lives. I always explore this in metaphorical terms with clients and ask, *"Then where are you taking your guilt to?"* When they say their grave, I will simultaneously drop an image of a cartoon gravestone onto the screen. People often look astounded, saying, *"Oh my God, you've read my mind!"* I haven't, I just understand the rules of the metaphor and of guilt in this context. Without change work, guilt, along with shame and regret, can stay in place forever. Even with change work, some will choose not to put the burden (as it is often depicted) or responsibility down, and that is their prerogative.

There is another difference here with regards to guilt and shame. Along with the observer element leading to a differentiation, there is also the fact that guilt is something a person feels in response to what they did or didn't do. Thus, shame has more of an identity element. Hence, if I'm seen transgressing, I will feel shame for who I am or who I was.

We have seen in the time-based division that the regrets for past actions will be felt with consequence to self; e.g., *"I regret not studying harder for my exam now I don't have the grades for the course I want to do"*, or *"I regret that late night at the club as I've now lost my job as a result of arriving late again."*

Regret can also have a quality of life issue that can be left unspoken and un-dealt with, for example in the case of societal taboos; *"I regret marrying this person"* is one of the biggest taboos and can lead to 'guilt' about thinking this way and to untold misery for both parties. Regrets can have an impact on how we are being because we are unhappy with who have become. We often hear the Great Big 'If Only' statements from people with regrets. When working with PTSD, regrets can feature quite heavily in the inner dialogue and internal torment of those affected.

Remorse can be expressed when feeling bad about the consequence of breaking the rules and feeling bad for the consequence to others. As seen above, remorse tends to be the only emotion in this column that is truly time-dependent; i.e., it often has a lifespan of its own, so to speak. Hence, it will often fade with time regardless of the act, which is why it's not the best qualifier for parole and release from prison.

Future Column

People who are prone to these types of responses often do so as a result of a lack of rules. Or they may not be aware of what the rules of a certain situation, family unit or work environment etc. actually are. They will feel unsafe or even exposed without a set of rules to adhere to, and this can lead to extreme responses such as panic attacks. During the time of Covid-19, 'The Rules' governing our behaviours and safety seemed to be changing in some instances daily, and for a person prone to future overthinking and catastrophisation, this can seem like their version of hell.

Now a person unsure of the rules who is prone to feeling anxious may start to create rules in order for them to feel comfortable and less exposed. In terms of Metaphors of Movement, a person may feel exposed when they are out of their 'container'. They may start putting up metaphorical walls or creating boundaries. Containers usually have at least five walls or boundaries, or may be a cave or some other domed structure. Walls are obstructions and they represent the rules. Hence, a person unsure of the rules who starts to create rules will be doing so to make themselves feel more secure.

Have you ever met that person in a work environment who likes to boss others about, or comments out loud, or goes off and tells the line manager when something is done differently to 'the protocol'? This is likely to be an anxious person. Or the person who keeps telling a driver to stay within the speed limit? My husband says he definitely knows somebody who's like this... Or that person who likes to take the role of supervisor, receptionist, Girl Guide leader, and so forth? The one in the family who ensures everyone is catered for at Christmas, cooking diner for the whole family so that they can be in control and ensure everyone is on time and everything runs to time? They will be always thinking about worst-case scenarios, so planning for all future eventualities. These people think that by being in control, they will feel better. Until the next event, that is...

Also, we can have people with OCD who need to ritualise their lives in order to attempt to feel okay. They attempt to prevent the out-of-place feelings as facilitated by hyperactivity in the caudate and putamen, for example leaving the house or being germ-free. There is the person who may not have OCD but will be anxious about leaving the house or washing their hands enough, because what if they become ill or get hit by a car and die?

An anxious person will manifest their worry, catastrophising and increasing their stress, which in turn will lead to more anxiousness and affect the autonomic nervous system, which can trigger a full-blown panic attack in some cases. However, if they can make the rules in such situations, this will give them a bit of respite, if only temporarily. If their rules are broken, however, then we move into the next column.

Present Column

> ***"Anger is a sign that something needs to change."***
> **Mark Epstein**

There are many quotes on the subject of anger, most of them geared towards it being a bad thing. However, I have chosen the above from the psychotherapist and Buddhist Mark Epstein as it is geared more towards what we discussed earlier regarding anger. With reference to the Three Pillars, we are at the here and now, when a person is vexed because their rules are being ignored or broken. If anger does indeed indicate that something needs to change, then the person getting annoyed or angry is saying:

"You" have to change because "You" have broken my rules, so "You" will need to apologise and make amends / "I" need to punish "You" for your transgression.

A person prone to temper, anger and so forth is also likely to be running the Three Stage Abreaction Pattern of Chronicity (POC). In addition, as they often have an underlying or even overt issue with anxiety, worry, panic or catastrophisation, they are also likely to be running the *Great Big 'What If?'* POC, while being in the *At Effect Rather Than Being At Cause* POC. They might be intolerant of things that are not 100% perfect in their mind (whatever that means) and will be running the *Testing for Existence of the Problem Rather than Evidence of Change* POC. This is a great one for making an excuse to not do something rather than do it, or to change because this situation is not 100% as it should be. And finally, they could even be the person who finds it difficult to make decisions, procrastinate about things, and don't like to be pushed into giving an opinion. As a result, frustration, irritation, temper and eventually anger can result. If my rule is, for example:

> *"**I** don't like to be put on the spot for an answer on things, then **I** can get angry with **you** for putting **me** on the spot because **you** have broken one of **my** rules...(i.e., a rule belonging to **myself**)"*

The above is a good of example of how all the models of IEMT interrelate and the complexity of a seemingly simple emotion or statement. This type of integrated thinking can be hard for the novice IEMT Practitioner to get their head around. After all, *"I only came on the course to move eyes around and create change in the blink of an eye"*, to which of course the reply can be, *"That's right..."*

Working With the Three Pillars in a Client Session

There is no absolute right or wrong way to work on the emotions that a person is running in their emotional viscous cycle. However, the next graphic is the sequence that I generally work in. I tend to start with the Past Column emotions because these can have the biggest impacts on long-term mental health and can be related to past events that include trauma. A Lynchpin may need to be elicited with some of these emotions prior to eye movement work. I then tend work on the present column emotions, unless anger, for example, is in danger of overwhelming and sabotaging the session. PSAC work to reduce the state can be very useful here, as well as who I am being work; e.g., *"I'm a really angry person"*, *"She really irritates me"*, *"I get so frustrated with myself"* and so forth.

Once columns 1 and 3 are dealt with, we can look at specific Future column situations and anticipatory events if that is still required.

I hope this chapter has added some illumination onto the subject of the Three Pillars Model. It may also have shown that there is a lot more to this model than first meets the eye, and that we cannot take any part of IEMT in complete isolation because so many aspects feed into other areas, such as identity or trauma work. IEMT is not just about ameliorating a feeling with a bit of eye wiggling - it is so much more than that.

If you are interested in knowing more about how we listen out for and decipher autogenic metaphors in order to interweave this into our IEMT work, do book a place on one of my Level 2 Advanced IEMT courses or one of my introductory sessions to Metaphors of Movement.

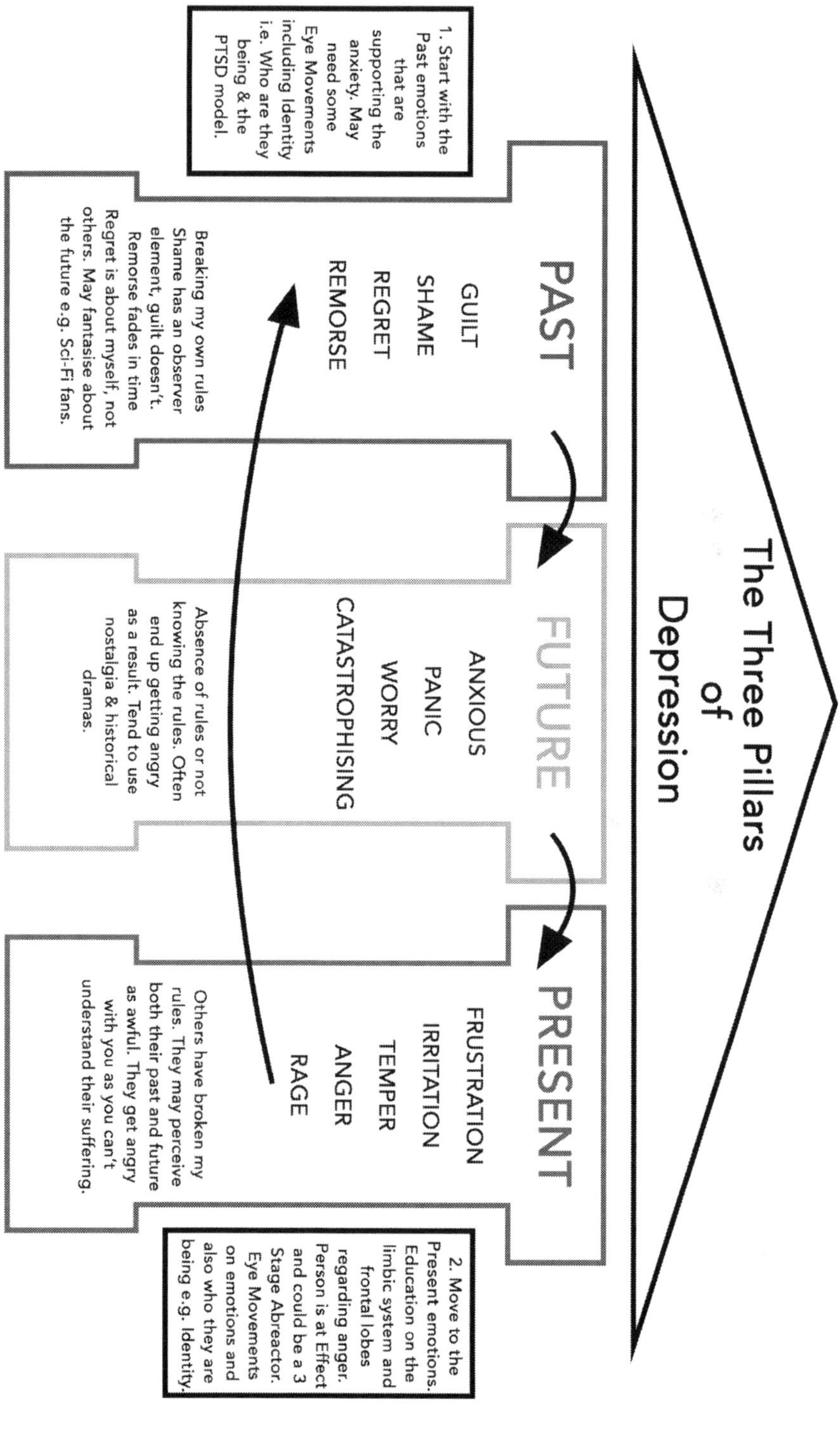

The Three Pillars of Depression
PAST
GUILT
SHAME
REGRET
REMORSE
Breaking my own rules Shame has an observer element, guilt doesn't. Remorse fades in time Regret is about myself, not others. May fantasise about the future e.g. Sci-Fi fans.
FUTURE
ANXIOUS
PANIC
WORRY
CATASTROPHISING
Absence of rules or not knowing the rules. Often end up getting angry as a result. Tend to use nostalgia & historical dramas.
PRESENT
FRUSTRATION
IRRITATION
TEMPER
ANGER
RAGE
Others have broken my rules. They may perceive both their past and future as awful. They get angry with you as you can't understand their suffering.
1. Start with the Past emotions that are supporting the anxiety. May need some Eye Movements including Identity i.e. Who are they being & the PTSD model.
2. Move to the Present emotions. Education on the limbic system and frontal lobes regarding anger. Person is at Effect and could be a 3 Stage Abreactor. Eye Movements on emotions and also who they are being e.g. Identity.

Chapter 14

Tips for Working Online

“Who’s Zooming Who?”

Aretha Franklin

A great song by the Queen of Soul and also one of the questions people are now asking each other when arranging a virtual meeting, be it business or social. Although Zoom isn't the only online platform providing meeting and conferencing facilities, it appears to be one of the most reliable and flexible. Anyone who bought Zoom shares prior to the Covid-19 pandemic must be laughing all the way to the sell button! In fact, the founder of Zoom's net worth has increased by more than $10bn since the virus hit in 2020, to more than $14.7bn in 2021 [(1)].

One of the things many practitioners were asking prior to the Covid-19 outbreak was whether IEMT could be conducted via an online platform. It has to be said that before that situation arose, The Association for IEMT Practitioners did not recommend performing IEMT virtually. There were some unknowns and concerns as to whether the integral eye movements would work on axial deviations to enable the required processing of the appropriate memories to enable consolidation and storage. This process is fundamental to the success of IEMT, so this needed to be trialled. Having trained IEMT in several different countries, I had been asked to work therapeutically with people online, so I decided this needed to be investigated and began to do some trials.

Asking for volunteers who were free of contraindications for IEMT, I set about testing whether IEMT could be introduced into online sessions. One of the concerning factors was whether staring at a screen for a lengthy period of time might increase some of the unwanted physiological responses that are sometimes reported with eye movement work such as EMDR and IEMT. This may include dizziness, nausea and headache. When doing this early online experimentation, Skype was still the platform most of us were using for virtual meetings. I also tried Go the Meeting and FaceTime with fellow Mac users.

The most important thing in providing this service was to ensure that the client's experience of IEMT would not be hindered and that they would be able to follow instructions via this medium, especially for the eye movement work. Full-length sessions of 90 minutes to 2 hours were trialled to see if they would be too much visually for clients. They turned out to be absolutely fine for all those who volunteered. Some practitioners may routinely undertake shorter sessions of 60 minutes, so this should be fine for most clients.

I use a whiteboard a lot during sessions, whether drawing out metaphors using MOM, writing up various identity statements, or drawing up images for the Three Pillars or the PTSD models. I use boards for other teaching purposes such as hypnobirthing, so the clarity of the writing and imagery through the screen needed to be tested. Drawing and writing on pieces of paper and showing these to the screen was also trialled. Both approaches appeared adequate. More recently, I have trialled virtual whiteboards and use one on my iPad. These have the great advantage of enabling the client or course attendees to annotate drawings, charts etc., improving interaction when working virtually.

For demonstrating eye movements, I also have two small whiteboards on which are drawn the straight line axes for the Kinaesthetic work and the 'lazy 8' circles for the Identity work. Before attempting any eye movements, these whiteboards are shown to the client to ensure they understand the type of movements we will be doing. The movements are also demonstrated and it is explained that, even though my hand may go off the screen, it is important they continue with the eye movements as far into the peripheries as they can. We establish visual points around the room the client is in so that they have markers for these peripheral movements.

I also explain that the speed for Kinaesthetic work is roughly one-second movements in one direction. You can practise to *"Picture This"* by

Blondie, which has the perfect tempo and, of course, the perfect lyrics for Kinaesthetic IEMT. With Identity movements, I tend to start off a bit slower, so the movement is roughly around 1.5 seconds per side. Again appropriately, a great song and tempo for these eye movements is *"Who Are You"* by The Who. Those of you who have trained with me will have heard these songs on the course at various junctures.

Both tracks have a 4/4 tempo and getting into a good rhythm is great for your work. Also, as humans are bipedal, we often favour the 4/4 tempo. Much of the modern music which stems from the Blues takes the 4/4 format. Humans respond to rhythm in a very visceral way. Play a person a piece of music and they will often start to move or tap a foot. This is called 'entrainment'; the ability of an organism to synchronise its movements to an external rhythm or pulse (150). Hence, axial deviations are a move away from this entrainment and as such a significant change in the brain. People who experience anxiousness are often unable to synchronise a rhythm very well, so teaching them self-IEMT with piece of 4/4 music as a reference can be really useful, as can throwing a small ball from hand to hand in time with the rhythm, which is easily taught online.

Sometimes, especially with straight line movements, I start directing the client with my fingers or a pen as normal, and once I am sure they are reaching the peripheries they are directed verbally. This is a great way of teaching them how to perform self-eye movement work. Only when there is an axial deviation will I point to the spot and ask, *"What was that?"* or similar and re-direct the movements to smooth them out. I sometimes even direct even this verbally. Occasionally, I ask the client to change direction verbally without directing them with my pen etc., by saying, for example, *"Now move your eyes along the top axis to the right corner and then move to floor on that diagonal - that's it, great keep going..."*

If you ensure that you speak clearly and confidently with your directions, there is usually no issue. Having the skill to direct people verbally with eye movements is also useful for those with impaired vision. It is also important to maintain a good tempo, so a little more interaction is needed if people are moving too slowly.

Some breathing techniques, visualisations and relaxations were also tested, with and without music, in hypnobirthing and some therapeutic sessions. First, I wanted to know if the sound quality was good enough, and second whether it was distracting. All feedback was positive, with clients preferring music during relaxations. After one complete round of eye movements, I ask people to take one or two calm breaths before were continue on to the questions. I also remind people prior to performing eye movements to remember to keep breathing. Occasionally, people start to hold their breath and I certainly don't want them keeling over! Another thing I ensure before a session is that people have a glass of water available. In addition, eye mist spray is highly recommended for IEMT work or any work that involves looking at a screen for a long period.

Although working with these techniques virtually seemed acceptable for clients, the Skype technology was not always robust. I have invested in an excellent wi-fi system and the speed is very good. However, not all clients have the same level of coverage and speed, so this needed to be considered. Once or twice this did become a problem with clients dropping off the internet. If we had FaceTime as a back-up, we would switch to this. If not, regaining the connection was sometimes problematic, and I had to complete a session over the phone on one occasion. This is why we switched permanently to Zoom for session work and IEMT online training. The training has been a huge success and every delegate has been able to successfully experience and perform eye movements via the screen.

With the people who were kind enough to volunteer to help me conduct these experiments, there were no adverse events physiologically. This obviously does not mean there never will be, and ensuring that any possible contraindications - such as recent eye injury or surgery, neurological and brain injury (e.g., tumours or stroke), psychosis, alcohol or drug use - are ruled out is key. However, even in face-to-face sessions abreactions can occur, especially if there is an amount of resistance to the process and to the rapid change that is experience by some people. Hence, this may occur on occasion during virtual sessions. It is also advisable when working remotely to have a full address for the client, contact numbers for a next for kin or person they live with, and a GP contact number. These are all standard on my client questionnaire form. It is highly unlikely that emergency measures will ever be needed, but nevertheless it is good practice.

Overall, the experience was promising and sufficient completed sessions were achieved to provide the confidence to offer online sessions. I am now able to work with clients from the UK and overseas, and to conduct trainee practitioners' post-training mentoring and case study feedback sessions for certification online.

In 2019, my husband convinced me to switch from Skype to Zoom. He conducts a lot of online meetings and webinars and has been using Zoom for several years as the reliability has improved a great deal over the years. It also benefits from a lot of useful additional functionality in comparison to the alternatives. Since switching I have never gone back to Skype. I like Zoom and feel the visual quality is excellent, which makes the client experience more comfortable and user-friendly. It is easy to install, and many clients have uploaded the free version to use with friends and family. One thing to consider is that there are frequent software updates, so it is important to be aware of these for optimal use.

Zoom is also great tool for hypnobirthing, especially for showing videos and presentations, use of a whiteboard and virtual whiteboard, deep relaxation work and guided visualisation. I also recommend that clients who have an Apple TV or similar use screen sharing to their television in order to enhance the session experience. When conducting eye movement work this is also very useful.

On the very rare occasion that my own Zoom service has struggled (only once thus far), the clients who had the free version were able to Zoom me, so we were able to complete our work. I always send some basic information on Zoom to a client before we work together and, as always, ensure they complete and return a full questionnaire, Ts&Cs and a consent form before a session.

Another great advantage of Zoom is the recording facility, which we use with the client's permission. Having the sessions recorded enables me to watch and listen more intently without needing to scribble down notes. Recordings are also available to clients on request. After a session, clients are always sent a follow-up email which includes learning points from the session. The recording is invaluable in providing this information. When doing relaxation, I usually make an extra audio recording of this part of the session on a Roland mini-recorder, also called a Zoom interestingly, or via Zoom itself which automatically provides an audio version when you record a session. This way, MP3 downloads of the relaxation can be provided for the client to listen to at home ongoing. I am fully aware that this technology does re-invent itself and often moves at quite a pace, however at the time of writing this, I am still using Zoom for recordings both video and audio.

On the subject of audio, I highly recommend that you have a good quality lapel microphone, or if not, a good quality multi-focal static microphone. Sound quality is important and in-built microphones on a device are usually not of a high quality, especially for recording purposes. I favour the RØDE Wireless Go system, which is very neat.

Camera quality is also an issue and again I favour an external camera which has better image quality that the in-built type. There are many on the market of varying price, and often you get what you pay for, so bear this in mind. You will also need to ensure it is compatible for your computer (as a Mac user, this isn't always so straightforward), and has a good field of vision. I also use a switching box to change from camera image to my laptop to show diagrams, videos etc. Luckily, I have a broadcast camera that ensures very low latency on images and audio. If you're using presentations and video for demonstrations, you may prefer to use a switch mechanism such as the Black Magic format. However, for many people conducting client sessions rather than training, Zoom's share screen options may be sufficient.

One of the things I still do when working virtually is offer a free consultation, which is useful to assess whether the client is in the right emotional place for IEMT. This is change work after all, not care and support like counselling. IEMT can be very direct and provocative at times, and this free consultation helps me to elicit some of the Patterns of Chronicity the client is running as well as check for any possible contraindications. I suggest that all practitioners do this before booking a therapeutic session; you can of course charge for this short consultation if you prefer.

Bullet points for online working:

- Ensure you have a good internet service and speed. Upgrade if needs be.
- Have a back-up such as Face Time, Skype or WhatsApp.
- Have a good microphone set-up if you can; don't only rely on the in-built device microphone.
- Use a good quality camera with a wide field of vision, good resolution and minimal latency in relation to the audio. A crisp clear image is important for eye movement work.
- Send clear instructions to clients on how to join the meeting and the set-up of their own environment.
- A plain backdrop is best. You may choose to use a green screen; if so, make the virtual background is uncluttered so as not to distract from the work you are doing.
- Ensure the client has a good-sized screen to work on; a phone is not sufficient for IEMT.
- Lighting in both rooms - yours and the client's - needs to be good.
- Improve your own set-up with a professional microphone and extra lighting and practice your set-up.
- Conduct the pre-session questionnaire, send out Ts&Cs, and a consent form should be signed and dated for each session.
- Have emergency contact details as a requirement.
- Upgrade your professional insurance for online working as required.

- For saving any contact details online, you will require an ICO certificate (in the UK: https://ico.org.uk/for-organisations/data-protection-fee)

- Work within your professional guidelines and qualification standards.

- Use props and a whiteboard for drawing out the models and demonstrate eye movements.

- When performing eye movements, ensure the client gets as close to the screen as possible to allow you to track for axial deviations.

- Record your sessions with your client's permission so that you can stay focused on the client rather than constantly looking down to write notes. Re-watching the video later is also an excellent learning tool for you.

- Ensure you and the client have water available.

- Schedule comfort breaks and stand up and move if sessions are lengthy; PSAC exercises are a good means of changing physiology and creating movement.

- Music can be useful to centre yourself pre-session and help regulate your own breathing. Perhaps steer clear of thrash metal or some frenetic punk unless you feel the need to be energised for the forthcoming session!

Chapter 15

Dealing With Abreactions in Training or Client Sessions

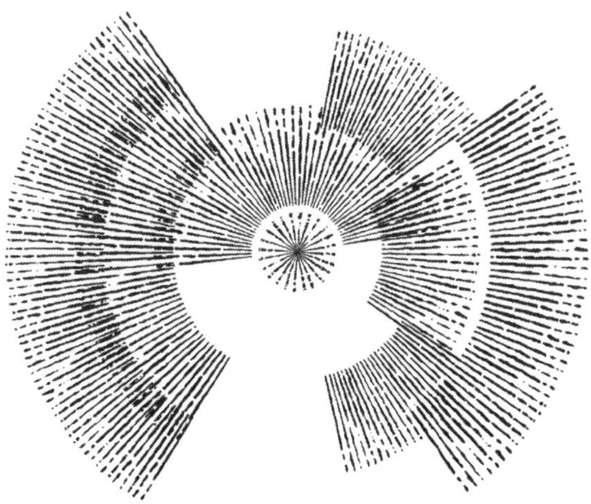

> **Emotional healing requires more than simply changing how you feel.**
>
> **Jessica Moore**

"Abreaction is a psychoanalytical term for re-living an experience to purge it of its emotional excesses – a type of catharsis. Sometimes it is a method of becoming conscious of repressed traumatic events." (1)

This psychoanalytical term abreaction was first coined by Freud in 1893, although it was thought to be formed via the influence of his mentor, Josef Breuer (1). It was first made public in their joint work, *The Studies of Hysteria* (1895) (2). The term was used to demonstrate that pent-up emotions associated with trauma can be discharged by talking about them. Freud likened it to a cathartic release by bringing *"a particular moment or problem into focus".* It used to be thought that abreaction was a vital part of therapy and the outpouring of emotion worked to release it, just like releasing poison by lancing a boil (3).

Shell-shocked survivors of World War 1 and later World War 2 were treated by a psychiatrist who is now famous (or should that be infamous) for his controversial work in electro-convulsant therapy (ECT) and deep sleep therapy. William Sargant's work with shell-shocked servicemen during World War 2 and his book *Battle for the Mind* explored the nature of the process by which our minds are subject to influence by others (4).

Affected personnel were encouraged to relive their trauma until 'the point of collapse', at which point the shell-shock/PTSD symptoms could be removed. This worked successfully only because the emotional collapse led to calm, and when the trauma was reviewed calmly for the first time the memory trace could be reassigned to the less emotive memory centres, lifting the PTSD. However, subsequent work on PTSD found that it was more effective to go directly for calm reviewing of troublesome memories, thus ensuring the safety and dignity of the person remained intact.

An abreaction may happen if a flashback of a traumatic event occurs. A flashback itself does not have the capacity to bring about processing of the memory experience and is of course traumatic in itself. An abreaction which also includes the emotional reaction may lead to healing and integration of the memory, but not always. A period of mounting internal pressure and conflict lasting for days or even weeks can result in an abreaction. This has been described in terms of part of the self holding onto unprocessed traumatic material from the initiating event, and this material then approaching the surface with an urgent need to release the experience. The internal pressure is due to an increasingly dangerous-feeling power struggle between this part and other parts which have been maintaining the dissociation.

Abreactions take several forms, but all involve some emotional reaction, often an outburst of emotion; i.e., agitation, tapping feet, wringing of hands, tears, anger, shouting, laughter, nausea, dizziness, headaches. Some clients may have a gentle release of tears, others a more intense or dramatic reaction. Someone may abreact if something in the environment - which includes the practitioner, their consulting room and/or words - reminds them unconsciously of an uncomfortable, unpleasant or traumatic event.

If someone abreacts, give them time. If their eyes are closed, don't hurry them to open them. Give them time and space to work the emotions out, so don't rush at them with a box of tissues. If you are working in person (rather than online), do not touch them. Find an appropriate time when the charge has begun to decrease to offer some words and/or tissues and remind them to take a drink of water.

If they are in your consulting room, reassure them that they are in an environment where it is safe to let out whatever it is they need to. This may be different if the client is at home and you are working online with them, so choose your words carefully. During lockdown, I worked online with people who were sharing a home with someone they had split from because they had not been able to move out due to Covid restrictions. So be mindful of the circumstances you are dealing with.

Get them to focus on something in the room - abreaction can be a hypnotic phenomenon, so we need to get them back with us. For example, you might say, *"Okay now just take a moment to think about your breathing and notice that as it calms right down again. Notice your hands and your feet now as your body becomes more relaxed again... thoughts become clearer."*

Avoid emotive words like, 'feel' or 'emotional'. Use language of the less emotional variety, i.e., left brain-like, such as *"think", "notice", "assess", "what are your thoughts on..."*, and so forth. The much-used therapeutic linguistic staple, *"How do you feel?"* can ignite the situation by directing attention further towards feelings, when in fact things need to be calming down. 'Think' words mobilise the 'thinking brain' (and therefore dilute emotion) and 'feel' words get the emotions going even more.

In my years of practice, I have mostly encountered abreaction with childbirth issues, but not exclusively and only in the minority of these cases. If it does happen, it's vital to stay calm and give the client time to deal with it. Interestingly, it's amazing how quickly people can calm down again.

Remember that when seeing clients, you should only work within your qualification framework knowledge and experience. Therefore, if you have no training in dealing with severe sexual trauma, for example, refer the client to someone who has. Obviously, we don't always know this is the case when somebody comes to see us to deal with, e.g., procrastination, wanting to lose weight, etc. However, if an abreaction occurs unexpectedly, staying calm and dealing with the situation as described will usually help to bring reassurance and calmness back for the client.

Please note that not all abreactions are a result of the client re-living an event. The reaction may be a sudden feeling of guilt or remorse based on an action or set of actions, or from not doing something they feel that they should have. It may be the result of sheer relief from freeing negative emotions such as guilt or remorse that has caused a sudden, physical outpouring or reaction.

Sometimes, the abreaction occurring is the Pattern of Chronicity known as the Three Stage Abreaction. This can be one of the indicators that a person, despite what they may be saying, is not happy or willing to change. This can occur for many reasons, the most obvious being that the behaviour or problem they are exhibiting or identifying with somehow affords them some special status or attention. This is known as 'secondary gain'; i.e., the issue they have come to see a therapist to 'change' may, consciously or unconsciously, be keeping them stuck in the same place. There can be a type of inner conflict; i.e., part of them wants to let it go, but another part is quite comfortable holding onto the problem. For example, a smoker says they want to give up, but part of their brain believes cigarettes are the only thing that help them to relax and thus they can't or won't quit. Some so-called secondary gain is actually a coping mechanism to help a person deal with the discomfort of their situation, so dismissing responses as mere secondary gain can be unhelpful at times.

When we are challenging people's beliefs and values, these are what we call 'highly charged states' and thus can cause an outpouring of emotion when challenged. IEMT can cause change rapidly and some people may not be prepared for this, as suddenly their comfort blanket has been removed. This may lead to a Three Stage Abreaction, and if you miss the initial signals, they may appear jump straight to Stage 3.

Dealing with this type of abreaction (as opposed to the trauma, flashback type) is no different. Give the person the time and space to do their own transderivational search of their thoughts, feelings, internal dialogue, etc. Then, when the emotional charge begins to dissipate, use some form of interaction to bring the person back into the here and now, to rationality and self-control. It may be appropriate at this stage to continue with IEMT, as you have possibly just hit a real nugget of change. However, I always ask the client if they want to continue. Never push on regardless, even if you think you are on the edge of a result. Also, never force a client to disclose anything they have experienced after an abreaction. Some will want to talk, others won't, so respect their decision. The beauty of IEMT is that it can be a completely content-free modality.

Learning to differentiate between a 'regular' abreaction and a Three Stage Abreaction is important for the IEMT Practitioner. If a client is prone to this Pattern of Chronicity and regularly attempts to manipulate or control others by this sort of behaviour, this will be causing disruption in their relationships. They may be having difficulties at work or with loved ones and may have no idea why that may be. Others will be blamed, so these clients need some training as well as therapy. Working with this pattern can be tricky because they may attempt to control you and the session. Learn to react with the agreement protocol so that you don't get emotionally dragged into their often zero-sum game cycle. Protecting your own emotional and mental health as an IEMT Practitioner is very important so that you don't burn out. Ensure that you take breaks, practise mediation and/or yoga, take some exercise, have some mentoring now and again with a trainer and join a practice group such as those I run for practitioners in order to discuss tricky cases, and get and give some support.

It is important to be able to spot the Three Stage Abreaction POC within the interactions that you have with clients prior to the actual session. Practitioners and therapists of all modalities can put themselves under great pressure in the belief that they must offer everyone who contacts them a session, even if the initial offer of a session and the subsequent interactions have the client demonstrating obvious irritation, frustration, or annoyance with the practitioner or their proposed way of working. In other words, they are doing one or more stages which signal: "*You need to change your therapeutic approach to make me feel better because I like to dictate what I require and like people to do exactly as I want at all times, even though I have no qualifications or experience in this particular field of work.*"

Remember that your own mental health and wellbeing is of paramount importance. If you are not on top of your game or as near to it as possible, working with people who have mental health issues runs the risk of affecting your own wellbeing. It has not happened very often, but I have on occasion cancelled sessions and refunded fees prior to a session if I feel that the client is trying to dictate the terms of the session or that they are ignoring any instructions such as my terms and conditions, or advice pre-session.

Always remember my mantra that your emotional state must be stronger than the client's problem state. If you like and use affirmations, work with this phrase in the present tense:

> *"My emotional state is always stronger than the client's problem..."*

Repeat it a few times prior to the session and get into the habit of mental and physiological practice and preparation. Notice your own physiology - if you feel tense or a tad anxious, how you are holding your body and how you are holding your jaw is often a giveaway; so do some tweaks in order to release the tension.

If you don't do any preparation with a client questionnaire/intake form before client sessions, then get into the habit of doing so, as it can assist you to pick up on Patterns of Chronicity as well as important identity statements. This is also why I do a free Zoom assessment session, as so much useful information can be gleaned before doing any therapeutic work, and potential abreactions of both kinds can be spotted or may even arise during this session, in which case the above procedure is followed in the same way.

Afterword

I hope that both experienced practitioners and those coming to IEMT for the first time have discovered new insights and useful information in this book. The great thing about Level 1 IEMT is that it is extremely user friendly, simple in its application, and can create desirable long-term change for the self and others.

Some readers may now wish to explore more on this subject and take their skills and knowledge to the next level. For example, in addition to one-to-one work, IEMT can be applied in group settings and in relational issues such as personal relationships, work and business relationships, and other group scenarios. Those who wish to progress further will find Level 2 (Advanced) IEMT an intriguing set of models and skills.

In Level 2, we take Level 1 models and expand them beyond their initial basic use, working more specifically with certain issues, be they emotional and/or identity-based. We also look at overlapping and integrating some of the skills I have acquired from related models, creating bespoke approaches for issues such as anxiety, eating and food issues, identity-based issues, pain, sleep issues, and trauma. We then continue with some psycho-education that can be passed onto clients for their own learning.

This comprehensive body of work deepens practitioners' knowledge base while increasing their understanding and application of skills and techniques which can create real-time remedial and generative change.

There will be a follow-up book on Advanced Techniques and Applications of IEMT, so do look out for this. Also, please visit the website for information on full course training dates, masterclass courses, private mentoring, and IEMTea Party events:

https://integraleyemovement.com

Many thanks for choosing this book.

Sonia Richards

"The future depends on what you do today."

Mahatma Gandhi

References

Chapter 1

1. T. Hoobyar. et al, (2013) **'Eye Movement Integration Therapy'** in The Guide to NLP. William Morrow.
2. S. Andreas, (2021) **Eye Movement Integration Therapy**. Real People Press. http://www.realpeoplepress.com/movement-integrationdvd-p-39.html
3. D. Grand, (2003) **What is Brain Spotting?** https://brainspotting.com
4. F. Shapiro (1989), **'Efficacy of the eye movement desensitization procedure in the treatment of traumatic memories'**. Journal of Traumatic Stress, 2, 199-223.
5. D. Beaulieu, (2020) **Comparison of EMI and EMDR**. http://www.academie-impact.com/en/imo_emdr.php
6. F. Shapiro, (1989) **'Eye movement desensitization: A new treatment for post-traumatic stress disorder'**. Journal of Behavior Therapy and Experimental Psychiatry, 20, 211-217.
7. F. Shapiro, (2001). **'Eye Movement Desensitization and Reprocessing: Basic Principles, Protocols and Procedures'** (2nd edition). New York: Guilford Press

Chapter 2

1. A. L. Yarbus, (1967) **'Eye movements and vision'**. New York: Plenum Press.
2. FAQ 9 - **Is the NLP "Eye Accessing Cues" Model Really Valid?** http://www.bradburyac.mistral.co.uk/nlpfax09.htm
3. Bandler R, Grindler J (1975) **The Structure of Magic**. I. Palo Alto, CA: Science and Behavior Books.
4. Bandler, R., & Grinder, J. (1979) **Frogs into Princes**. Moab, Utah: Real People Press.
5. Bolstad R., **Eye Movement Research: Core NLP Hypothesis Vindicated**. 2015. http://www.transformations.net.nz/trancescript/eyes.html
6. James, W. (1950) **The Principles Of Psychology (Volume 1 and 2)**. Dover, New York.
7. Gardner, H. (1993) **Frames Of Mind: The Theory Of Multiple Intelligences**. Basic Books, New York.
8. Nate, S. (2004) **Eye Accessing Cues: A Study in Storage and Retrieving Information**. Anchor Point Volume 18, No 4.

9. Andrillon, T., Nir, Y., Cirelli, C., Tononi, G., and Fried, I. **"Single-neuron activity and eye movements during human REM sleep and awake vision"**, Nature Communications, 11 August (2015) Volume: 6, Article number: 7884,.

10. Rahul Kumar **"The Anatomy and Physiology of Eye Movements"**. Health And Medicine, February 2014.

11. No Author Given **"Positive Neuroscience: 3 Ways to Wire Your Brain"** Positive Psychology Programme, September 2015. https://positivepsychologyprogram.com/positive-neuroscience/"

12. Terao, Y. , Fukuda H., 2 and Hikosaka O., **"What do eye movements tell us about patients with neurological disorders? — An introduction to saccade recording in the clinical setting"** Proc Jpn Acad Ser B Phys Biol Sciv.93(10); 2017 Dec 11.

13. Parker A., Parkin A. and Dagnall N. **"Effects of Saccadic Bilateral Eye Movements on Episodic and Semantic Autobiographical Memory Fluency"**. Frontiers in Human Neuroscience. 7: 63, 2013.

14. Sue Langley, **"The neuroscience of change: Why it's difficult and what makes it easier."** The Langley Group, May 2012. http://blog.langleygroup.com.au

15. I . P. Howard, (1995) **'Binocular vision and stereopsis'**. New York: Oxford University Press. p.32. ISBN 0-19-508476-4.

16. N. Wolchover, (2012) **'How Far Can the Human Eye See?'** http://www.livescience.com/33895-human-eye.html

17. Pierrot-Deseilligny, C; Milea, D. Muri, R. M. (2004) **'Eye movement control by the cerebral cortex'**. Current Opinion in Neurology 17 (1): 17–25

18. Krauzlis R.J. (2005). **"The control of voluntary eye movements: new perspectives"**. The Neuroscientist 11 (2): 124–37

19. Tehovnik E.J., Sommer M.A., Chou I.H., Slocum W.M., Schiller P. H. (2000) **"Eye fields in the frontal lobes of primates"**. Brain Res. 32 (2-3): 413–48.

20. **'Anatomy of the Eye'**. American Association for Pediatric Ophthalmology and Strabismus. Updated 2019. http://www.aapos.org/terms/conditions/22

21. **'The Cranial Nerves. (Organization of the Central Nervous System) Part 4'**. What-when-how. In Depth Tutorials and Information (2020 http://what-when-how.com/neuroscience-the-cranial-nerves-organization-of-the-central-nervous-system-part-4/

22. Purves D, Augustine GJ, Fitzpatrick D, et al., editors (2001). **'The Actions and Innervation of Extraocular Muscles'**. Neuroscience. 2nd edition. Sunderland (MA): Sinauer Associates; Available from: http://www.ncbi.nlm.nih.gov/books/NBK10793

23. M. Horowitz. **'Cranial Nerve Functions'**. http://pabrainspine.com/media/presentations/Cranial20Nerve20Functions.pdf

24. M. Rubin (2020) **'Palsies of Cranial Nerves That Control Eye Movement. Brain, Spinal Cord and Nerve Disorders'**. http://www.msdmanuals.com/en-gb/home/brain,-spinal-cord,-and-nerve-disorders/cranial-nerve-disorders/palsies-of-cranial-nerves-that-control-eye-movement

25. **The Human Memory**. http://www.human-memory.net/types.html

26. **Brain 101**. Neuroscience. University of California. http://memory.ucsf.edu/brain/memory/episodic

27. Kim Ann Zimmermann. Live Science Contributor, February 25, 2014. **Episodic Memory: Definition and Examples**.

28. Roger Johansson and Mikael Johansson. (2013) **"Look Here, Eye Movements Play a Functional Role in Memory Retrieval"**. Psychological Science.Walker, M.P.; Stickgold, R.; Alsop, D.; Gaab, N.; Schlaug, G. (2005). **"Sleep-dependent motor memory plasticity in the human brain"**. Neuroscience 133 (4): 911–7

29. Jessica Hamzelou. (2015) **"Darting Eyes in REM Sleep are Seeing Objects in Your Dreams"**. The New Scientist.

30. Rosalind Cartwright (2017 **The Science of Sleep: Regulating Emotions and the 24 Hour Mind.** https://fs.blog/2017/03/twenty-four-hour-mind-rosalind-cartwright/

31. Norman Doidge, (2007). **The Brain that Changes Itself**. Viking Press

32. **What is Neuroplasticity?** 2010. http://www.whatisneuroplasticity.com/history.php

33. Michael Abrahams and Dan Winters (2003). **"Can you see with your tongue?"** Discover Magazine.

34. Edward Taub (2014) Foreword for **neuroplasticity and neurorehabilitation**. Front Hum Neurosci. 2014; 8: 544.

35. Michael Merzenich. **Brain HQ**.http://www.brainhq.com

Chapter 3

1. Closer to the Truth. **"Are the mind and brain the same?"** http://www.closertotruth.com

2. Marcelo R. Roxo et al. (2011) **"The Limbic System Conception and It's Historical Evolution"**. Scientific World Journal; 11: 2428–2441

3. Green CD. (2003) **"Where did the ventricular localization of mental faculties come from?"** Journal of the History of the Behavioural Sciences; 39(2):131–142.

4. Del Maestro RF (1998). **"Leonardo da Vinci: the search for the soul"**. Journal of Neurosurgery; 89(5):874–887

5. Finger S. **"Paul Broca (1824–1880)"**. Journal of Neurology. 2004;251(6):769–770.

6. Ekman P. (1973) D**arwin and Facial Expression A Century of Research in Review**. New York, NY, USA: Academic;

7. Cannon WB. (1987) **"The James-Lange theory of emotions: a critical examination and an alternative theory. By Walter B. Cannon, 1927"**. The American Journal of Psychology;100(3-4):567–586.

8. Hayman LA, Rexer JL, Pavol MA, Strite D, Meyers CA. (1998) **"Kluver-Bucy syndrome after bilateral selective damage of amygdala and its cortical connections"**. Journal of Neuropsychiatry and Clinical Neurosciences;10(3):354–358.

9. Rajmohan V. and E Mohandas. (2007) **"The limbic system"**. Indian J Psychiatry. Apr-Jun; 49(2): 132–139.

10. Maclean PD. (1990) **The Triune Brain in Evolution: Role in Paleocerebral Functions**. New York: Plenum Press.

11. Ambrosia Lorenzi C.G. et al. (1997) **"Analysis of mnemonic processing by means of totally reversible neural inactivations"**. Brain Res Brain Res Protoc. Oct;1(4):391-8

12. Bailey, R. **Anatomy of the Brain**. About Education. December 2014. http://biology.about.com/od/humananatomybiology/a/anatomybrain.htm

13. Swenson R. (2006) **Review of Clinical and Functional Neuroscience**. Dartmouth Medical School.

14. Barker, R. A., Cicchetti F. and Neal, M. J. (2012) **Neuroanatomy and Neuroscience at a Glance**. Fourth Edition. Wiley-Blackwell.

15. Masaki Tanaka and Jun Kunimatsu. (2012) **Thalamic Roles in Eye Movements. The Oxford Handbook of Eye Movements**. Edited by Simon P. Liversedge, Iain Gilchrist, and Stefan Everling. Oxford Handbooks On-line.

16. **Hypothalamus**. No Author given. Modified 2006. www.neuroanatomy.wisc.edu/coursebook/neuro2

17. Bart J. A. Hollander E. **Oxytocin and experimental therapeutics in autism spectrum disorders**. Prog Brain Res. 2008;170:451-62.

18. Shen Helen. **New Oxytocin Neuroscience Counters "Cuddle Hormone" Claims**. Scientific American, June 2015

19. Tomasi D. et al. **Sex differences in sensory gating of the thalamus during auditory interference of visual attention tasks**. Neuroscience. 2008 Feb 19; 151(4): 1006–1015.

20. Joseph, R.G. **Neuroscience**.http://brainmind.com/Cingulate.html

21. Casey B.J. et al. **Behavioural and neural correlates of delay of gratification 40 years later**. PNAS July 2011 vol. 108 no. 36

22. Lehman M. **The Brain Anatomy and Function – Anatomy** http://www.brain-maps.com/index.html

23. Yücel M. et al. Anterior cingulate dysfunction: **Implications for psychiatric disorders?** J Psychiatry Neurosci. 2003 Sep; 28(5): 350–354

24. Wright Anthony. Chapter 5: **Limbic System: Hippocampus**. Dept of Neurobiology and Anatomy, The University of Texas Medical School. http://neuroscience.uth.tmc.edu/s4/chapter05.html

25. Amaral D., Lavenex P (2006). Ch 3. **Hippocampal Neuroanatomy**. In Andersen P, Morris R, Amaral D, Bliss T, O'Keefe J. The Hippocampus Book. Oxford University Press.

26. Moscovitch M et al. **Functional neuroanatomy of remote episodic, semantic and spatial memory: a unified account based on multiple trace theory**. J Anat. 2005 Jul;207(1):

27. Teyler T.J., DiScenna P., Behav Neurosci. **The hippocampal memory indexing theory**. 1986 Apr;100(2):147-54

28. Teyler T.J, Rudy J.W. **The hippocampal indexing theory and episodic memory: updating the index. Hippocampus.** 2007;17(12):1158-69.

29. Reas Emile. **Important new theory explain were old memories go**. October 2013. Scientific American

30. Maguire E.A., Woollen K. and Spiers H.J. **London taxi drivers and bus drivers: a structural MRI and neuropsychological analysis**. Hippocampus. 2006;16(12):1091-101.

31. Joseph E. LeDoux. **Amygdala. Scholarpedia**, 2008 3(4):2698

32. Anthony Wright. **Chapter 6: Limbic System: Amygdala** http://neuroscience.uth.tmc.edu/s4/index.htm

33. Gregory J. Quirk and Devin Mueller. **Neural Mechanisms of Extinction Learning and Retrieval. Neuropsychopharmacology**, 2008 Jan; 33(1): 56–72.

34. Michael G. Garelick and Daniel R. Storm. **The relationship between memory retrieval and memory extinction**. PNAS, June 2005 vol. 102 no. 26

35. Larry W. Swanson, Gorica D. Petrovich. **What is the Amygdala?** Trends in Neurosciences, August 1998, Volume 21, Issue 8, p323–331

36. Markowitsch, H. (1998) **Differential Contribution of Right and Left Amygdala to Affective Information Processing**. IOS Press. 11(4), 233–244.

37. Hamann, Stephan. **"Sex Differences in the Responses of the Human Amygdala"**. Neuroscience (2005). 11 (4): 288–93.

38. Carlson, Neil R. (2012) **Physiology of Behavior**. Pearson Press.

39. Blair, H. T. et al. **"Synaptic Plasticity in the Lateral Amygdala: A Cellular Hypothesis of Fear Conditioning"**. Learning & Memory (2001) 8 (5): 229–242

40. Hutcherson, Cendri A.; Seppala, Emma M.; Gross, James J. **"Loving-kindness meditation increases social connectedness"**. Emotion (2008). 8 (5): 720-4

41. Bickart, Kevin C; et al. **Amygdala volume and social network site in humans**. Nature Neuroscience (2010). 14 (2): 163–4.

42. Mormann, F. et al. **Neurons in the human amygdala encode face identity, but not gaze direction**. Nature Neuroscience. 2015. 18 (11): 1568–1570

43. Malkin, B. Man arrested for **'having sex with lamp-post'**. The Telegraph, 6 March 2008.

44. Stanisław Kwiatkowski, et al. **Neuropsychological characteristic of post-traumatic Klüver-Bucy Syndrome**. Archives of Psychiatry and Psychotherapy (2011); 4 : 59–65

45. Blumberg H.P. et al. **Amygdala and Hippocampal Volumes in Adolescents and Adults With Bipolar Disorder**. JAMA Psychiatry (December 1, 2003); Vol 60, No. 12

46. The Overlook Blog. **Differences Between Emotional Memory and Event Memory** April 21 (2017). https://www.overlook-mass.org/2017/04/differences-between-emotional-memory-and-event-memory/

47. L. A. Bean, L. Ianov, and T. C. Foster. **Estrogen Receptors, the Hippocampus**, Memory. Neuroscientist (2014) October; 20(5): 534–545

Chapter 5

1. Chong-Hwa Hong, et al (1995) **Localized and Lateralized Cerebral Glucose Metabolism Associated With Eye Movements During REM Sleep and Wakefulness:** A Positron Emission Tomography (PET) Study. Sleep, Volume 18, Issue 7. Pages 570–580.
2. Sandusky L.A. et al **"Elevated glucose metabolism in the amygdala during an inhibitory avoidance task"** Behav Brain Res. 2013 May 15; 245: 83–87.
3. Nofzinger E.A., et al **"Human regional cerebral glucose metabolism during non-rapid eye movement sleep in relation to waking."** Brain. 2002 May;125(Pt 5):1105-15.
4. Sarah Newman. **"The Importance of Getting Comfortable with Discomfort"** Psych Central July 8, 2018 https://psychcentral.com/blog/the-importance-of-getting-comfortable-with-discomfort/
5. Shawn M. Burn. **"Is Empathy your greatest strength or your greater weakness?"** Psychology Today. June 2019.

Chapter 6

1. Amelia Aldao, **"Why labelling emotions matters"** Psychology Matters Aug 2014. https://www.psychologytoday.com/gb/blog/sweet-emotion/201408/why-labeling-emotions-matters

Chapter 7

1. de Voogd et al, **"Eye-Movement Intervention Enhances Extinction via Amygdala Deactivation"**. Journal of Neuroscience 3 October 2018, 38 (40) 8694-8706.
2. Shravani Sur and V. K. Sinha **"Event-related potential: An overview"** Ind Psychiatry J .2009 Jan-Jun; 18(1): 70-73. ****
3. Simola J. et al **"Eye movement related brain responses to emotional scenes during free viewing"**. Front. Syst. Neurosci., 20 August 2013.
4. Hannula, D. E. & Ranganath, C. (2009). "**The Eyes Have It: Hippocampal Activity Predicts Expression of Memory in Eye Movements"**. Neuron 63: 1-8. DOI: 10.1016/j.neuron.2009.08.025.
5. Christopher Bergland. **"12 Ways Eye Movements Give Away Your Secrets".** Psychology Today, May 07, 2015 https://www.psychologytoday.com/gb/blog/the-athletes-way/201505/12-ways-eye-movements-give-away-your-secrets

Chapter 8

1. René Descartes. **"Cogito, ergo sum"**. https://en.wikipedia.org/wiki/Cogito,_ergo_sum
2. Jean-Paul Satre. **"La Transcendance de l'ego: Esquisse d'une description phénomenologique"**. https://en.wikipedia.org/wiki/The_Transcendence_of_the_Ego
3. Eckhart Tolle. (2005) **A New Earth: Awakening to Your Life's Purpose.** Penguin Books.

4. Leana Wen. **"6 Lessons We Can Learn From Eastern Chinese Medicine"**. Jan 2013 https://www.psychologytoday.com/intl/blog/the-doctor-is-listening/201301/6-lessons-we-can-learn-eastern-chinese-medicine

5. Christopher P. Austin. **"The Difference Between Eastern & Western Medicine"**. February 2017. https://www.youtube.com/watch?v=YfFePhczgGs

6. Deepak Chopra. **"The Fundamental Differences Between Eastern and Western Thought"**. August 2016 . https://www.youtube.com/watch?v=YfFePhczgGs

7. Erik Erickson https://en.wikipedia.org/wiki/Erik_Erikson

8. Kendra Cherry and Steven Gans. **"Erik Erikson's Stages of Psychosocial Development"**. September 2019. https://www.verywellmind.com/erik-eriksons-stages-of-psychosocial-development-2795740

9. Erik Erikson's **Theory of Psychosocial Development** .2019. https://www.psychologynoteshq.com/erikerikson/

10. Andrew T. Austin. **Metaphors of Movement. 2010**. https://metaphorsof-movement.co.uk

11. Mark Dixon. **"Cire Identity - Reprise. March 2013**. http://www.discovering-identity.com/2013/03/29/core-identity-reprise/

12. Wizemann TM, Pardue ML, editors. (2001) **Exploring the Biological Contributions to Human Health: Does Sex Matter?** Chapter 3 - Sex Begins in the Womb. National Academies Press.

13. Robert Preidt. **About 1 in 1,000 Babies Born 'Intersex,' Study Finds**. May 2019. https://www.webmd.com/parenting/baby/news/20190503/study-about-1-in-1000-babies-born-intersex

14. Kath Woodward. (2002) **Understanding Identity**. Oxford University Press.

15. Frances Mao. **Dissociative Identity Disorder: The woman who created 2,500 personalities to survive**. September 2019. BBC World News. https://www.bbc.co.uk/news/world-australia-49589160

16. **Dissociative Identity Disorder (Multiple Personality Disorder)** February 2019. https://www.psychologytoday.com/gb/conditions/dissociative-identity-disorder-multiple-personality-disorder. Referenced from the American Psychiatric Association. Diagnostic and Statistical Manual of Mental Disorders, Fifth Edition.

17. **Dissociative Disorders - Symptoms and Causes. November 2017**. https://www.mayoclinic.org/diseases-conditions/dissociative-disorders/symptoms-causes/syc-20355215

18. **What's the difference between dissociative identity disorder (multiple personality disorder) and schizophrenia?** 2015. Canadian Mental Heath Association.https://www.heretohelp.bc.ca/q-and-a/whats-the-difference-between-dissociative-identity-disorder-and-schizophrenia

19. Mary V. Seeman. **"Identity and schizophrenia: Who do I want to be?"** 2017 Mar 22; 7(1): 1–7. World Journal of Psychology

20. R. D. Laing **"The Divided Self: An Existential Study in Sanity and Madness"** August 1960, Penguin Books.

Chapter 9

1. Carol Wilson. **The Work and Life of David Grove.** October 2017. Troubadour Publishing.
2. Hildegunn Fandrem. **Friendship During Adolescence and Cultural Variations**. In - International Encyclopedia of the Social & Behavioral Sciences (Second Edition) 2015. https://www.sciencedirect.com/topics/social-sciences/identity-formation
3. M.S Merry. **Identity.** In - International Encyclopedia of Education (Third Edition) 2010. https://www.sciencedirect.com/topics/social-sciences/identity-formation
4. Robert Dilts and Stephen Gilligan **"What is generative change?"**. https://generative-change.com/generative-coaching/what-is-generative-change/
5. **What are Reflexive Pronouns?** - https://www.grammar-monster.com/glossary/reflexive_pronouns.htm
6. Catherine Traffis. **What is a Reflexive Pronoun?** 2019. https://www.grammarly.com
7. Melinda Smith and Lawrence Robinson. **Narcissistic Personality Disorder.** December 2019. https://www.helpguide.org/articles/mental-disorders/narcissistic-personality-disorder.htm
8. Courtney Ackerman. **What is Self-Concept Theory?** A Psychologist Explains. August 2019. https://positivepsychology.com/self-concept/
9. Mateusz Woźniak. **"I" and "Me": the self in the context of consciousness.** Frontiers in Psychology. 04 September 2018
10. Carey et al. **Narcissism and the Use of Personal Pronouns Revisited**. Journal of Personality and Social Psychology . American Psychological Association 2015, Vol. 109, No. 3, e1–e15
11. James Pennebaker. **Your Use of Pronouns Reveals Your Personality**. Harvard Business Review. December 2011 issue.

Chapter 10

1. Herman, Judith Lewis. (1992) **Trauma and Recovery: The Aftermath of Violence - from Domestic Abuse to Political Terror**. New York: BasicBooks
2. Neil Baldwin (2015) **Marvellous: Neil Baldwin - My Story**. John Blake Publishing.

Chapter 11

1. Matthew J. Friedman, MD, PhD. **PTSD History and Overview. 2013**. https://www.ptsd.va.gov/professional/treat/essentials/history_ptsd.asp
2. **DSM History** (2021) American Psychiatric Association. https://www.psychiatry.org/psychiatrists/practice/dsm/history-of-the-dsm
3. NHS - **Symptoms of Post Traumatic Stress Disorder**. (2018) https://www.nhs.uk/conditions/post-traumatic-stress-disorder-ptsd/symptoms/

4. Matthew Tull. **Why People With PTSD Use Emotional Avoidance to Cope**. March 2020. https://www.verywellmind.com/ptsd-and-emotional-avoidance-2797640
5. **Theory of Mind**. https://en.wikipedia.org/wiki/Theory_of_mind
6. **Theory of Mind**. Spectrum News (2020). https://www.spectrumnews.org/wiki/theory-of-mind
7. Atsushi Senju, Victoria Southgate, Sarah White, Uta Frith. **Mindblind eyes: an absence of spontaneous theory of mind in Asperger syndrome**. (2009) Science. Aug 14;325(5942)
8. S Baron-Cohen, A M Leslie, U Frith. **Does the autistic child have a "theory of mind"?** Cognitions (1985) Oct;21(1):37-46.
9. **Post Natal Depression Overview**. https://www.nhs.uk/conditions/post-natal-depression/
10. Czarnocka, J., & Slade, P. (2000). **Prevalence and predictors of post-traumatic stress symptoms following childbirth**. British Journal of Clinical Psychology, 39(1), 35–51.
11. George Maxwell. (2020) **Birth Trauma and Post Natal PTSD**. https://depression-innewdads.com/
12. Carolyn Spring. (2011) **Powerlessness**. https://www.carolynspring.com/blog/powerlessness/
13. Porges S.W. (2011) **The Polyvagal Theory**. W.W Norton & Company
14. Blessing B. & Ginnins I. **Autonomic Nervous System**. http://www.scholarpedia.org/article/Autonomic_nervous_system
15. Ross D.C. (2018) **Book Summary: The Pocket Guide to the Polyvagal Theory** by Porges S.W. (2017) https://traumaedessentials.com/blog/porges-polyvagal

Chapter 12

1. Porges S.W. (2011) **The Polyvagal Theory**. W.W Norton & Company
2. Amy Cuddy Ted Talk **"Tiny Tweaks"**: https://www.ted.com/speakers/amy_cuddy

Chapter 13

1. Sydney Banks (1998) **The Missing Link: Reflections on Philosophy and Spirit**. Lone Pine Publishing C.A
2. Rosemary K.M. Sword & Philip Zimbardo. **Remorse**. Psychology Today. (September 2018) https://www.psychologytoday.com/gb/blog/the-time-cure/201809/remorse
3. Martin E.I. et al (2009) **The Neurobiology of Anxiety Disorders: Brain Imaging, Genetics, and Psychoneuroendocrinology**. Psychiatr Clin North Am. 32(3) 549-575

4. Allana Akhtar (2020) **11 science-backed ways your parents' behaviors shaped who you are today**. Business Insider. August 21, 2020. https://www.businessinsider.com/how-your-parents-behaviors-shape-who-you-are-today-2019-7?r=US&IR=T
5. Graham C.L. Davey (2017) **Helicopter, Snowplow, and Bubble-Wrap Parenting How is anxiety transmitted from parents to their children**? May 23, 2017. Psychology Today: https://www.psychologytoday.com/us/blog/why-we-worry/201705/helicopter-snowplow-and-bubble-wrap-parenting
6. Andrew T. Austin. **Help for Flashbacks**. https://helpforflashbacks.com
7. No author given: **What happens when we get angry?** Science Daily June 2010 https://www.sciencedaily.com/releases/2010/05/100531082603.htm
8. Dyer K.F.W. et al (2009) **Anger, aggression, and self-harm in PTSD and complex PTSD**. 12 August 2009. The Journal of Clinical Psychology.
9. Clayton M. (2012) **What is Entrainment? Definition and applications in musical research**. The Music & Science Lab, Durham University. Empirical Musicology Review Vol 7 No. (1-2)

Chapter 14

1. **Insider**. https://www.businessinsider.com/meet-zoom-billionaire-eric-yuan-career-net-worth-life

Chapter 15

1. **Abreaction**. https://en.wikipedia.org/wiki/Abreaction
2. Freud S., Bauer J. **Full Text of Studies on Hysteria**. https://archive.org/stream/studiesonhysteri037649mbp/studiesonhysteri037649mbp_djvu.txt
3. Murphy T., Llewelyn S., **Companion to Psychiatric Studies (Eighth Edition)**, 2010. https://www.sciencedirect.com/topics/nursing-and-health-professions/abreaction
4. William Sargant https://psychology.wikia.org/wiki/William_Sargant

Appendix 1

Use the following IEMT Tree of Knowledge as a quick guide to your work. If you want to add further checks, list them on the page below.

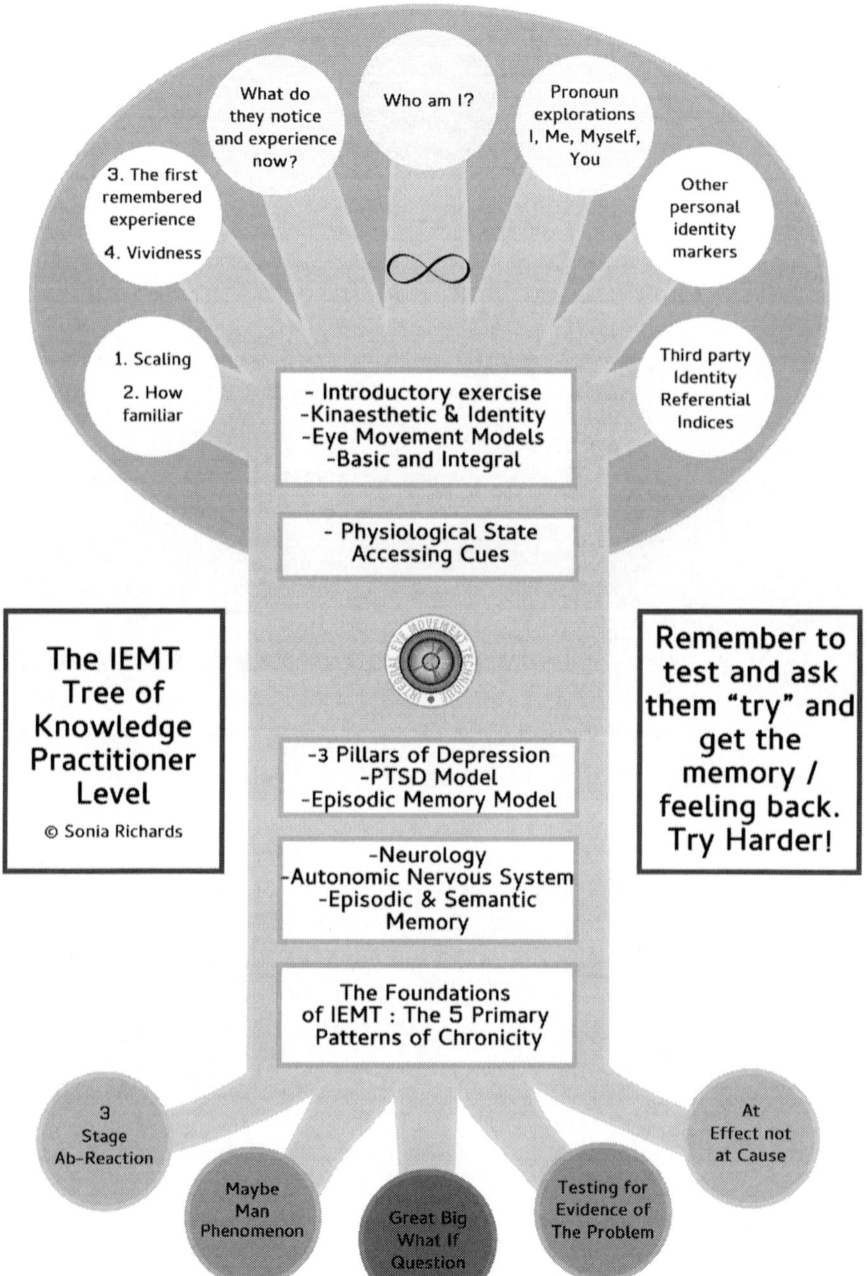
What do they notice and experience now?
Who am I?
Pronoun explorations I, Me, Myself, You
3. The first remembered experience
4. Vividness
Other personal identity markers
1. Scaling
2. How familiar
Third party Identity Referential Indices
- Introductory exercise
-Kinaesthetic & Identity
-Eye Movement Models
-Basic and Integral
- Physiological State Accessing Cues
The IEMT Tree of Knowledge Practitioner Level
© Sonia Richards
Remember to test and ask them "try" and get the memory / feeling back. Try Harder!
-3 Pillars of Depression
-PTSD Model
-Episodic Memory Model
-Neurology
-Autonomic Nervous System
-Episodic & Semantic Memory
The Foundations of IEMT : The 5 Primary Patterns of Chronicity
3 Stage Ab-Reaction
Maybe Man Phenomenon
Great Big What If Question
Testing for Evidence of The Problem
At Effect not at Cause
© Sonia Richards Training

Appendix 2

Self-use of IEMT

Self-use of IEMT is an important part of understanding the eye movement process in order to change feelings, ways of being and identity issues.

Self-use (i)

The following is an extract from the course work of a Level 1 Practitioner Training Course attendee who wishes to remain anonymous. The trainee, who is now a Practitioner, chose to work on some identity pronouns and Patterns of Chronicity, and this is a great example of how to use IEMT for personal use:

As I was conducting and reviewing the case study, I was aware that I used the word '*you*' a lot when I meant '*I*' and also used the words '*about*' and '*probably*' a large number of times. This indicated that I use the Maybe Man pattern of chronicity. I decided to focus on Identity and indecisiveness in self-use of IEMT.

As I have now attended the IEMT Practitioner course several times, not completing the coursework initially was linked to issues of self-doubt. Rather than read the examples and write up the work, I put off completing the task. Because using a video format was new to me, I chose to procrastinate rather than download the video immediately. I was also self-critical watching myself on video. As a result I put myself under unnecessary pressure. This links directly to the Maybe Man Pattern of Chronicity. I now realise that I can never be certain about the outcome of decisions I take, but I can be decisive in making those decisions.

I wondered if there was a link with my use of '*you*' as a distancing technique, and this indecisiveness.

Firstly I looked at self-doubt in terms of Identity using the IEMT Identity Protocol:

Identity Pronoun	Identity Pronoun	Identity Pronoun	Identity Pronoun	Identity Pronoun
I	Heart	57	Taking early retirement and voluntary redundancy from work, school closing.	Yes
Me	Gut	54	Issues around being a parent and grandparent	
Myself	Head and Shoulders	67	Uncertainty about the future after the pandemic	
You	Arm's length away in front	62	Recovering from plural infusion and completing my M.A.	

I noticed that all four responses were about times when I felt uncertain about the future and anger/frustration or sadness about the issues around me. I used the IEMT Integral Pattern around 'I' at 57.

Identity Pronoun	Where Is I Now?	How old is I?	What is happening around......I....?
Before	Heart	57	Taking early retirement and voluntary redundancy from work. Feeling anger and resentment at the way school is being closed.
After Round 1	Throat	59	Health issues- feeling weak, scared and resentful.
After Round 2	Chest	62	In Scotland, having difficulty breathing despite the air being clean.
After Round 3	Teeth	65	Really bad chest infection feeling frightened in case the illness has come back. Clenching my teeth – angry at self for being ill again and for putting weight back on.

As the anger and fear were palpable and 'I' is only 2 years off my actual age, I decided to do the Integral Kinaesthetic Pattern on Anger.

I realised I was angry with myself for being ill again and for putting weight back on after losing 5 stone in 2016.

SUD 8 – Quite Familiar

Various visions:

After round 1 - SUD 5 – Feeling sadness

Various visions:

After Round 2 - SUD 3

I had learned to self-soothe with music and distraction.

I decided that as the SUD had decreased to 3, I would leave it there.

At the end of this exercise I have learned that I have a pattern of getting frustrated with myself if I am overweight or ill. At the moment I feel accepting towards self and I am making a commitment to being kinder to self.

As a result of this I have submitted my coursework, despite my many reservations about my own performance on the videos. Now I have completed it I feel more confident in what I need to do in order to improve the work in future, which is:

i. Clear instructions to the client.

ii. Complete the process and learn to accept my features and voice.

I will use PSAC to change my state until I become more accepting. For example, if I notice my jaw tighten, I will loosen it by trying different positions until the state changes. If my voice is weak, I will make different sounds or use breathing techniques to strengthen it. If I hear my internal voice of doubt, I will remind it to be decisive, to choose. I will check in daily to monitor changes towards self-compassion.

Self-use (ii)

The following is extracted with permission from course work submitted by Inese Zvingevinca-Gravane, our first IEMT Practitioner from Latvia. She uses several aspects IEMT very successfully with her family, including PSAC work.

I chose to use IEMT for a feeling that I get fairly regularly from a situation I encounter reasonably regularly.

I dislike and get a feeling of anxiety when driving with passengers. I never feel anxious if I am driving with no passengers. If I do drive with passengers, I have a running internal dialogue; i.e., *"They are going to judge me"* and *"they think I am bad at driving"*. I also experience physical symptoms of anxiety; my body tenses up and sometimes my legs shake.

I decided to use this feeling associated to driving with passengers as something to work on with IEMT:

First imprint: anxiety

IEMT Kinaesthetic Pattern

SUDS Scores:

7/10 – Feeling very familiar and memory very vivid.

6/10 – Memory still there but feeling less intense.

4/10 – Less vivid memory and feeling less intense and quite different.

3/10 – Feeling was felt more as an uncomfortableness that was manageable.

The memory was more difficult to access and was broken up and did not bring about any emotion. When the broken-up memory was accessed it caused a neutral response and I now didn't have any feelings connected to it.

Next time I took my housemate out in my car, I did not worry about the journey beforehand, which usually I would have done.

When we were actually in the car, I was much more relaxed both in mind and body. My legs did not shake, I was not worrying about what the passenger was thinking or how they felt. I was able to drive confidently and without worry.

Note: Of course, there are other approaches that Inese could have used here, such as PSAC, and even to look at whether there were any supporting emotions cycling around as per the 3 Pillars; however, this brief use has worked well in this instance.

Appendix 3

IEMT with family members, by a practitioner in the USA

I had the pleasure of training Lori at the HypnoBirthing© Conclave in Las Vegas, 2014, and the passage below is reproduced with her kind permission.

Since becoming trained in IEMT, I have used it fairly regularly with pregnant moms who are attending my HypnoBirthing® childbirth education classes and who express a need for additional fear-release work beyond what I already provide in my classes. However, I had the opportunity recently to use IEMT with two of my three daughters, and it brought about amazing results.

In October 2014, my 11-year-old daughter, my 7-year-old daughter and I were in a very bad car accident. Our car was damaged beyond repair, and my girls and I felt emotionally fragile, traumatised and physically beaten up. For weeks after the accident, my 11-year-old, who is usually very emotionally stoic, cried regularly and followed me around the house. She wanted to be in the room with me, no matter what I was doing, and she repeatedly said through her tears: *"I thought you were going to die, mama."* She and I had many tear-filled cuddle sessions in the weeks following the accident.

While all three of us started chiropractic care within a couple of days of the accident, the emotional side of the accident weighed heavily on all of us; and although I am a hypnotist as well, I did not feel well enough myself to help my own kids. I started seeking out therapists for them to see, but before I got very far with my research, I thought to myself, *"I should use IEMT with the girls and see how that impacts their emotional state."*

After one session with each of them, both girls felt balanced and grounded, and neither one of them had any more crying jags about the accident. In fact, my youngest daughter started chuckling about the accident as she mused: *"That was one of the most ridiculous ways to have a car accident that I can imagine."*

Days later, when I mentioned to my 11-year-old that I was thrilled that she was feeling emotionally safer and independent again, she said, *"I never followed you around the house while crying, Mama. What are you talking about?"* I was a bit stunned by her reaction, but I realised that she was not denying those feelings; she just truly had a different physical and emotional reaction to the entire accident - all from our one IEMT session! It was amazing!"

Lori Nicholson, IEMT Practitioner, Master Hypnotist at Well Awakened Living

Appendix 4

Wider uses of IEMT

I had the pleasure of training Dr Nick Wright in both the Practitioner and Advanced Practitioner levels of IEMT. Please note that ordinarily neurological conditions such as Alzheimer's disease are on the contraindicated list unless, as with Nick, you are qualified and specialise in working in this area.

Neurological Disorders and IEMT

Neurological disorders are diseases of the central and peripheral nervous system. In other words, the brain, spinal cord, cranial nerves, peripheral nerves, nerve roots, autonomic nervous system, neuromuscular junction, and muscles. Together they control all the workings of the body. When something goes wrong with a part of the nervous system, a person can have trouble moving, speaking, swallowing, breathing or learning. They can also have problems with memory, senses or mood.

These disorders include epilepsy, Alzheimer's disease and other dementias, cerebrovascular diseases including stroke, migraine and other headache disorders, multiple sclerosis, Parkinson's disease, dystonia, Bell's palsy, essential tremor, neuro-infections, brain tumours, traumatic disorders of the nervous system such as brain trauma, and neurological disorders as a result of malnutrition.

There are more than 600 known neurological disorders and conditions that affect the human nervous system and for many of them treatment options are extremely limited. In addition to the physical and mental toll these conditions take on patients, their families and carers, they also have an enormous economic impact, resulting in millions of pounds annually in lost productivity.

As therapists we are well-placed and have a unique opportunity to offer help in a number of these conditions. Not only in helping with the stress, lack of confidence and self-esteem that results, both in the patient and also their immediate family, but also in helping the patient to regain some control over the condition itself. Disorders such as Parkinson's disease, dystonia, Bell's palsy, essential tremor, to name a few, are well within our reach.

I have worked with such conditions for the past eight years and in the last year have introduced IEMT into my treatment protocol with excellent results. One common denominator of a large number of these conditions is the presence of some kind of traumatic event at some point prior to the onset of the condition. Remember that for many of these conditions there is no definitive differential diagnosis and often the final diagnosis is as a result of negative results being returned for other conditions that present with similar symptoms. This means that any diagnosis often occurs quite some time after the first onset of any symptoms.

I have found that by identifying the trigger, i.e., the traumatic event, and de-sensitising it, there is very often a reduction in the presenting symptoms, in these cases, tremor and or muscle rigidity. IEMT is, in my experience, an invaluable therapeutic tool, not only for helping to find that trigger but also for helping the client to deal with it. But it goes much further than this.

For the client, anxiety, depression, worry for the future are all presenting symptoms. These very often evolve into anger and sometimes feelings of guilt, especially with the thought of loved ones having to care for them in the future. That big 'what if' and 'if only' are often present.

All these issues are within the scope of IEMT and clients see it as a gentle intervention that produces rapid and lasting results by not only reducing the stress and anxiety that naturally accompanies these conditions but by having a positive impact on the tremors themselves. It is an invaluable tool for conditions where general medical treatments are often very limited and is now the first port of call for me with any client.

Dr. Nick Wright, Doctor of Osteomyology, Advanced Practitioner of IEMT

Appendix 5

Remember, the foundation of the IEMT model is not just to ameliorate feelings, but to deal effectively with the behavioural patterns that can get in the way of life, sabotage change, keep people repeating mistakes or leave them stuck in a rut. These patterns, which we term the Patterns of Chronicity, primarily set IEMT apart from other eye movement-based models. IEMT practitioners are taught the significance of these patterns and how to familiarise themselves with them. Thus, they can closely observe the verbal, visual and written indications from clients that often defeat the most competent of therapists unaware of the existence of these patterns.

Use the diagram to the right as a checklist, and list your own Patterns of Chronicity below.

IEMT The 5 Patterns of Chronicity

1. Three Stage Abreaction process

A person's pattern of escalating emotional behaviour to create or force a change in the external environment. They want others to change, because they don't want to. This often occurs in 3 stages, of which some may be very subtle.

Solution: *"That's right"....* or *"Your emotional state does not dictate my response."*

2. The Great Big 'What if...' question

The use of a single counter-example that sabotages and counteracts any therapeutic generalisation. Future-paced, anxiety, loop-around, beliefs, and/or catastrophisation.

Solution: *"Then... Deal with it..."*

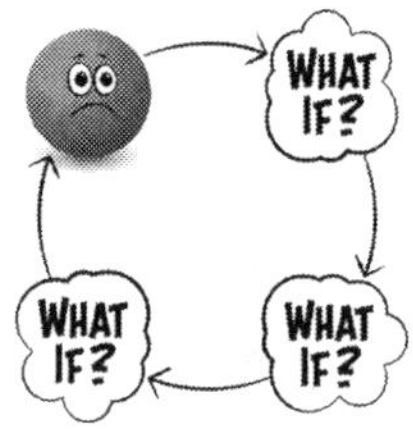

3. The Maybe Man phenomenon

The Maybe Man is uncertain of their own experience and this leaks out into their language. They do not commit to their genuine experience or to their identity by remaining uncertain and without precision, and thus inadvertently sabotage effective therapy.

Solution: Ask them to be specific. IEMT on feelings of uncertainty.

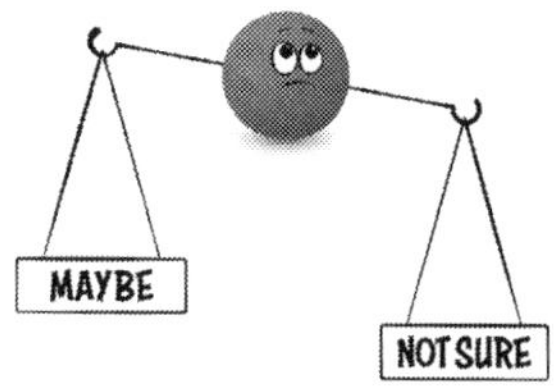

4. Testing for existence of the problem rather than testing for change

Even though 99% improvement might be made, if the person with this chronicity is able to locate just 1% of the problem existing, this will generally be seen as representative of 100% of the problem existing. (Metaphor) Some people only ever see a problem.

Solution: Reframe the problem, deal with the emotion of the problem, Kinaesthetic IEMT, and perform some Identity IEMT.

5. "Being at Effect" rather than "Being at Cause"

By being "at effect" the person experiences emotional problems happening to them, rather than being something that happens by them. A person "at effect" will seek 'treatment' rather than seeking 'change'. (Magic wand) Most clients are in effect!

Solution: Deal with cause IEMT, PSACs - solutions and resources

Appendix 6

IEMT PTSD Lynch Pin Model

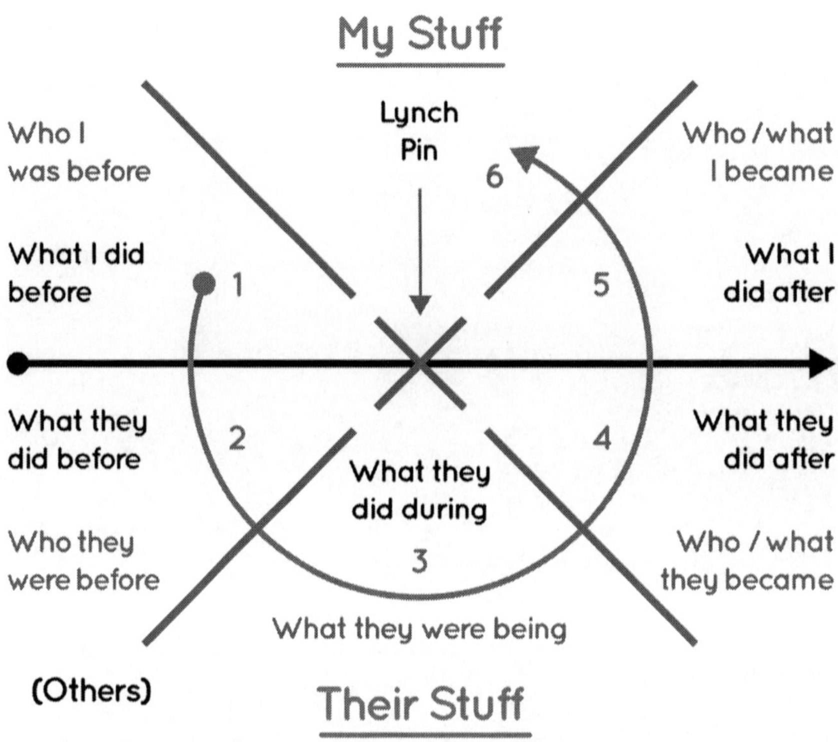

Printed in Great Britain
by Amazon

12953218R00203